MW00559989

تو چون نسیم لطیفی برای دیدن باران

تو استواری چو کوهی بوقت غرش طوفان

بلند همت و راسخ مثال شاهینی

بشکرانیز دمنان شدت پشتیبان

درون آینه شخصی تماشا میکند خود را نسیم آهسته تر بگذر

بابا – فروردین ۱۳۹۷

Sofreh

Sofreh

A Contemporary Approach
to Classic Persian Cuisine

NASIM ALIKHANI

With Theresa Gambacorta
Photographs by Quentin Bacon

ALFRED A. KNOPF NEW YORK 2023

THIS IS A BORZOI BOOK
PUBLISHED BY ALFRED A. KNOPF

Copyright © 2023 by Nasim Alikhani
Photographs copyright © 2023 by Quentin Bacon

All rights reserved. Published in the United States by
Alfred A. Knopf, a division of Penguin Random House LLC,
New York, and distributed in Canada by
Penguin Random House Canada Limited, Toronto.

www.aaknopf.com

Knopf, Borzoi Books, and the colophon are registered
trademarks of Penguin Random House LLC.

Library of Congress Cataloging-in-Publication Data
Names: Alikhani, Nasim, author. | Gambacorta, Theresa, author. |
Bacon, Quentin, photographer.
Title: Sofreh / Nasim Alikhani; with Theresa Gambacorta;
photographs by Quentin Bacon.
Description: First edition. | New York: Alfred A. Knopf, 2023. |
Includes index.
Identifiers: LCCN 2022014632 | ISBN 9780593320747 (hardcover) |
ISBN 9780593320754 (ebook)
Subjects: LCSH: Cooking, Iranian. | LCGFT: Cookbooks.
Classification: LCC TX727.I7 A45 2023 |
DDC 641.5955—dc23/eng/20220707
LC record available at https://lccn.loc.gov/2022014632

Cover photograph (dish) by Quentin Bacon
Cover design by Rozhia Tabnak

Manufactured in China
First Edition

For my mother, Giti Joon,
and my father, Reza Ali,
who gave me the tools and the foundation
from which to build my life.

And for my husband,
Akis, who provided the safety and structure
from which to realize my dreams.

I whispered to my grapevine, "You are fine, just as you are:
your roots are deep, you bear fruit each season, what more could
you possibly want?" "But why stop now," answered the grapevine,
"when there is such immense joy in my reaching for the sun."

Contents

What Sofreh Means to Me

Sofreh is a word that exists in Farsi as both a literal expression and a symbolic act. When used literally, *sofreh* refers to the sometimes ornate, boldly colorful, and often beautifully hand-embroidered table coverings that serve as backdrops for food.

Specific *sofreh* mark seasonal feasts, celebrations, and religious ceremonies, such as *sofreh-aghd*, used for wedding ceremonies, or *sofreh haft-seen*, for Nowruz, the Persian New Year. In my Prospect Park, Brooklyn, restaurant, Sofreh, as you travel down a set of stairs to the downstairs garden entrance and dining area, you'll pass the Farsi names of several ritual *sofreh* cast into the cement walls. The larger-than-life Farsi calligraphy symbolizes the immensity of my desire to share Persian cuisine and culture with my customers. My Greek husband, Akis, did the casting. The joke in our house is that he is Iranian, he just doesn't know it!

Rather than naming the restaurant after any particular literal reference to one of these celebratory *sofreh*, I took on the name for its symbolic meaning. "To sit at the *sofreh*" also refers to setting the table with a spread of delicious, vibrant, soul-satisfying Persian food to be shared with family and friends. As I hope you do with the dishes in this book.

I am speaking of women, whose names alone
are equal to a miracle.
Giti, Mihan, Masi,
and Innocent Soul, an angel
whose way of life was bravery,
and she received eternal life.
She taught me
stay the course,
fear has no place in life.
These women showed me
stay strong like a mountain,
just being a woman
is bigger than a miracle.
I dedicate this to all the strong women of my life:
My friends, my relatives,
Sofreh belongs to all of you.

—Translated from the Farsi dedication
that hangs at Sofreh

Introduction: Welcome Home

Isfahan, Iran, 1992. I am feverish. Not the kind of fever brought on from illness; it's a psychogenic fever caused by the anxiety of my long-awaited homecoming. I've spent the last nine years separated from my extended family and friends, culture, and native Iran. And, now that I have finally landed from New York with my new husband, Akis, I am overwhelmed with emotion. I'm about to face more than two hundred and fifty relatives and acquaintances who've been invited to my parents' home for a wedding party that has been arranged by my mother, Giti Joon.

I use my fever as an excuse to park myself in the back of my parents' home, un-showered and still wearing my American T-shirt and jeans. A flurry of activity swirls around me; here come the chairs, now the tent, and flower deliveries. I don't lift a finger to help anyone. Instead, I am staring at the elaborate setup of massive pots and the outdoor catering kitchen that the *a'ashpaz* (chef) and his crew are organizing. Giti Joon has raved to me about this *a'ashpaz*, the revered head chef at a big hotel. I can tell that I am annoying him. As much as I am sure he'd like to ask me to take a hike, he can't because I'm the guest of honor. He and his kitchen crew make certain, however, that I remain on the periphery of their circle, so I can't get close enough to see their professional cooking tricks and secrets. I hover stubbornly for hours, captivated and curious. I want to know how the hell they are going to pull off this elaborate feast.

My mother has organized such a luxurious overdose of food for our wedding party that it looks as if these guys can feed our guests twice over. There are two incredibly tender, stuffed whole lambs, along with several celebratory *polo,* layered rice dishes, including jeweled rice, studded with the glow of tiny crimson barberries, slivered almonds, pistachios, and raisins, and *shirin polo,* sweet rice laced with bright carrots and candied orange peel. There are massive, steaming trays of lamb and beef *kababs* served with a variety of thick yogurts, as well as a splendid array of vegetable-based yogurt dips called *borani.* There are our most beloved, traditional stews that capture distinctly sour flavors unique to Persian cooking, such as *khoresht-e fesenjan,* a stew whose base is made from rich ground walnuts and dark, sour pomegranate molasses. And, of course, *ghormeh sabzi*, our national dish, with its base of earthy-sweet fried herbs, tender pieces of beef, hearty kidney beans, and the zing of dried limes. All of these dazzling dishes and more will be brought to the table in one *whoosh* for our guests to enjoy.

I can still vividly see myself standing alone, watching the cooks in my father's garden, my identity as a chef still unformed. But in the days that follow, during my return home, my family and the abiding love of my community of neighbors and friends will usher in my rebirth—both culinarily and emotionally—and set me on course for a twenty-six-year journey, from Isfahan to the opening of my restaurant Sofreh in Brooklyn.

IT IS IRANIAN WOMEN WHO SET THE TONE IN HOMES. THEY COOK, HOST, AND FEED OTHERS, TASKS THAT ARE A SYMBOL OF LOVE, OF CARE FOR ONE ANOTHER.

I was born in Isfahan, a province in central Iran bound by the Zagros mountain range to the west and the Varzaneh Desert to the east. While the areas of the province along the desert's edge are arid, and the western edges along the mountains can be cold, the capital city of Isfahan, located on the central plateau, is a fertile desert oasis. The Zayandeh Rud, the largest river of Iran's central plateau that cuts east to west through my city, has, for centuries, provided a significant water source for urbanization and agriculture. Plums, apples, peaches, and grapes, along with quinces, pears, and muskmelons, flourish in this oasis. Unlike our Middle Eastern neighbors, much of Iran, including Isfahan, experiences four distinct seasons that provide the climate necessary for a profusion of fruits, herbs, vegetables, legumes, and nuts indigenous to each province. It is no wonder that Iranians are food-obsessed!

It is Iranian women who set the tone in homes. They cook, host, and feed others, tasks that are a symbol of love, of care for one another. Giti Joon, a teacher and later a principal, was also a dedicated and talented home cook. I'd wake for school each morning to the enticing smell of her herb stews. She'd rise early, before her workday, to ready them in time for lunch for me, my father, and my two younger brothers, Hamid Reza and Amir.

While most nine-year-old girls would be content to run off and play, I preferred the company of my mother's circle—her sisters, friends, and neighbors—so I would help with summer pickling and preservation projects. I mostly picked and washed herbs, but no matter how small the task, I devoured every bit of food-related information and direction they gave me. I had a strong sense of flavor, and a discerning sense of smell;

I'd skip past my neighbors' homes on my way home from school, and play a guessing game of feasts and flavors. Sweet-smelling, slowly cooked onions and pungent turmeric would waft through their windows, intensified by the desert air, and I'd think, "Oh, they're having *koofteh ghelgheli* today," imagining humble, comforting lamb and chickpea flour meatballs being rolled out and dropped one by one into the broth. From my early childhood helping my mother, to later, in my teenage years, helping her raise my two younger brothers, cooking for extended family and guests provoked in me a feeling that I can describe only as having a song in my heart.

When I was growing up, Iran had been under the rule of Shah Pahlavi. He and his beautiful wife were the picture of glamour, wealth, art, and fashion; many felt they had fallen out of touch with the struggles of the everyday Iranian. By the time I had reached high school, tension was bubbling beneath Iran's glossy, pro-Western surface. There was a widening socioeconomic gap between rural and urban areas, a push and pull between secularism and religious conservatism and myriad social issues that arose from a rapidly advancing culture whose roots were in antiquity. Many Iranians were angry, but their public opinions were suppressed by the Shah's secret police, called SAVAK, who censored the media and brutally oppressed dissenting voices.

I had always been an outspoken kid—my family joked that instead of being like my name, Nasim, which translates as "gentle breeze," I was instead more like thunder! While I was in high school, I fought with my teachers, taking a stance on issues that we were forbidden to discuss in the classroom. Any other ordinary kid would have surely gotten into trouble with SAVAK, but my teachers cut me a lot of slack, because they knew my mother. Whether it was swimming competitively, or going head-to-head with teachers, and later my parents, I was fueled by an inborn will and determination to win, no matter the project or cause.

I left my home in Isfahan in 1977 to study law at the University of Tehran. But I wasn't content to become a lawyer. I wanted to be a judge and had a mind-set for fighting oppression. It was the first time that I had ventured so far from home and experienced firsthand the vastness of my country. I came to understand that there exist as many tribes, languages, regional dishes, and customs as there are climates in Iran. At that time, the University of Tehran was a place where the seeds of civil resistance were being sown by student movements. As culturally diverse as the kids were, so were their political ideals; my school was a mix of both secular and Islamist students, as well as those who identified as religious progressives, leftist, communist, and socialist, and a wealthy minority who quietly supported the Shah.

On the third day of my freshman year, I remember a huge political demonstration at school. Factions of students unified and stormed out of a building, only to be met with a counterattack by SAVAK and the university police. During that first semester, one student strike followed another, making my freshman year pretty much a bust. During one of my final exams, for a class that I had barely attended, I remember tearing up the exam sheet, standing up, and storming out for a strike. I was having a ball! I fell in fast with new friends and, like many of my colleagues at school, I fervently expressed my desire for change.

While at school, I realized that I hated studying law. But I also knew that a career change would not only be socially unacceptable but impossible, because I would have to leave school, then take another national reentry exam. My inner turmoil mirrored the tension happening around me, and the only thing that brought calm and purpose to my young angst was cooking. I hosted parties for my friends, arranging get-togethers in my dorm room, hoping to make life beautiful through food. One incredulous friend said, "Nasim, bullets are flying outside and you're in here frying eggplant?"

By 1978, students at schools weren't the only ones demonstrating. A wide cross section of Iranians—teachers, oil factory workers, and more—joined the cause to depose the Shah. Demonstrations rapidly intensified. The movement, which had started in Tehran, now included other major cities, such as Shiraz and Isfahan. The political unrest was like hot lava bubbling over. However, secular factions in these cities lacked the ability to reach the villages and more rural parts of Iran, so instead, local mosques emerged as the leadership in the movement for change.

By November 1978, the face of Ayatollah Khomeini, a religious cleric who had been exiled to Iraq after opposing the modernizing reforms of the Shah in the 1960s, was seen everywhere, striking fear in the hearts of older Iranians. My father's generation understood that the mullah (religious cleric) and his movement would remake Iran in his fundamentalist Muslim image. Still, his faction successfully took charge of the revolution, and in December 1978, the Shah left Iran, ending a series of Persian monarchies that had lasted more than 2,500 years. By the spring of 1979, a new Muslim-led government put forth a national referendum that left little choice but for people to vote for the Islamic Republic.

You could feel the change immediately. The new government forced women to wear a *hejab* (hair covering) regardless of religious identity and attacked women's rights. In schools, textbooks were purged to remove references to the West and Iran's history of monarchies. Giti Joon returned home early from work one day to tell us that she'd been forced to retire at forty years old, because she would not conform to the new regime's sweeping curriculum changes. I was crestfallen that my mother, a respected and brilliant career woman, as well as a masterful homemaker, had lost *her* heart song.

Throughout this time, my relationship with my father was tumultuous. I was a fierce young woman who had high hopes of changing the world, and I clung to my ideals regardless of the price I might pay. My father, a very wise man, tried to warn me. He knew that if I continued to participate in protests, I'd ultimately end up placing not just myself but the lives of my two younger brothers in danger. Defiantly, I left home and estranged myself from my family.

Every few months, while on my own, I'd visit Isfahan, under the cover of darkness, where my aunt, or my mother, would give me a little money and allow me to stay for a night or two in my grandfather's house. One summer night, I asked my aunt for *beryuni,* a singular Isfahani specialty. It's a rich mince of lamb seasoned with cinnamon, turmeric, and black pepper, then shaped into a patty. It's grilled, topped with a fatty, succulent dice of lamb lungs, and served on *sangak* bread to soak up its rich juices. Eating *beryuni* was all I could think about that summer, and when I asked my aunt if she could bring me some, she looked at me as if to say, You're out here on your own, struggling to survive, and all you're thinking about is *beryuni*? If there is any dish that says "I am Isfahani," it's *beryuni*. But in Isfahan, no one eats *beryuni* alone—except perhaps for a few construction workers on their break; it's the kind of dish that you eat with a troop—aunts, uncles, cousins, and parents, sisters and brothers, and grandparents, gathering one and all for lunch at long community tables. I hungered for the feeling of *beryuni*.

In 1980, the new regime closed all universities, and by the fall, Iraq launched an invasion of Iran, starting a full-scale war. I had satisfied every ounce of my willful protesting and by now had come to terms with the fact that I was just lucky to be alive. Along the way, I had lost friends to execution and imprisonment, so I returned to my family in Isfahan, scared for my safety and humbled. With universities shut down, and the roles for women diminishing, I knew I had no choice but to leave my country. I begged my father to help me find a way out.

It took more than a year, but eventually, my father's coworker arranged for me to stay with some of his family in Jersey City, New Jersey. On the day of my departure, at the airport, my father held me tightly. I was a twenty-three-year-old twig of a girl, leaving behind my family and my country in the throes of war. I was a basket case of loss and anger for countless friends whose lives were shattered, or lost, and I was terrified, hopeful, and grateful. I had no idea what was waiting for me on the other side of the world, or if I would ever see my family again.

I arrived alone in New Jersey in 1983 with two small suitcases that my mother had packed. One was filled with dried herbs—saffron, turmeric, and dried dill. So much dill. Too much dill. I think my mother has a thing about dill! And she filled the other with *maviz*—dark, sweet, long raisins; dried plums, barberries, and *kashk,* a type of whey that is full of protein and makes a delicious base for a nutritious pot of *a'ash* with noodles and beans. I didn't pack many clothes, because we didn't know the weather, but Giti Joon made sure I had a well-stocked pantry.

I REACHED ACROSS THE FLOODS OF FLAVOR MEMORIES TO RE-CREATE THE TRADITIONAL, HOME-COOKED STEWS AND RICE DISHES FROM MY IRANIAN CHILDHOOD IN MY LITTLE NEW YORK APARTMENT.

Our family acquaintance picked me up at the airport and brought me to his overcrowded two-bedroom apartment. He handed me a subway map with two destinations circled—my location in New Jersey and Queens College, so that I could find my way to English classes the next day. He then gave me two weeks to find my own place. Eventually, I found a job at my school and later, my own apartment in Queens. I didn't have time to waste on despair. Instead, I summoned my determination and immediately accepted that New York was my new home. My sole motivation at that time was survival.

One day, I ventured to the only Iranian grocery store in New York City at the time and picked up an Iranian newspaper. My eyes landed on a NANNY WANTED ad. An Iranian woman, just three years older than me, was looking for someone to care for her two small children. I landed the job, and as it turns out, she wasn't thrilled with her role as a homemaker. So, in addition to nannying her kids, I was put in charge of her family's meals. I had never felt so lucky! I replaced the kid-friendly canned foods that filled her cupboards and lovingly prepared the nutritious, home-cooked fare I had enjoyed as a child. Her trust allowed my kitchen confidence to flourish, and soon after, she hired me to cook Persian meals for her extended family. That increased my income and gave me more financial stability.

During these early years, I called home to my mother as often as I could. I reached across the floods of flavor memories to re-create the traditional, home-cooked stews and rice dishes from my Iranian childhood in my little New York apartment. Our conversations sometimes made my head spin. *(Sabziha ro khord kon. / Prep your vegetables. Badan ghusht ro ezafe koon. / And after, add your meat. Piyaz yadet nare. / But don't forget onion.)* But how much onion, Mom? *(Be ghushtet nega koon. / Look at your meat.)* But how much meat? *(Be piyazet nega koon. / Look at your onion.)* I marked the

Persian New Year by making *reshteh polo*—an aromatic noodle and rice dish redolent of cardamom and saffron. Each time I cooked a traditional dish from home, I was searching for a way to water my roots so they wouldn't die. But with greater ease than I think even I anticipated, I began to fall in love with New York. Most significantly, Brooklyn.

There are two critical things you should know about me during those early days as an immigrant. First, I longed to reclaim the sense of beauty that I had left behind in my ancient city of Isfahan, where the majesty and splendor of some of the world's great monuments were right outside my door. Second, I longed for a sense of belonging and community, a pocket of New York where I could see a reflection of myself. And so, it was in the brownstone Brooklyn of the 1980s where I wandered the streets, in neighborhoods like Park Slope, Fort Greene, Cobble Hill, and Prospect Park, taking in the tall stoops, the looping archways of the doorway entrances, and the swirling, carved designs in the sandstone facades. The best part of my meanderings, however, was the people. In the diversity of Brooklyn, I felt like I fit in.

When I was twenty-seven, I met Akis, a professor at the New Jersey Institute of Technology, and I was drawn to his wonderful "nerdy professor" sense of humor and his understanding of good food. He brought me to a very fancy restaurant for our first date, and when the bill arrived, it put me to shame. I was still a student and cash-strapped. So, I proposed a deal. To continue dating, we'd have to alternate dining out with home-cooked meals from my cooking repertoire. And so, as our bond over food grew, I introduced him to the flavors of the Persian pantry, such as nigella seeds, hogweed seeds, and a whole range of spices—some still from my suitcases—as well as fresh herbs and vegetables. In turn, he introduced me to the fine-dining scene that was in full swing in New York City. Within six months, I had moved in, and we eventually married. At one point, I was working in a copy shop, but owing to Akis's business smarts, he helped me open my own copy store. After we married, two more years passed before I was finally able to return to Isfahan and introduce him to my family. And it was during the early days of our trip that the roots that I had been consciously and subconsciously watering revealed their depth to me.

The day after my wedding party, my fever broke as quickly as it came on. All that week, Akis and I would return home to my parents' house from sightseeing in Isfahan's Nagshe Jahan Square to discover that my friends and neighbors had brought us food gifts. Sometimes, two or three visitors a day would arrive with jars of shimmering marmalades and jams, sour pickles, and their own "famous" meticulously decorated, over-the-top pastries—offered with such pride, as a showcase of their tradition and expression of their love. Even though I had never stopped cooking in New York, the dishes I had been making were basic in comparison with this onslaught of flavors, colors, and textures.

Akis, floored by the barrage of gifts, said, "I have never seen such generosity like this." "Yes. Yes," I told him, "this is what we do." And for the first time, I felt released from the pain of separation. "This is who we are," I said. And I began to understand myself, once again, as part of my community.

During these days, I was also able to see my parents, especially my father, in an entirely different light. Giti Joon's resentment over the loss of her job had fallen away. She'd softened, and I marveled as she commanded my wedding party with such joy and pride. I watched her accumulate the empty bowls, after we'd devour all that our neighbors brought, and fill them up with something extraordinary from her home kitchen. For my dear aunts and close friends, she filled the bowls with freshly cut flowers from my father's garden. And sent me off to thank them in person. Her generosity and thoughtful reciprocity moved me.

I WATCHED MY MOTHER ACCUMULATE THE EMPTY BOWLS, AFTER WE'D DEVOUR ALL THAT OUR NEIGHBORS BROUGHT, AND FILL THEM UP WITH SOMETHING EXTRAORDINARY FROM HER HOME KITCHEN.

And I noticed for the first time this ritual of my father's: he'd arrange all kinds of leftovers from our meals in separate containers—the rice would go for the birds, the bones and fat would go for the cats and dogs, and all the vegetables would go to his friend, a crow named Crow, who would follow him around. And finally, any thick, dry bread crumbs from what we ate would feed the hundreds of fish in his pond. I remember as a child watching him in wintertime, spreading the food across dry land, with Crow flying, then striding, alongside him, birdsong flooding the air as other birds swooped in, pecking around for their share. And then, the circling of stray cats and dogs around my father, awaiting their turn. Watching him again, I almost couldn't believe the fights I'd had with him when I was a teenager. Ten years later, and through the lens of a hard-won maturity, I really *saw* my father and was blown away by his kindness. I was able to finally piece together everything he had sacrificed to give me a chance at a new life in America. I found out that he had sold everything he had—properties, his car, and personal possessions—to help me leave Iran. My sense of debt to him was enormous. And my reconnection with him, once I was home and in his loving presence, healed me.

In those days of homecoming—which had never been guaranteed—we gathered around the *sofreh* with extended family. At my aunt Mihan's house, mostly I think to impress Akis, my aunt set her *sofreh* with regional northern dishes she had incorporated into her fabulous cooking. I fell in love with her *mirza ghasemi*, a smoky charred eggplant sauce, layered with garlic, turmeric, and tomato. And for the first time, at her house, we tasted an indelible fish stew called *ghalieh mahi*, whose base of silky sweet-sour sauce of fried, musky fenugreek, flavored with the sour punch of tamarind, she had learned to cook from her neighbor.

These and other dishes from home made me realize how much I had to learn about Persian food. I returned to New York with a heart full of appreciation for the vitality, exciting flavors, and deep well of tradition I had rediscovered. But I also returned with a renewed sense of self. I was no longer broken, or disconnected. And whether I was conscious of it or not, I had been set on a new course.

Around the time of this first return to Iran with Akis, nouvelle cuisine was taking New York City by storm. Akis and I enjoyed our early, child-free years making a home together, working, and dining out in a New York that was growing more fascinated with the world cuisines of Thailand, China, and India. But mostly everyone seemed unaware of the unique character of Persian home cooking beyond *kababs*. Conversations between Akis and me turned around how we could bring Iran's incredibly old, rich, and vast cuisine center stage. Soon, I began telling everyone, "I am going to open a restaurant one day." I was thirty-three years old with zero restaurant experience. Sure, I had cooked for my husband and a few friends, but now, I am opening a restaurant one day?! I had been only scratching the surface of Persian cooking; I needed to practice and learn more. I was determined to do just that.

My plans were put on the back burner when I became pregnant with our twins, Soshy and Noony. I threw myself into the labor of motherhood (if there is one thing you should know about me, I am a mother first and a chef second). I channeled my passion into home-cooked meals to nourish them, and brought them with me each year on return trips home to Isfahan. While our children played on the streets where I grew up, I took on purposeful research, uncovering my Persian roots, still driven to open my Persian restaurant. I went to my Iranian neighbors' homes to collect recipes, take pictures, and capture the voices of Persian grandmothers whom I was introduced to. But each time I asked someone for a recipe for their specialty, they would be so happy to share their family's history, or the name of who taught them to make their splendid offering, or even to nail down the date, year, and time of day for the feast or wedding that they cooked it for, that I came away with much more than just an ingredient list.

When we'd return to New York after each trip, I'd replicate the new dish, from whatever information I had, coupled with the fundamentals of good Persian cooking and my home cook's common sense. Then, I would invite my mostly non-Iranian friends over to taste my discovery. Even if they didn't comment, I just had to look at their faces and empty plates to surmise that they enjoyed it, and I took a ton of notes.

While raising my twins, I carved out massive cooking and baking projects for school functions. I fed growing, hungry boys and girls on my kids' soccer and basketball teams. And because I had been so fortunate to have a great kitchen and stable finances, I donated my time and money to catering charitable events, executing Persian feasts for hundreds of people. Cooking and offering food were such an incredible source of joy that I couldn't imagine a day without nourishing people. By the time my kids were heading to high school, Akis and I decided that the time had come to search for a special restaurant space. I wanted to blur the lines between home and restaurant. I wanted people to feel the *whoosh* of love and community that forms the foundation of the way food is cooked and offered—with generosity, abundance, and love—in Iran.

When I began searching for restaurant spaces, I endlessly drove around my favorite Brooklyn neighborhoods, but a building at 75 St. Marks Avenue found *me* one early morning while I was dropping off my nephew Sapand at day care in Prospect Heights. There I stood, enamored with its raw beauty. And its potential. Not just the building but the potential to bring my life full circle; although Akis and I had already been living in Manhattan for more than twenty years, I wanted to plant my Persian roots in the New York neighborhood that I had always wished to call home.

Organically, morsels of my life were incorporated into the look and feel of Sofreh. Before you even enter, ornate wrought-iron door handles greet you. They look much like the door knockers you'll find on the most ancient gates outside of homes in Iran, representing traditional "masculine" and "feminine" energies. Knock the thick, masculine-looking metal bar on the right, and you get a deep male tone. Lift the feminine one on the left for a lighter pitch. In Iran, these communicate to whomever is home the gender of the guest at the door. If a male knocks, a woman host should be prepared to cover herself accordingly in her *hejab*. Growing up, my friends and I would purposely use the masculine knocker to have the old ladies in my village greet us at the doors all wrapped up. I hunted the door knockers down at the Grand Bazaar of Isfahan and carried them back to New York. For me, they embody my and Akis's energy and personality, which brought Sofreh to fruition.

Sofreh's creative director and interior designer, Rozhia Tabnak, conceived the gentle archways that loop over my bar. Rozhia drew inspiration from historical cities of Iran, where arches, and domes, are cornerstones of their architecture. We built the bar twice and knocked it down each time to get it right! Akis built a prototype first on the third try to help bring Rozhia's distinct vision to life. What emerged was a bar with arches that resonate with me, as they are a nod to those in the receiving room at my great-grandmother's house. Her house was crumbling down in her later years, and those arches were a glimpse into her past. Rozhia covered the wall of Sofreh's bathroom with pulpy movie posters featuring 1970s' pre-revolution Iranian cinema. I had collected these images for years, and she curated them in such a hip way that they have become a popular Instagram backdrop. These elements, and my preference for Iranian pop music's catchy rhythm, transport me to the days of joy before I left my homeland for New York. Throughout Sofreh, Rozhia's signature style of balancing traditional silhouettes with a minimal modern twist is expressed using memories of my life.

Turn the corner at the bottom of the staircase that leads to a downstairs dining room and you'll find hanging on the walls the timeworn but treasured pictures of the inspirational women in my family. Look into their eyes, and what do you see? Matriarchs. You can imagine their homes, where they bustled around to call together those they love for comfort. And good food. They showed me the way.

It took a lifetime of journeying for Sofreh to be born. From the time we purchased the building to the time we opened our doors, six years passed. Our children had gone from high school to college graduation. And I was fifty-nine years old.

Sofreh celebrates the delectable flavors, aromas, textures, comfort, and bounty of Iran's dishes. These recipes carry the love I have for cooking and are inextricably linked to the love of my family, friends, and even the world at large. My wish is that they will ignite or enhance your appreciation and understanding of Persian food and culinary techniques. I also hope that they deepen your understanding of the love and warmth of the Iranian people, too. Sofreh is a celebration of my roots in Isfahan, Iran, and the ones I have planted in Brooklyn, New York.

And you, my dear home cook, are invited to the party.

A Brief History of
Persian Cuisine

Persia or Iran?

I use "Persian cuisine," "Persian cooking," and "Iranian food"
interchangeably throughout this book. For the sake of clarity, Persia, the
name for Iran in the Western world until 1935, was once a vast-stretching
empire founded by Cyrus the Great in 550 BCE. The ancient city of
Persepolis, whose ruins are located in the modern-day Fars province,
was its seat. Ancient Iranian people migrated to the region known as
Persis. Thus, being Persian is an ethnicity among several ethnic groups
that compose the people of Iran today. You can be Iranian; however, you
might not identify as Persian. And you can be Persian, as well as identify
as Iranian. And then there are the Parsee people of India, who fled Iran to
escape religious persecution between the eighth and tenth centuries AD,
carrying ancient food traditions with them. I tasted their layered rice dishes
(*polo*) expressed as *pulau*, a host of meat *kababs*, dishes with dried fruits
and aromatic spices, their roots unmistakably in Iran. The Parsee people are
not Iranian, but their culture and food traditions have origins in Persian
history and culture.

Iran's Geography

The story of Persian cuisine begins with Iran's geography. Central to Iran
is an arid high-elevation plateau with interior lakes and rivers. To the east
of the plateau is a huge, uninhabitable salt desert—the Dasht-e Kavir. Two
major mountain ranges define Iran; in the north, the Alborz Mountains
curve west to east, following the southern shoreline of the Caspian Sea,
and the Zagros mountain chain runs parallel to Iran's western border. To
the south is the Persian Gulf, with a coastline that stretches more than six
hundred miles. The diversity of Iran's topography shapes our cuisine. For
centuries, lowland mountain ranges have been integral to animal husbandry.
And the range of temperature and varying climates have made it possible
for Iranians to cultivate a wide variety of fruits, herbs, spices, vegetables,

nuts, and grains for centuries. Dry, arid zones of the Iranian plateau, where water sources were scarce, have benefited from the development of *quanat*, underground wells, and water channels for thousands of years. First developed by ancient Persians and later improved on and expanded, the *quanat* used gravity to direct mountain water from high elevations to arid regions. The availability of a water source for drinking and agricultural work allowed the oasis of Isfahan and other village settlements to form.

The Silk Road and Isfahan

The Silk Road, initiated by China in 130 BCE, and in use to trade goods until the Middle Ages in AD 1453, was a four-thousand-mile-long network of land and maritime routes. These routes wended and crisscrossed through the Middle East, North Africa, and Europe. By land, caravans of merchants traveled on camels in packs, in a relay system, dropping off wide-ranging precious goods: silk, teas, and spices—black pepper, saffron, ginger, nutmeg, cumin, and cinnamon—as well as gems that came from China. Persia was central to the Silk Road; the importance of its role as a center for trade and the exchange of culture and ideas unfolded over hundreds of years; the ancient monotheistic religion of Zoroastrianism is believed to have influenced Judaism, Christianity, and Islam. As eggplants, citrus, and rice made their way from China *to* Iran, apples, spinach, saffron, pistachios, and almonds made their way west to Europe *from* Iran.

Because of its fertile land and the power and wealth of the Persian empire, Iran was constantly under attack from foreigners, most notably Alexander the Great in 334 BCE, the Arabs in the seventh century, and later the Mongols in the thirteenth century. These foreign conquests of Iran meant that their food traditions, flavors, and ingredients were carried across the world, leaving their imprint on the cuisines of the Mediterranean and India. When the Arabs later conquered Sicily in the ninth century, they brought the eggplant, preservation methods for fruits and vegetables, and candied fruits, all from Iran. The Mughlai cuisine of northern India has its origins in the medieval conquest of Iran by the grandson of Ghengis Khan. These Perso-Indian foods of north India are redolent with ground spices, saffron, and black pepper, and include *kababs,* Persian lamb preparations, and rice dishes full of nuts and dried fruits.

Much of what we know about the roots of modern-day Persian cooking can be traced back to the Safavid dynasty's royal court cuisine. Two cooking manuals with recipes detailing the flavor-packed stews called *khoresht*, layered with luscious fruits, survived. Profusions of herbs, hearty vegetables, and legume-based *a'ash*, and slow-cooked *kuku* egg dishes, are chronicled, as well as the emergence of celebratory, extravagant rice dishes (*polo*) that made use of precious spices and fresh and candied fruits. Many recipes remain unchanged. Eventually, the cooking manuals and recipes moved out of the courts and into the kitchens of the common people. Shah Abbas moved the capital of Iran to Isfahan in the sixteenth century, placing it at the main crossroads of the Silk Road trade and securing a trading monopoly. He set up mercantile factories and commercialized the production of Persian rugs, which were traded to Europe. And he ushered in a period of glorious architecture. Isfahan's nickname became *"Isfahan nesfe Jihan"* ("Isfahan is half the world").

The ingredients and foods laid out in this book are found today on the *sofreh* in homes across Iran's thirty-one provinces and among many ethnic groups, both religious and secular. This cookbook does not attempt to categorize the regional foods of Iran, although many are respectfully mentioned. Many of the regional dishes I have included are expressed differently, from home to home—much in the same way you can knock on ten different people's doors in Italy and discover ten variations of the same traditional pasta dishes. Regional ingredients unique to the climate and topography and local customs of the people find their way into kitchens and preparations. These variations are, in my opinion, the mark of love by the home cook. Many of the recipes are from my home province of Isfahan. Other dishes I have cooked in my travels or have experienced in homes across Iran. I offer them through the lens of my personal experience; they reflect my taste and personality and have been influenced by my experience as a chef, cooking for my beloved community of guests.

Pantry

In Iran, the most magnificent homes in the centers of the old cities of
Kashan, Yazd, and Isfahan have modest exterior walls and humble wooden
doors. Behind the doors, however, are long corridors that lead to aromatic,
flower-filled gardens, with towering trees, reflective pools of water, brightly
colored windows, and intricate, brilliant tile motifs. Once inside these
homes, you'll find treasures and decor showcasing each owner's unique
sense of Persian culture, history, family, and tradition. Think of the seven
Pantry Essentials listed below as inviting and as easy to approach as the
humble doors to a mansion. Following that, you'll find an overview of
Other Items that lend authenticity, depth, color, texture, and layers of
flavors to my dishes—a robust "garden" of ingredients—and a hint at
what lies ahead. Once you journey into the pages of this book and explore,
chapter by chapter, you'll discover entire "rooms" of ingredients, such as
Dairy, Rice, and Herbs, in my house of Persian cooking, with several of
the spices and ingredients introduced here further spotlighted.

I love to think of you standing in front of my pantry door, saying,
"Let me knock and see what is inside!"

Pantry Essentials

You can purchase many of these pantry items at good markets everywhere.
For a list of markets specializing in the Persian ingredients mentioned
throughout this book, see Resources (page 317).

First, a note on oil and fat: I use light olive oil for sautéing onions and
herbs, and neutral oil, such as vegetable or canola oil, in those recipes that
require frying. I reserve good-quality extra-virgin olive oil for finishing
dishes and making Mint Oil (page 196). Clarified butter, also called *ghee*,
is butter from which water and milk solids have been removed, leaving
only the butterfat. I use it or melted salted butter poured over a rice dish
to enhance the flavor before serving. And I also use both salted butter and
neutral oil in baking and making sweets.

ONIONS *(Piyaz)* Onions are the number-one building block of Persian cooking, and at Sofreh I use more than two hundred pounds of onions per week. Onions have been cultivated in Iran for more than five thousand years. Wild onions thrive in the northern provinces surrounding the Caspian Sea; virtually every province has its own varietal that has adapted to the local climate. There are more than a dozen dishes in this book, and many more in Persian cooking in general, whose foundation begins with onions combined with turmeric. I use yellow onions in my kitchen. They are strong in flavor and firm, which makes them hold up to sautéing over medium heat until golden and soft, their edges gently browned. Every morning at Sofreh, I stand over multiple giant pots of onions, stirring so the onions don't burn. Your onions will take a much shorter cooking time, but give them great care and, in return, you will get great flavor from their sweetness. In addition to using onions in cooking, we use sautéed onions as a garnish, either leaving them soft and dark, or frying them until they are crispy and golden (see Crispy Fried Onions, page 194), depending on the taste of the cook. Iranians also love to eat small, raw, tiny onions with their meals, and for this I recommend cipolline onions because they are mild and sweet. I also use raw red onions, thinly sliced and marinated with sumac and salt, as a garnish or for stuffing in sandwiches. Grilled and raw, red and white onions are also eaten with *kababs* (see pages 151–157).

GARLIC *(Sir)* Garlic grows throughout Iran, and its cloves, leaves, and flowers have been used in cooking and for medicinal purposes for centuries. I use plenty of garlic cloves in my cooking, adding them to my base of sautéed onions. When I add them in large amounts, I stare at them, just like my onions, so they don't burn, but allowing them to take on some color and release their aroma. Crispy Garlic Chips (page 195) are wonderfully fragrant for garnishing *a'ash* (see pages 189–209). Pickled garlic, called *torshi seer,* is a delicacy; whole cloves age over months in a vinegar brine, growing mellow and sweet, before serving.

TURMERIC *(Zardchobe)* Turmeric is the root of the *Curcuma longa* plant in the ginger family, and is native to tropical South Asia, including southern India. The taste of turmeric is earthy, a touch bitter with a hint of peppery ginger. It's bright yellow and is often known as Indian saffron because India is its largest exporter. Turmeric also has a well-documented history of use for medicinal purposes, and its health benefits are reaching a wider audience; you may now notice it in its root form. When cooking with it, I use it as a ready-ground spice. Before using turmeric, you'll see that I refer to "blooming" it first in the bottom of the pot, always adding a bit of oil, so that it doesn't burn. When ground turmeric comes into contact with gentle heat, the heat brings turmeric's flavor and aroma to their fullest expression.

TOMATO PASTE *(Rob-e Goje Farangi)* Iran boasts plenty of indigenous fruits and vegetables, but for those that were introduced for cultivation from other parts of the world, such as *goje farangi* (tomatoes), *nokhad farangi* (peas), and the more recent *toot farangi* (strawberries)—introduced more than a hundred years ago—they carry the name *farangi*, which means "foreigner" in Farsi. During my childhood summers, my mother would make her own tomato paste, but nowadays, it is usually store-bought. I use good-quality San Marzano tomato paste to lend a deep, savory richness, described as umami, and color to the foundation of a stew or sauce.

SAFFRON *(Zafaran)* Saffron threads are the bright orange-red stigmas of the *Crocus sativus,* also known as the saffron flower. The crimson-red upper filament of the flower's stigma is the most prized part of the flower and the part that is processed and packaged for home use. Its flavor is earthy, musky, and slightly sweet. Currently, Iran is the world's leading producer of saffron, with cultivation occurring mainly in the northeastern Khorasan province. The labor-intensive production of saffron is in the hands of families of farmers who grow the purple-blossomed flowers and then painstakingly handpick the three stigmas that each flower yields. It takes the cultivation of about 150 flowers to produce one gram of saffron, making it, by weight, the world's most expensive spice. I use a lot of saffron in my cooking, but I treasure it and don't allow it to go to waste. Someone once told me that I am a "philosopher cook," meaning that my approach to how I live my life imbues my cooking. If I am, so be it. To me, every ingredient I work with is precious—from cheaply bought bags of potatoes or onions to "pay through your nose" saffron, each deserves care and respect.

SAFFRON WATER

makes ¼ cup strong saffron water

Throughout these recipes, you will find saffron water called for. Note that it needs to be prepared or "bloomed" before starting the recipe. To bloom saffron means to expose it to liquid, drawing out its optimum color and aroma before use. Saffron must always be bloomed from its powder form and never from its threads. Although you can buy saffron powder, to ensure optimum quality, I advise purchasing saffron threads and grinding them yourself into powder form using a small mortar and pestle. I prefer blooming my saffron powder over ice. It takes longer but better preserves the beautiful color and aroma.

¼ teaspoon saffron powder

2 ice cubes or ¼ cup (60 ml) room-temperature or hot (not boiling) water

Note Three to 4 tablespoons of saffron threads, ground in a mortar and pestle, will yield 1 teaspoon of saffron powder. I store small amounts of saffron powder in a mini marmalade jar in the freezer. Saffron water will hold in the refrigerator, in an airtight container, for about 1 week, so if you make more than you need for a recipe, you can save it for later use.

If using ice Sprinkle the saffron powder over 2 ice cubes and allow it to slowly melt at room temperature.

If using water If you're in a rush, place the saffron powder in a mug and pour ¼ cup room-temperature or hot water over it. Steep for 10 minutes until dark orange in hue.

ROSEWATER *(Golab)* The first thing you'll notice in an excellent-quality bottle of rosewater is its potent floral aroma. But taste it, and you'll discover that it is soft, clean, and delicately floral on the palate and not cloyingly sweet. Much of the production of rosewater in the world happens in the towns of Kashan and Ghamsar, both located in the north of the Isfahan province, where the warm climate and rich soil nurture the cultivation of roses. Farmers pick the roses first thing in the morning, before their powerful aroma soars away in the breeze. The cultivation of damask roses, the varietal bred for Iranian rosewater and the extraction of rose oil for perfume, reaches back to the Sassanid dynasty that ruled Persia for four centuries until the Arab conquest in the seventh century AD. In the tenth century, the medieval philosopher and scientist Avicenna is credited with inventing the steam distillation process of extracting essential oils from plants and herbs, among them rosewater. Rosewater has been used for cooking and for medicinal and cosmetic purposes, has been sold in the bazaars since antiquity, and has been traded along the Silk Road. When my beloved grandmother would kiss me good night after telling me a story and tucking me in, I could smell the fragrance of rosewater on her cheeks—she used it to cleanse her face—and it would comfort me. Although rosewater is essential in making sweets (*shirini*) (see pages 221–241), it permeates every aspect of my cooking. I add a bit of rosewater to my Saffron Water (page xxxiv) when garnishing my Saffron Basmati Rice (page 56) and even add a few drops over my stews before serving. Rose petals (*barg-e gol*) are decorative, and their aroma and beauty enhance sweet and savory dishes; I use them and rosewater spray (see Resources, page 317) for a special touch over Sofreh cocktails (see pages 295–311).

WHOLE AND POWDERED SUN-DRIED LIMES *(Limoo Amani)* Dried limes are made by boiling limes in a salt brine before drying them in the sun, yielding a hollow, hard, walnut-size fruit. They are an essential souring agent for our national stew, *Ghormeh Sabzi* (page 103), and many other dishes. They range in color from light to dark black, with the dark dried limes preferred because they yield a more intense flavor. Because Isfahan is located at high altitude, I am very mindful of the cooking times for dried limes and beans, such as for my *a'ash* (see pages 189–209). So, on that note, if you are also cooking at a high altitude, dried limes need to be soaked in cold water the day before; otherwise they will not soften. Also, cutting them in half with a serrated knife, or cracking them with a mallet, before adding them to a stew allows their flavor to be released. Dried lime powder makes for a good substitute when dried whole limes are not available. I use it in herb stews, as well as as a rub to lend a bright, tart flavor to shrimp (see Fish and Seafood, pages 175–187), and even a bit on the rim of a glass for a uniquely Persian spin on a margarita, called *Limoo* Mezcal (page 304).

Other Items

Spices

Persian dishes are highly aromatic. In my kitchen, as is tradition, I use prodigious amounts of warm, earthy ground spices and their seeds and bark. In addition to turmeric and saffron, I use cumin, cardamom, cinnamon, and the citrus zing of ground sumac throughout these recipes. The slightly bitter onion taste of nigella seeds, and mild nuttiness of sesame seeds, are featured on my breads, including Sofreh Bread (page 271). And hogweed seeds and coriander seeds feature prominently in pickling. In addition to these spices, I treasure the warmth of freshly ground black pepper, and I have a heavy hand with it. I understand that it can be off-putting if you're not accustomed to it, especially when cooking for younger kids, so, I have scaled back my typical amounts of pepper a bit throughout these recipes. As a general rule, regardless of the spice I am using—but especially with saffron, cardamom, and cinnamon—when I stick my head in the pot, I want to be enveloped by the dish's heady aroma. I do not buy prepackaged spice blends, called *advieh*. Instead, I buy my spices fresh and, where applicable, I grind them in a spice grinder. In addition to the aforementioned dried spices used throughout this book, red chili flakes are important in the flavor profile of southern Iran, where their dishes are spicy, and I use them in those regional dishes I have included here, where spicy heat is appreciated.

Fruits

As well as being aromatic, Persian cooking has a tart and sour punch! The role of fruit figures prominently in expressing the sourness we appreciate and crave in our food. Fresh fruit is abundant in Iran, owing to its diversity in climates. Our love for fruit reaches back to antiquity and forward to the modern day, with Iran currently among the top three producers in the world of pomegranates, watermelons, cherries, dates, apricots, and kiwis. While you wouldn't store fresh fruit in your pantry per se, the inclusion of both fresh and dried fruit in combination with meat in our one-pot, slow-cooked stews, or dried fruit in our rice dishes, is unique to Persian cooking. In addition to whole sun-dried limes *(limoo amani)* and dried lime powder, my recipes include the use of jarred sour cherries in syrup, as well as fresh sour cherries, when available. Fresh pomegranate seeds, tart apples, and sour plums are used, as are sour grapes in brine. Dried fruits, such as barberries, prunes, golden raisins, and dates, are called for in many recipes, and I love them. Candied fruits, such as Candied Orange Peels (page 53) and Candied Barberries (page 52), lend beauty and a touch of sweetness to rice. And I use blocks of dried, pressed tamarind to make a thick Tamarind Paste (page 181) for use in dishes that originate in the southern and eastern coastal regions of Iran.

In addition to cooking with fresh and dried fruits, we use fresh lemon and lime juice as souring agents. In Iran, a guy comes to your house with a few cases of lemons and limes and squeezes the fruits for you, so bottled lemon and lime juice are always at the home cook's fingertips. I call for store-bought bottled lemon juice throughout my recipes, for convenience mostly, because the amounts used range from ¼ cup to 1 cup or more, depending on your preference for the taste of lemon in your food. I also use fresh lime and lemon wedges for squeezing over my dishes for a touch of brightness. *Abgooreh,* a type of verjus, made from the juice of unripe sour grapes, lends a soft acidity. Fruit molasses or pastes called *rob* are widely used in Iran; the best known among them is pomegranate molasses. They give an incredible tart dimension to stews, the most famous being *fesenjan* (page 285). Occasionally, grape molasses and bitter orange molasses are called for.

A season's bounty of fruit is preserved in the form of *lavashak,* an Iranian fruit leather that is enjoyed for snacking, and in marmalades and jams (see *moraba,* pages 257–260), or in fruit pickles (see *torshi,* pages 247 and 251). For drinking, freshly squeezed fruit juices are extremely popular. So is the use of fresh fruit to make syrups as the base for nonalcoholic *sharbat* (see pages 295–301).

Nuts

Pistachios, almonds, and walnuts are a huge part of Iranian culture, and their flavor, variety, and beauty are incomparable. In homes, salted varieties of nuts to munch on are always on offer for guests to enjoy on arrival. Throughout this book, they also appear as integral components or garnishes in a multitude of forms—whole, crushed, ground, and slivered.

Flours

I use all-purpose flour and whole wheat flour for baking, and semolina or wheat germ for dusting when making bread. Instead of bread crumbs, I use chickpea flour as a binding agent for my tender beef *koofteh* (meatballs; see page 147) and *Kabab Shami Lori* (page 131) meat patties, because I love its soft, delicate texture. Chickpea flour and rice flour are widely used in Iran, and I use them to make my Nowruz cookies (see pages 239–241). And finally, salep, a powder made from the roots of an orchid, is used to give Saffron-Rosewater Ice Cream (page 231) its stretchy texture.

Legumes and Grains

Lentils are used in my *kateh*-style Lentil Rice with Dates (page 58), a simplified, homey version of the two-step rice-making process, as well as in thick, nourishing, legume-rich *a'ash* (see pages 189–209), where I also use bulgur wheat, barley, and a host of dried beans, which I prefer over canned; these include chickpeas, cranberry beans, yellow split peas, kidney beans, and mung beans.

Equipment

When I moved to New Jersey, I had a basic setup with one pot, one pan, and a single burner. And I turned out great meals, even hosting friends in my tiny apartment. You most likely have essential kitchen equipment at your disposal—plenty of towels and wooden spoons—but for cookware, I recommend good-quality stainless-steel, heavy-bottomed pots, and sauté pans with tight-fitting lids. For making Persian rice (see pages 45–83), I recommend an 8-quart (7.6-liter) nonstick pot and a large colander. A food processor is great for chopping large amounts of onions and garlic, but a good chef's knife is essential for chopping herbs by hand, so that I can control their size and texture. A standing mixer is used for baking. While I use a spice grinder to grind large amounts of spices at Sofreh, at home a small mortar and pestle is great. A *ghusht kub*, a traditional, wooden "meat masher," is referenced to render the uniquely stretchy texture of *haleem* (see page 23), and it comes in handy (see Resources, page 317). But you can just as easily rely on an empty wine bottle to do the job. And above anything else, I feel strongly that your nose, eyes, ears, and hands are your best kitchen tools.

Notes on Cooking with Me

First, trust yourself. As you read each recipe, employ your best kitchen instincts and judgment, and engage your senses. Second, and more important, engage your heart. If you can, thoughtfully and abundantly share what you make with others. For me, food doesn't make sense unless you tell me my kids are coming, or I am cooking for guests at Sofreh, or someone's friend or mother has passed away, and I need to make a food offering. Or, if you can, thoughtfully make food gifts to share with people. Whenever possible, use these dishes to spark connection and community; for that is at the heart of food for me.

And if you are not Iranian, along the way, ask yourself, Who are these people who make this bread? These stews? This rice? I share much about the people and places of my home throughout these recipes and stories. Use this book as a springboard to dig deeper and ask questions about the Iranian people, our food and our culture.

If you are new to the kitchen, I encourage you to set aside time to practice, at least in the beginning. Unless, of course, you are one of those people who jumps into exercise by doing one hundred push-ups a day. Wait, are you? If so, get a grip. When cooking a new dish for the first time, be patient. If you burn your *tahdig* on your first go-round, good job! Essential to deepening your understanding of cooking, regardless of the culture from which that dish originates, is trial and error. I will give explicit directions for each recipe, but at the end of the day, your mistakes have more to teach you than I ever can about cooking. Go and do it again. On the flip side, if your first *tahdig* comes out perfectly crispy, oily, and delicious and your mouth is swimming with pleasure, wonderful. Go and do it again.

And if you are an experienced home cook, and you've been feeding family and friends for years, I wish for the foundation of these favorite dishes to liberate you and be a source of inspiration in your kitchen, as they are in mine. Once you've gotten the hang of *kateh*-style Lentil Rice with Dates (page 58), start tweaking and changing it. Throw open your pantry to perhaps use mung beans, or how about black beans? They aren't even

Iranian—and that's good! Merge your own roots with the fundamental Persian cooking techniques that I share with you. I want you to see possibilities to create new flavors at every turn.

And finally, if you are Iranian, perhaps you'll experience a wave of nostalgia provoked by the tender beef, hearty kidney beans, and dried Persian limes of *Ghormeh Sabzi* (page 103). But then you think to yourself, "Hey! My mother never made *ghormeh sabzi* this way." To you, I say, bring me your mother's *ghormeh sabzi* so that I may taste it. Perhaps there is something I can learn. And then cook my *ghormeh sabzi* for your mother. Perhaps there is something she can learn, too! There is room for both in the world.

Garmi and *Sardi*

There is a traditional food practice in Iran that divides foods into two categories, *garmi* (hot or "warming foods") and *sardi* (cold or "cooling foods"). This practice has its roots in thousands of years of ancient medicine. It is believed that eating the right balance of each food type is optimal for your body's metabolic processing. Too much of one *garm* or *sard* food category in one sitting, such as a bowl of rice (cold), mixed with pickles (cold), and yogurt (cold)—which is one of my favorite snacks— may not be best for your health or temperament. As I was growing up, I always thought the food classifications were contradictory. And, when I began cooking for others, I didn't like telling people what foods they could or could not eat and in what amounts and what combination with one another. So, I don't subscribe to *garmi* and *sardi,* nor do I address them in my cooking. Instead, I focus on the inherent deliciousness of foods when offered together.

Measurements

I have provided both imperial and metric measurements for ingredients in each recipe. I strongly advise using the metric unit of the measurement supplied when baking bread and desserts, as metric measures are more precise, and precision is important when baking.

Layout of Chapters

Meals in Iran do not follow the familiar three-course dining experience of the Western world. From family lunches to casual dinner parties and celebratory wedding feasts, home cooks and hosts bring a chorus of dishes, in abundant portions, all at once to the *sofreh* for sharing. The earthy depth of fried herbs gives way to sour edges in our stews in each mouthwatering bite. But when further enjoyed with the coolness of yogurt, the tang of pickles, the clean crunch of fresh herbs, and accompanied by the airy lightness and fragrance of our rice, balance and beauty, texture and aroma are enhanced and revealed by the spoonful. So, in this book, you will not find recipes arranged as appetizers and salads, main-course proteins, vegetable sides, and desserts. Instead, I've placed the dishes in order of their importance—the ingredients and foods—on the Iranian table.

In the final chapter, called Sofreh (see pages 263–311), you'll see how the ingredients, foods, and traditions that I have journeyed with now provide the foundation of the new Persian dishes at my restaurant in Brooklyn.

And because her name is always on my lips when I speak of food, Iran, and my heart song of cooking, the words of my mother, Giti Joon, sometimes appear throughout *(in parentheses)*.

BREAD NAAN

When I was five, my father brought me to visit my grandparents on their farm in the small, lush, green village of Dehagh, about sixty miles from Isfahan. I remember the smell of refreshing, damp earth mixed with hay wafting through the air of their wheat field nearby. Also, I recall the taste of the tiny, sour Dehagh apples from dozens of fruit trees that filled their garden. The apples and the air are enough to nail down the fact that it must have been late July or August, nearing harvest time. There was a shed that they had set up under the shade of their grapevines to keep us cool from the sun, and a massive dog with matted fur running around that wasn't allowed to come into the house. Although, on second thought, he may not have been all that big. I was just so small that he *felt* so big. But for sure, I heard the squabble of chickens and the bleating of sheep. Because the sights, sounds, and smells of my grandparents' farm were so new and wonderful to me that first night there, I couldn't sleep a wink.

I tiptoed out of bed around sunrise the following day. Someone was moving around. "Khanoom?" I whispered to my grandmother. I saw outside that she already had a fire going, and her slight body was hunched over a clay oven baking bread. Her deep, dark, arresting eyes and her smile held me captive as I moved to sit beside her. Her beautiful face was framed by two long, thick, black braids that hung out of her perfectly white headscarf. I watched her poke at each piece of dough with a small stick, and then, as the loaves turned light brown and crusty, she pulled them out one at a time and stacked them up. As the stacks grew higher and their baked, wheaty fragrance grew more irresistible, my little hand reached for a broken piece of bread to taste. But before I could get a torn piece to my mouth, my grandmother held my hand back and instead offered me a perfect, unbroken piece, whispering, "Here, take this one. You are my guest, and only *the best* goes to a guest." I felt cherished.

Years ago, while researching the history of lavash, I came across a passage in a book describing how women from all cultures would keep a piece of dried-up starter tucked away, hidden safely in their headscarves. During times of war, they'd flee with their children and once safe, they would rehydrate the bread starter, and along with flour and water, they had food for their family. That image stayed with me, and I fantasized over the years that my grandmother was among them. Even though I know that she never kept her starter in her kerchief, to me she epitomized the life-affirming potential that is bound up in bread. And the quite literal power of a "mother."

NAAN IS THE PRIMARY PILLAR OF OUR CUISINE. THERE IS NO MEAL, NO GESTURE OF WELCOME, NO EXPRESSION OF LOVE THROUGH FOOD WITHOUT IT.

You'll find bread as the first chapter in one of Iran's oldest surviving cookbooks from the seventeenth century, but, of course, bread is not unique to Persian cooking. It has been the primary source of nutrition for thousands of years among all ancient civilizations, including the Egyptians, Greeks, and Romans. Because processing cereals and baking bread for sustenance were at the center of sedentary life, bread fueled the formation of societies and allowed them to expand and thrive. The intense labor involved in ancient practices of cultivating cereals and wheat laid the foundation for the more advanced agricultural methods that followed.

As much as bread has been placed at the center of every meal in Iran for centuries, so too culturally bread draws the line that divides the tasks of men and women. In my home, while Giti Joon would rise early to prepare our home-cooked lunches, my father, Reza Ali, would awaken just as early, do his stretches with military discipline, then set off on a walk to join the other men waiting in line for hot bread at the bakery. Perhaps it was the belief that the darkness of early morning was unsafe for women—or maybe it was because being a baker, just as being an *a'ashpaz* (chef), is a role that was traditionally for men. Perhaps the task of thrusting long, heavy, and unwieldy paddles of dough into brutally hot ovens was a show of strength that only other men, or boys, could appreciate. Regardless, my father would return home and wrap the bread in a clean kitchen towel for our breakfast before leaving for work. For my mother, cooking showed her love. For my father, heading to the bakery signaled his drive for life. At ninety-three years old, he still walked to the bakery each morning to buy fresh bread for himself and my mother.

And then there is the right of passage for boys who are sent—and the girls who send them—to the *noonvai* (bakery). One day, when I was a teenager, my mother put me in charge of preparing lunch. She left me money to send my younger brother Reza for warm bread, as is customary. So, with great seriousness about my task, I did my calculations and sent him off to buy three pieces. But when he returned home with less than two and a half, I was mortified. "We don't have enough bread!" I yelled. A woman who was helping us at home gently pulled me aside. "Nasim," she said. "Whenever you send a boy to the bakery, have him buy one extra piece, because they'll always eat some on the way home." That day, I learned an important unwritten rule. I mean, really, what was I thinking?

Because bread is central to every meal, we'd often have excess. And every Iranian will tell you that wasting bread feels like committing an eternal sin. It's virtually unheard of to throw bread away. After large affairs, such as weddings, when a ton of bread may be left over, it's donated to the poor, or bagged up and placed outside with the understanding that someone less fortunate can come by to pick it up and resell it. In my home, my mom would use leftover bread to thicken soups. And any dry, hard pieces would go to feed the fish in my father's pond. To this day, at Sofreh, if I drop a hot piece of bread while transferring it from oven to workstation, I pick it up, put it on the grill to clean it, and that piece gets wrapped up and comes home with me. Ali, my trusted chef de cuisine at Sofreh, after witnessing me do this for the first time, thought I was nuts. But for me, any ingredient, from the humblest crumb to the remnants of precious and expensive saffron that cling to the side of my grinder, has value. And I don't take it for granted.

"WHENEVER YOU SEND A BOY TO THE BAKERY, HAVE HIM BUY ONE EXTRA PIECE, BECAUSE THEY'LL ALWAYS EAT SOME ON THE WAY HOME."

To trace the history and evolution of *naan* through to today is the stuff of academic research. You'd have to sift through countless ethnic, traditional, local variations on the simple combination of flour, water, and salt, variations that reflect the merging of centuries of languages and cultures and local customs, to account for the differences in shapes, textures, colors, and flavors expressed from region to region. However, at the center of this bread map, four typical breads emerge from antiquity to modern-day Iran. They are *naan-e sangak, naan-e barbari, naan-e lavash,* and its smaller, thicker version called *naan-e taftoon.* In addition to these four breads, you'll also find variations of comforting milk bread, called *naan-e shirmal,* that is colored with saffron and slightly sweet in flavor. Each of these breads can be found in both urban and rural areas of Iran's thirty-one provinces.

Naan-e sangak is our national bread and is primarily composed of whole wheat flour and a sourdough starter. Its size is around three feet in length and one foot wide, and its texture is super crispy, owing to a wet dough method of bread making. The dough is so hydrated that bakers in Iran scoop it up with both hands before laying it on a flat peel, then slathering it with more water. They bake it in a wood-burning oven lined with river stones (*sang* means "stone" in Farsi). It's the hot water hitting the hot surface of the stone that gives the *sangak* bread its signature crispy bottom. *Sangak* is often sold plain or topped with nigella seeds. And it's this beloved bread that most often accompanies an Iranian lunch spread. The Sofreh Bread (page 271) recipe that I perfected with Ali is a unique bread with the taste of *naan-e sangak* and the look of the thick flatbread called *naan-e barbari*. Like my other collaborations with Ali that I celebrate in the Sofreh chapter (see pages 263–311), Sofreh bread belongs to the special world of Sofreh in New York.

In this chapter, you'll find my recipe for *Naan-e Barbari* (page 9), whose crispy exterior, soft, chewy interior, and incredible aroma make it a favorite bread to savor with Iranian Breakfast (page 17). On page 6, you'll discover how simple it is to make piping hot *naan-e taftoon*, either on your stove top or in your home oven. It makes a great sandwich wrap, or you can layer it on the bottom of a rice pot for a crispy *tahdig* (page 49). Or use it for sopping up the juices from a *Kabab Chenje* (page 156). My recipe for the lovely, lightly sweetened milk bread called *shirmal shirin*—*shirin* meaning "sweet" in Farsi—is a perfect afternoon snack with an aromatic glass of black Persian tea. And lastly, I've included my savory, cumin and golden-colored turmeric milk bread called *Naan-e Shirmal Ba Zardchobe* (page 14), my loose interpretation of a bread from the northwest part of Iran.

For years, my father, my brothers, and I were always searching for the chewy, dark variation with the sourdough taste and whole grain depth of my grandmother's bread. Instead, Khanoom's *dehati* (villager) bread belongs to the sunrise of that summer morning on the farm and the dawn of my life's purpose. The memory of the smell, the sight of her, and the feeling she evoked in me was *my* chapter one on my road to cooking. Because there is more to bread than its nutritional value, it was the spirit of my grandmother's bread offering that has guided me through nourishing my family at home, and my guests at Sofreh. "This is how we move through life, Nasim," my grandmother seemed to say to my five-year-old self. "We greet people eye-to-eye with our warmth and offer the best pieces of ourselves to them. We give them our sustenance. And awaken them to life with a feeling of love."

Welcome to chapter one of Persian cooking, my dear.

NAAN-E TAFTOON

makes 6 to 8 flatbreads

Naan-e lavash and its variant, *naan-e taftoon,* are the most traditional unleavened flatbreads in Iran and across the Middle East. In the past, rural home cooks used *tandor* clay ovens, either relegated to a separate room or built outdoors, to bake bread. Khanoom's "villager bread" that I ate as a child when visiting my grandmother on her farm in Dehagh was almost certainly her version of *taftoon*. Today, most people rely on commercial bakeries that specialize in making only one type of bread. For *naan-e lavash,* the *noonva* (bakers) slap the dough along the sides of the oven where it bakes up quickly, yielding a long, paper-thin, crispy flatbread. The significant difference between *lavash* and *taftoon* is the inclusion of yogurt (some traditions call for milk), which yields a thicker flatbread. Also, sometimes, I like to use a ratio of ¾ cup (100 grams) whole wheat flour to 3¼ cups (400 grams) all-purpose white flour for added nutrition. A mixer is not necessary to make this bread; you can just as easily mix by hand, if you prefer.

1 Dissolve the yeast and sugar in ⅓ cup (80 ml) lukewarm water in a bowl. Cover with plastic wrap or an inverted plate, and allow the mixture to foam, about 10 minutes. Add the oil and mix.

2 Pour 1 cup (235 ml) lukewarm water into the bowl of a standing mixer fitted with the paddle attachment. Add the yeast water and mix to combine. Sift the flour into the mixture, add the salt and yogurt, and mix on low (to avoid a mess of flour flying everywhere) until incorporated. Increase the speed to medium and mix until a soft dough forms, about 5 minutes.

3 Turn out the dough into a greased and floured mixing bowl, cover the bowl with plastic wrap, and allow the dough to rise at room temperature until doubled in size, about 1 hour.

4 Turn out the dough onto a floured surface and punch it down with your hands to deflate. Divide the dough into 6 to 8 balls, each about the size of a small orange, and place them several inches apart on your work surface. Loosely cover them with plastic wrap and a clean kitchen towel and allow to rest for 30 minutes.

5 Move the oven rack to the lowest rung and place a pizza stone or an inverted rimmed baking sheet on the rack. Preheat the oven to 500°F.

6 Working with one ball at a time, use a rolling pin to gently roll it into a circle about 8 to 9 inches in diameter. Sprinkle a pinch of nigella seeds (or your choice of topping), if using, over the top and use the rolling pin to press the seeds into the dough. Brush the top with a bit of water (this helps the

½ teaspoon active dry yeast

¼ teaspoon granulated sugar

3 tablespoons neutral oil, such as vegetable or canola oil

4 cups (500 grams) all-purpose flour (see headnote), plus more as needed

1 tablespoon kosher salt

2 tablespoons full-fat Greek yogurt, store-bought

Several pinches of nigella seeds

Several pinches of sesame seeds (optional)

Several pinches of dried or fresh herbs (optional)

Several pinches of dried or minced garlic cloves (optional)

dough get puffy and golden), invert it onto the pizza stone or baking sheet, and bake for 1 minute, or until bubbles form in the center. Flip and continue baking until the other side gets some color, about 1 to 2 minutes more.

7 Continue with the remaining dough balls, stacking the *naan-e taftoon* on top of one another and keeping them covered with a clean kitchen towel to prevent them from drying out.

Note Traditionally, every villager uses a bread pillow to help stretch their dough, and I like to do the same. You can use any small, round decorative pillow that you might have lying around (about 6 inches in diameter is best) and wrap it in two clean kitchen towels. Also, as an alternative, you can use a flat, round Indian *tawa* (see Resources, page 317) or a round cast-iron skillet to make *naan-e taftoon* on the stove top. Preheat your preferred pan over medium-high heat and, working in batches, cook the rolled-out dough for about 30 to 40 seconds, until bubbles appear in the center. Flip and cook on the other side for more color, about 30 seconds more. Transfer to a plate and repeat rolling out and cooking the remaining dough balls, stacking the *naan-e taftoon* on top of one another.

Nigella Seeds *(Siadaneh)*

These tiny black seeds, also called *kalonji,* come from the flowering *Nigella sativa* plant—native to Iran and other parts of Asia, the Middle East, and Eastern Europe—and have been used for thousands of years for medicinal purposes. When sprinkled on bread and baked, their essential oils release a warm onion aroma that fills your home. They are also used in making *torshi* (see pages 247–256), where they add beauty, delightful crunchy texture, and herbaceous, oregano-like flavor.

NAAN-E BARBARI

makes 2 loaves

Naan-e barbari is a thick, oval-shaped ciabatta-like bread that is proofed twice. The high water content of the dough makes the crumb soft and airy. Before baking, bakers brush each oval loaf with a flour and water glaze called *roomal* that gives *naan-e barbari* its signature golden, crispy crust. At bakeries in Iran, the bread can be sold either plain or topped with sesame and nigella seeds. I like to include the seeds for both aroma and beauty. I recommend using bread flour for a softer texture, so that besides enjoying this bread at breakfast, it will also be easier to slice open to hold sandwich fillings. It reheats nicely the next day, too.

Note If the same amount of all-purpose flour is all you have on hand, it will still give you a crispy outer crust, but it will not yield as light and airy a crumb.

Semolina or wheat germ
for dusting

2½ teaspoons active dry yeast

1 teaspoon granulated sugar

4¾ cups (600 grams) bread flour

2 tablespoons kosher salt

1 ounce (25 grams) room-temperature clarified butter
or 1 ounce (25 grams) Crisco vegetable shortening

Pinches of nigella seeds (optional)

Pinches of sesame seeds (optional)

For the *roomal*

½ teaspoon granulated sugar

¼ teaspoon baking soda

1 tablespoon bread flour

1 Prepare two 8½ x 11-inch parchment sheets by dusting them with semolina flour or wheat germ. Set aside.

2 Dissolve the yeast and sugar in 3½ ounces (100 ml) lukewarm water in a bowl. Cover with plastic wrap or an inverted plate and allow the mixture to foam, about 5 minutes.

3 Combine about 4 cups (500 grams) of the bread flour and the salt in a bowl. Using your fingertips, work the butter or shortening into the flour mixture until fully incorporated and the texture is sandy.

4 Add about 1¾ cups (400 ml) water to a standing mixer fitted with the dough hook. Add the yeast water, followed by the flour mixture. Knead, stopping often to gradually add about 6 tablespoons (50 grams) of the remaining ¾ cup (100 grams) bread flour to the bowl, about 5 minutes. (This is a very wet dough, so it needs a lot of kneading to develop the gluten.) Stop the motor, flour your hands, and shape the dough into a sticky ball.

5 Turn out the dough into a greased and floured mixing bowl, cover the bowl with plastic wrap, and allow the dough to rise at room temperature until doubled in size, about 1 hour.

6 Meanwhile, prepare the *roomal:* Combine the sugar, baking soda, flour, and ½ cup (100 ml) water in a small saucepan and cook over low heat, stirring occasionally, until thickened, about 2 minutes. Set aside to cool.

7 Move the oven rack to the lowest rung and place a pizza stone or 2 inverted rimmed baking sheets on the rack. Preheat the oven to 400°F. $\rightarrow$

8 When the dough has almost doubled in size, punch it down, transfer it to a lightly floured work surface, and knead by hand, gradually incorporating the remaining 6 tablespoons (50 grams) bread flour. Return the dough to the bowl, cover the bowl with plastic wrap, and allow the dough to rise for 30 minutes more.

9 After the second rise, gently remove the dough (so it doesn't deflate) to a lightly floured work surface and divide it in half. Shape each half into about a 13 x 7-inch-long oval. Use the *roomal* to assist in stretching and shaping the dough, working it evenly over the top, starting from the center and moving outward to shape an oval.

10 Transfer each oval to the prepared parchment sheets. Use your fingers to make 2 parallel lines of indentations down the length of each oval, sprinkle the top with a generous amount of seeds, if using, and slide the parchment sheets onto the top of the pizza stone (both should fit) or baking sheets. Bake until slightly risen and the tops are light golden and crusty, about 10 to 14 minutes.

SHIRMAL SHIRIN

SWEET MILK BREAD | *makes 1 large, round loaf*

Sheer is the Farsi word for "milk," and *mal* refers to the process of kneading. In almost every European culture, you'll find a sweet bread made with milk and eggs. The French have slightly sweet, rich brioche; Italians have tall, golden Christmas *pandoro;* and Greeks have braided, challah-like *tsoureki.* But instead of a fluffy, high-rise, or braided version, Iranians press down their sweet bread into a round circle. You can leave the top smooth or, to make it more interesting, in the final step, use your fingers to make impressions in it and add nigella seeds for a touch of perfume and spice to contrast with the bread's light sweetness. Enjoy for breakfast or as a snack with tea. See the photograph on page xlii.

1 Stir together the milk, whole egg, butter, and sugar in the bowl of a standing mixer fitted with the whisk attachment. Sprinkle the yeast over the top, cover the bowl with plastic wrap, and set aside for 10 minutes.

2 Switch to the dough hook. In a separate bowl, combine the flour and salt, then add it to the wet mixture in two batches. Knead until the dough comes together, about 6 minutes. Cover the bowl again with plastic wrap and allow the dough to rise at room temperature until doubled in size, about 1 hour.

3 Preheat the oven to 325°F.

4 Place the dough on a baking sheet, and using your hands, flatten it into a large, round circle, about ½ inch thick and 12 inches in diameter. Brush with the egg yolk, sprinkle nigella seeds, if using, on top, and bake for about 35 to 40 minutes, until the top is golden brown.

1 cup (235 ml) warm whole milk

1 large egg, plus 1 large egg yolk lightly beaten, for brushing

3¼ ounces (92 grams) salted butter, melted

½ cup (100 grams) granulated sugar

1 tablespoon active dry yeast

3¾ cups (450 grams) all-purpose flour

1 teaspoon kosher salt

2 tablespoons nigella seeds (optional)

NAAN-E SHIRMAL BA ZARDCHOBE

TURMERIC MILK BREAD | *makes 8 pieces*

This savory flat milk bread is my version of bread from the Azerbaijan province, home to a large diaspora of Turks, where it's commonly eaten for breakfast. It's typically called *komaj,* and you'll find versions of this bread that incorporate dried fenugreek, oregano, and other herbs into the dough, as well as variations stuffed with dates and tahini. I make it as a simple flatbread, adding turmeric and cumin seeds for color and a toasty, earthy flavor.

1 Dissolve the yeast and sugar in 2 tablespoons lukewarm water in a bowl. Cover with plastic wrap or an inverted plate and allow the mixture to foam, about 15 minutes.

2 Combine the flour, turmeric, and salt in a large mixing bowl and set aside.

3 Combine the egg yolk, milk, and 7 tablespoons (3½ ounces/100 grams) of the melted butter in the bowl of a standing mixer fitted with the paddle attachment and mix to combine. Next, add the yeast water and mix to combine.

4 Slowly add the flour mixture and mix until the dough forms a ball around the paddle. Transfer the dough to a greased and floured bowl, cover with a clean kitchen towel, and set aside in a warm spot until doubled in size, about 2 to 3 hours.

5 Divide the dough into balls the size of tennis balls, about 4 ounces (112 grams) each, and set them aside on a baking sheet to rest. Cover with plastic wrap, followed by a clean kitchen towel, for 30 minutes more.

6 Preheat the oven to 400°F.

7 Transfer the dough balls to a large, parchment-lined baking sheet. Sprinkle the cumin seeds on the balls, so they stick to the dough, and using a rolling pin, or your hands, flatten them to about ¼ inch thick and 6 inches in diameter. Use a fork to poke holes in the tops of the flatbreads and bake for 15 to 20 minutes.

8 Brush with the remaining 3 tablespoons (50 grams) melted butter before serving.

1 tablespoon active dry yeast

1 tablespoon granulated sugar

4 cups (500 grams) all-purpose flour

2 tablespoons ground turmeric

1 teaspoon kosher salt

1 large egg yolk

1 cup (235 ml) whole milk

10 tablespoons (5 ounces/ 150 grams) salted butter, melted and cooled

2 tablespoons cumin seeds

Baba's
Garden

I was in my father's garden,
when I savored, for the first time
THE BUTTER AND CREAMY CRUNCH
OF *GERDOO* (WALNUTS) from the tree that
stood majestically in the center. And in the
VEINS THAT RAN FROM STEM TO TIP
OF THE GRAPEVINE LEAVES, I SAW THE
CRACKED HANDS OF MY GRANDMOTHER
KHANOOM, AND TRACED THE ROOTS OF
MY STORY IN ITS VINES. I savored the
velvety tang of apricots, the tart of wild apples,
the orange glow of persimmons, the heft of ripened
pears, and husky mulberries called *shah toot,*
"THE KING OF BERRIES." They are deeply dark,
and juicy-sweet, and at their feet
my father planted rows of gillyflowers, and
hyacinth that by day offered beauty, and by night
released an intoxicating fragrance that blanketed
the neighborhood. "WHERE'S THAT SMELL
COMING FROM?" I heard a voice from
the street whisper. I had woken up and
tiptoed to the garden to breathe in as much as
I COULD BEFORE MORNING CAME AND
THEIR FRAGRANCE FADED AND
I LEFT AGAIN FOR NEW YORK.

Iranian Breakfast

Breakfast in Iran is best described as an event rather than a meal—you sit at the table at seven in the morning and don't get up for at least two hours! Warm *Naan-e Barbari* (page 9) is enjoyed with salty chunks of feta cheese, fresh herbs, summertime tomatoes, and cucumber. Or, in cold weather, handfuls of earthy, creamy black Iranian *gerdoo* (walnuts), and on special occasions, hard-boiled eggs. On the *sofreh*, you'll find rich clotted cream, called *khameh* (see page 41), and sweet *moraba* (jams and marmalades; see pages 257–261). On return visits to Isfahan, Giti Joon would set out big bowls of her homemade preserves, along with *khameh*. When the preserves ran low, she'd make more *khameh* appear. Then, as the *khameh* ran low, she would compensate by topping off the bowls of preserves until Akis would throw up his hands and cry, "No more!"

In the morning, with our breakfast, we drink our first and second glasses of loose-leaf *chai* (aromatic black Persian tea) sweetened with sugar. And as the day progresses, any occasion to sit with multiple glasses of tea served in transparent glasses (the better to see its dark red-amber color) follows: just before lunch, after lunch, after a snack, when a neighbor pops by, after dinner, and again before bed. And after heavier meals, a rock candy crystal sugar called *nabat*, saffron tinged or plain, is swirled into our tea as a digestif. When I began dreaming of a place to share Persian food and culture in New York, I initially wanted to have a little café in my East Village neighborhood where I could serve Iranian bread, Persian tea, pastries, and specialty cookies from home. Things didn't unfold as planned once I became a busy mother. But who knew that the seed of my idea would blossom into Sofreh? Even today, I still harbor a dream of opening a little spot where people from all walks of life can taste and enjoy the comfort of home-style Iranian breakfasts, drink tea, play backgammon, and hang out with friends.

PERSIAN STREET SMOOTHIE

MAJOON | *makes 4 servings*

Majoon, which loosely translates as "special," is an insanely thick, sky's-the-limit, thousand-calorie energy smoothie that hardly anyone makes at home. People will travel far to get their favorite *majoon,* waiting in line at juice bars as much for the entertainment of watching a laundry list of ingredients going into the blender as for the taste. My recipe is a light version that I used to make for my kids for breakfast. Add as many ingredients as you wish, but know that, in my opinion, a great *majoon* always starts with a base of dates, milk, bananas, and pistachios.

1 Place the dates and milk in a blender and mix until combined.

2 Add the frozen bananas, rosewater, and a generous pinch of salt and continue blending until the bananas are well incorporated. Next, add the yogurt, honey, walnuts, pistachios, sesame seeds, cinnamon, and instant coffee, if using. Blend until thoroughly combined and creamy.

3 Divide among 4 glasses, and if you wish, garnish with more pistachios, sesame seeds, and banana slices. Serve immediately.

8 large Medjool dates, pitted

½ cup (120 ml) whole milk

2 large frozen bananas, plus 1 fresh banana, sliced on the diagonal, for garnish (optional)

1 tablespoon rosewater

Kosher salt

1 cup (285 grams) Homemade Yogurt (page 32) or store-bought Greek yogurt

2 tablespoons honey

⅓ cup (33 grams) walnuts

⅓ cup (42 grams) pistachios, lightly ground

¼ cup (35 grams) sesame seeds, plus more for garnish (optional)

1 tablespoon ground cinnamon

1 tablespoon instant coffee (optional)

Walnuts (Gerdoo)

The Persian walnut tree (*Juglans regia*) is native to Iran, and its walnuts are beloved for their giant size, meaty texture, and incomparable sweet and rich flavor. Walnut trees grow throughout the thirty-one Iranian provinces, and only pistachios are more widely cultivated. We eat them by the handful for breakfast, and in combination with almonds, pistachios, and dried fruits, they are an integral part of snacking. Finely ground walnuts and pomegranate molasses form the base of the tart sauce called *fesenjan* (see page 285). Walnuts add texture, flavor, and body to everything from herb and walnut stuffings to egg dishes such as a Persian Herb Fritatta (page 214) or as garnishes for yogurt-based dishes. They also figure prominently in cookies, pastries, and sweets (*shirini; see* pages 221–241).

SPINACH "NARCISSUS" EGGS

NARGESI ESFENAJ | *makes 2 servings*

This dish of sunny-side up eggs nestled in green spinach is named for the beautiful paper-white petals, bright yellow corona, and green stalks of the Persian daffodil flower called *narges.* It makes a great all-day meal when paired with warm bread, feta cheese, and a handful of walnuts. I like to use curly-leafed, dark green savoy spinach for my *nargesi esfenaj* rather than flat-leaf spinach leaves, because savoy has a heartier texture that's better for cooking and a slightly bitter, earthy flavor that I love. Kale and Swiss chard also make good substitutes for savoy spinach.

Note If using prewashed, bagged, flat-leaf spinach leaves, they do not need to be precooked, and you may skip step 1.

1 Add the savoy spinach, ¼ cup (60 ml) water, and a pinch of salt to a pan set over medium heat. Cover and cook until the spinach wilts and is softened, about 10 minutes. Remove from the pan and strain any remaining liquid.

2 Meanwhile, add the onions and 4 tablespoons olive oil to a large, heavy-bottomed pot and sauté over medium heat, adding more oil if needed, so that the onions turn golden, their edges darken, and they soften, about 5 to 7 minutes. Make a well in the center of the pot, add the garlic and a bit more oil (so that the garlic doesn't burn), and sauté until fragrant, about 3 minutes more. Add the turmeric, a bit more oil, and stir, allowing the turmeric to bloom and release its fragrance, about 1 minute more. Set aside some of the onions for garnish, leaving the rest in the pot.

3 Add the cooked savoy spinach (or if using flat-leaf spinach, add it now), 1 teaspoon salt, the pepper, and a little more oil, and sauté until well combined and the spinach darkens in color, about 4 minutes. Taste for seasoning.

4 Create 4 to 6 evenly spaced wells in the pot, crack an egg into each one, and season the yolks with more salt, if you like.

5 If you prefer your eggs fully cooked, cover the pot, lower the heat to low, and cook for about 8 minutes. Or if you are like me, and like your eggs runny, continue cooking, uncovered, for about 4 to 5 minutes.

6 Serve the eggs garnished with the reserved fried onions, adding crushed walnuts and crumbled feta cheese, if you like.

10 to 12 ounces (283 to 340 grams) fresh curly-leaf spinach, such as savoy, washed, drained, and roughly chopped (see headnote)

Kosher salt

1 medium yellow onion, thinly sliced

Light olive oil

5 garlic cloves, very finely chopped or grated

1 teaspoon ground turmeric

1 teaspoon freshly ground black pepper

4 to 6 large eggs

A handful of crushed walnuts for serving (optional)

Feta cheese for serving (optional)

DATE SCRAMBLED EGGS

OMLET KHORMA | *makes 2 or more servings*

Iranians love dates for their sweetness, nutrients, and because they are rich in fiber, making them a perfect, wholesome snack. Pairing excellent-quality dates with soft and silky scrambled eggs enriched with a bit of cream and seasoned with the warmth of black pepper has been one of my favorite breakfasts since my mom's Shirazi cousin made this for me on a visit south when I was a teenager.

1 Add the onions and 4 tablespoons olive oil to a large, heavy-bottomed pot with a tight-fitting lid and sauté over medium heat, adding more oil if needed, so that the onions turn golden, their edges darken, and they soften, about 5 to 7 minutes. Add the turmeric, a bit more oil, and stir, allowing the turmeric to bloom and release its fragrance, about 1 minute more. Remove some of the onions to reserve for garnish, leaving the rest in the pot.

2 Add the butter, dates, and 2 tablespoons water (to help soften the dates) to the pot, and sauté over medium heat for 1 minute.

3 Whisk the eggs with the cream in a mixing bowl and add them to the pot, along with the salt and pepper. Lower the heat, cover the pot, and cook for a few minutes, taking care not to overcook the eggs.

4 Serve the eggs garnished with the reserved onions, and toasted walnuts, if you like.

1 large yellow onion, thinly sliced

Light olive oil

1 teaspoon ground turmeric

2 tablespoons (¼ stick/28 grams) salted butter

8 large Medjool dates, pitted and thinly sliced

4 to 6 large eggs

2 tablespoons (30 ml) heavy cream

1 tablespoon kosher salt

1 tablespoon freshly ground black pepper

2 tablespoons chopped walnuts, toasted, for garnish (optional)

OMLET-E GOJEH FARANGI

TOMATO SCRAMBLE | *makes 2 or more servings*

After landing in Tehran, Akis and I face a long drive home to Isfahan. On one trip, our driver pulled over to a favorite roadside stand to get us breakfast. He returned to the car with a panful of scrambled eggs in excessive amounts of butter and rich tomato paste, with fresh bread set on top. We were so tired and hungry, and the simplicity of using the bread to soak up all the juicy fat and fresh local eggs was so divine that to this day, the memory of that *omlet-e gojeh farangi* remains Akis's all-time favorite breakfast. While roadside cafés use tomato paste, home versions typically use fresh tomatoes. I try to capture that roadside flavor and use a combination of both. Choose a very large pan that leaves enough room for the fresh tomato juices to evaporate. And if you like, you may omit the butter.

Note Skin the tomatoes by blanching them, then transferring them to an ice water bath where the skins will slide right off.

1 Add the diced onions and 4 tablespoons olive oil to a large, heavy-bottomed pot and sauté over medium heat, adding more oil if needed, so that the onions turn golden, their edges darken, and they soften, about 5 to 7 minutes. Add the turmeric, a bit more oil, and stir, allowing the turmeric to bloom and release its fragrance, about 1 minute more. Remove from the pot and set aside.

2 To the now-empty pot, add the chopped tomatoes and cook over medium heat until the tomato juices have evaporated, about 5 minutes.

3 Add ¼ cup (60 ml) more oil, the butter, if using, and tomato paste, and cook, stirring occasionally, until the color of the tomato mixture is deep and shiny, about 2 to 3 minutes more.

4 Add the reserved onions and cook for another minute. Add the salt, black pepper, red chili flakes, and paprika, and taste and adjust the seasonings.

5 Crack the eggs into the sauce, but don't mix them. Just allow the yolks to set, about 2 minutes. If you start mixing the eggs before then, they will become tough, and the dish will look messy. After 2 minutes, gently break the egg yolks.

6 I like to turn off the heat while the yolks are still runny, letting the eggs sit in the hot pot for a few minutes before serving. Garnish with the hot peppers and serve with the sweet onions.

1 small yellow onion, medium diced

Light olive oil

1 tablespoon ground turmeric

2 pounds (907 grams) good-quality tomatoes, skinned and finely chopped (see headnote)

2 tablespoons (¼ stick/28 grams) salted butter (optional)

½ cup (112 grams) tomato paste

2 tablespoons kosher salt

Freshly ground black pepper to taste

½ teaspoon red chili flakes

½ teaspoon paprika

6 large eggs

Fresh hot peppers, your choice, thinly sliced, for serving

A few sweet onions, such as Vidalia, peeled and thinly sliced, for serving

BREAKFAST HALEEM

LAMB AND WHEAT PORRIDGE | *makes 10 or more servings*

Haleem is a thick wheat and meat porridge that dates from the sixth century. It's known as a farmer's breakfast because it's the kind of nutritious, high-calorie meal you'd eat the first thing on a cold winter's morning before a long day of physical work. I've made *haleem* over the years with lamb neck, for my kids' school events, but I grew to love making it with leftover turkey from my Thanksgiving get-togethers. It all started when Rozhia Tabnak, the interior designer of Sofreh and a treasured part of my family, began receiving fat turkeys as holiday gifts. The first time she brought one to me, I just stared at it; turkeys in Iran run wild and are skinny. I made it part of my Thanksgiving repertoire, along with my roasted leg of lamb (see page 141), but no one even glanced at it. Still, year after year, it was understood that Rozhia would bring me a giant, farm-raised bird to serve, and I would get to work, one year glazing it with pomegranate molasses (that at least elicited some compliments!). Inevitably, though, I would have so much leftover turkey that I figured, Let's make turkey *haleem*! Because a large pot of porridge requires an audience, I began throwing a brunch party, inviting everyone, again, back to my house the Sunday after Thanksgiving; after all, who really is in the mood for more eating on the Friday and Saturday following?

1 Add half of the diced onions and 4 tablespoons olive oil to a large, heavy-bottomed pot with a tight-fitting lid and sauté over medium heat, adding more oil if needed, so that the onions turn golden, their edges darken, and they soften, about 5 to 7 minutes. Add 3 teaspoons of the turmeric, a bit more oil, and stir, allowing the turmeric to bloom and release its fragrance, about 1 minute more.

2 If using leftover turkey meat: Place the turkey in a medium pot with a bit of water and warm through, over low heat, until it is soft enough to shred. Remove the turkey from the pot, reserving any liquid, and using two forks, shred the meat and set aside. Skip the next step.

3 If using lamb: Add the lamb to the onion mixture and sauté for about 5 to 7 minutes. Next, add 1 tablespoon of the salt, the cinnamon stick, bay leaves, and 4 cups (1 liter) water. Raise the heat to high and bring to a boil, then lower the heat, cover with the lid, and allow to simmer, about 3 hours, or until the liquid is reduced to about ½ cup (120 ml) and the meat is falling apart. The lamb will give out its fat while slow-cooking. Discard any fat rising to the top as it cooks. Remove the meat from the pot, reserving the remaining liquid, and separate the meat from the bones and remove the fat, if any. Shred the meat and set aside. →

2 large yellow onions, medium diced

Light olive oil

4 teaspoons ground turmeric

1 pound (454 grams) leftover cooked turkey or 2 pounds (907 grams) bone-in lamb neck

2 tablespoons kosher salt

1 large cinnamon stick (about 3 inches long)

4 to 5 whole dried bay leaves

1 pound (454 grams) extra fine bulgur

8 tablespoons (1 stick/112 grams) salted butter, cut into small pieces, for garnish

Granulated sugar for garnish, plus ½ cup (100 grams) for serving

Ground cinnamon for garnish, plus 2 tablespoons or more for serving

4 Meanwhile, in a separate large pot, add the remaining onions and
4 tablespoons olive oil and sauté over medium heat, adding more oil if
needed, so that the onions turn golden, their edges darken, and they soften,
about 5 to 7 minutes. Add the remaining 1 teaspoon turmeric, a bit more
oil, and stir, allowing the turmeric to bloom and release its fragrance, about
1 minute more.

5 Add the bulgur to the onion mixture and sauté for a few minutes.
Add 12 cups (3 liters) water, or more if necessary, to cover the bulgur by 3 to
4 inches. Add the remaining 1 tablespoon salt, bring to a boil, then lower the
heat and cook, uncovered, stirring frequently because the bulgur will stick to
the bottom of the pot, for about 1½ hours. The resulting mixture should
be more liquid than ready-to-eat oatmeal.

6 Working with 1 cup at a time, add the bulgur mixture to a blender and
puree until it has a farina-like texture. Repeat with the remaining mixture.

7 Working in batches, add the pureed bulgur, along with some of the
reserved shredded turkey or lamb neck, back to the pot with the reserved
liquid, and using a *ghusht kub* (see page xxxviii), or the bottom of a clean
wine bottle, mash to thoroughly incorporate.

8 Return the pot to the stove and cook over medium heat, stirring
occasionally, for 30 minutes more.

9 When ready to serve, make sure that the *haleem* is very hot. Transfer to
a large serving bowl, scatter some of the butter pieces on top, and garnish
generously with sprinkles of the sugar and cinnamon. Set out a small bowl
of the remaining butter pieces, along with more sugar and cinnamon on the
side, for guests to add, to taste. Some people like their *haleem* sweeter.

Alternatively I put very little salt in this sweet version of *haleem* because I
garnish it with butter, a generous amount of cinnamon, and sugar, plus more
on the table to taste. But you can also make savory *haleem*, if you like. Just
increase the amount of salt in the water to season the bulgur, and garnish
with fresh lemon juice instead of cinnamon and sugar. Also, feel free to cut
the recipe in half if you have a smaller group.

SAVORY BREAKFAST A'ASH

A'ASH SABZI SHIRAZI | *makes 6 to 8 servings*

We were once invited to my cousin's wedding in Shiraz in the south of Iran. Shiraz is a city best known for being the birthplace of the poets Saadi and Hafiz and for its public gardens that date back to the Middle Ages. So, we had poetry, the intoxicating perfume of flowers, and all the love of extended family and friends. And then there was my weary, jet-lagged husband, Akis. He had to stay behind for work in New York and flew into Tehran on the wedding day, only to have to rush and catch a flight to Shiraz to join us. And just when you thought the guy might catch a break, my cousin picked him up at the airport with a car full of empty pots. Before bringing Akis home to meet us, my cousin was in charge of collecting a type of breakfast *a'ash* called *a'ash sabzi Shirazi* for the forty family members who had gathered that morning.

A'ash is a one-pot meal with a texture between that of a soup and a stew (see *a'ash*, pages 189–209). Because portions for purchase at the *tabaakchi* (a take-out place for cooked dishes) are limited to one pot per person, my cousin needed Akis to stand in line with him. My cousin knew that if he brought a bleary-eyed Akis with him and announced, "We have a *khaarejee* here!"—a foreigner—the shopkeeper would bend the rules to have the pleasure of impressing and welcoming an outsider, offering up more than the normally allotted amount of *a'ash sabzi Shirazi* to buy. The *tabaakchi* owner sent Akis and my cousin home with plenty of *a'ash,* as well as a bag of cut limes, as is tradition. They know that no one is up to the task of cutting copious amounts of limes at seven in the morning.

The warmth of the lime along with plenty of black pepper are the signature flavors of this breakfast, as is the thick, stretchy texture that comes from the lamb neck. (If you can't find lamb neck, beef or lamb stew meat will also work well.) Years ago, I tried using a food processor or handheld immersion blender, and the results were disappointing. So, shred the cooked meat by hand for the best results—using a fork and knife to work the meat into small pieces.

To garnish, Crispy Fried Onions are on page 194. But here, you can sauté the onions instead, if you prefer, adding most to the pot and reserving the rest to top your *a'ash*. If you prefer a crispier texture to your onion garnish, spread the sautéed onions on a baking sheet and place them in a 350°F oven for a few minutes to crisp. Or, if you like, you can continue sautéing the remaining one-third of the onions for a few minutes more to allow them to get very crispy.

Note You will need to soak the beans for a minimum of 4 hours and up to overnight before making this recipe. $\rightarrow$

1 Place the kidney beans, white beans, pink beans, and chickpeas in a large bowl and cover with water by 2 inches. Soak for a minimum of 4 hours and up to overnight.

2 Add the diced onions and 4 tablespoons olive oil to a large, heavy-bottomed pot with a tight-fitting lid and sauté over medium heat, adding more oil if needed, so that the onions turn golden, their edges darken, and they soften, about 5 to 7 minutes. Add 1 tablespoon of the turmeric, a bit more oil, and stir, allowing the turmeric to bloom and release its fragrance, about 1 minute more.

3 Pat the lamb dry and add it to the pot with the onion mixture. Season with 1 tablespoon of the remaining turmeric, 1 tablespoon of the salt, and the pepper. Cover with the lid, lower the heat to low, and cook, allowing the meat to release its juices, about 5 minutes. Remove the lid, give the mixture a stir, raise the heat to medium-high, and continue cooking, uncovered, until the meat is glossy and any remaining liquid in the pot evaporates, about 6 minutes more. Add 1½ cups (360 ml) water, return the lid, lower the heat to low, and cook until the meat is fork-tender, about 1½ hours. Once the lamb is cooked, separate the meat from the bone and, using a fork and knife, shred the cooked meat, working it into very small pieces, and set aside in its liquid.

4 Meanwhile, drain the soaked beans and place them in a large pot. Cover with cold water and bring to a boil, then lower the heat to low and cook for about 1 hour, until the beans are cooked but still retain a bite. Season with the remaining 1 tablespoon salt in the last few minutes of cooking. Remove the beans from the heat and set aside in their cooking liquid.

5 Place the lentils in a small pot with a tight-fitting lid with enough water to cover. Cover with the lid and bring to a boil, then lower the heat and simmer until tender, about 25 minutes. Drain, rinse (so that the color of the water doesn't discolor the *a'ash*), and set aside.

6 Put the rice into a large pot and cover with 5 cups (1¼ liters) water. Bring to a boil over medium-high heat and cook until it is very soft, and the water is absorbed, about 30 minutes. Remove from the heat and add about two-thirds of the chives, reserving the rest for later, and the dried tarragon.

¼ cup (45 grams) dried red kidney beans

¼ cup (45 grams) dried white beans

¼ cup (45 grams) dried pink beans

1 cup (200 grams) dried chickpeas

2 large yellow onions, 1 medium diced, 1 thinly sliced on a mandoline

Light olive oil

2 tablespoons plus 1 teaspoon ground turmeric

1 pound (454 grams) bone-in lamb neck or beef neck

2 tablespoons kosher salt

1 tablespoon freshly ground black pepper, plus more to taste

½ cup (100 grams) lentils, rinsed

½ cup (92 grams) jasmine rice, rinsed twice

10 ounces (283 grams) Asian chives, roughly chopped

10 tablespoons dried tarragon

6 to 8 or more limes, cut into segments, for garnish

7 Meanwhile, add the sliced onions and 4 tablespoons olive oil to a large, heavy-bottomed pot and sauté over high heat, adding more oil if needed, so that the onions turn golden, their edges darken, and they soften, about 10 minutes. Add the remaining 1 teaspoon turmeric, a bit more oil, and stir, allowing the turmeric to bloom and release its fragrance, about 1 minute more. Remove from the heat and set aside.

8 Use a slotted spoon to reserve 1 cup of the cooked beans and set aside. Add the remaining beans, all of their liquid, the reserved lentils, the shredded meat and its juices, and two-thirds of the sautéed onions, reserving the remaining one-third for garnish (see headnote), to the pot of rice.

9 Cover and cook on low for 30 minutes, stirring occasionally so that it doesn't stick to the bottom of the pot, adding more water if necessary. Next, add the reserved chives, the reserved beans, and 2 cups (470 ml) water. Taste and adjust the seasoning, adding more pepper to taste. The texture of this *a'ash* should be like a thick stew.

10 Garnish with the remaining one-third of the onions and serve with lots of fresh lime segments and plenty more freshly ground black pepper.

DAIRY LABANIAT

I was around twelve when I made *maast* (yogurt) for the first time. I had watched my great-grandmother, Nane Joon, make hers numerous times with ewe milk, bringing it to a rolling boil and constantly aerating it with her spoon until it began to foam. She would cool it down and then temper a bit of existing yogurt from a previous batch with her boiled milk and add it to the pot before wrapping it and setting it aside. One day, she looked at me and said, "Your turn." And she left me alone, assuring me that I knew the steps by heart. I gently poured the culture into one corner of the pot; then, as I had seen her do, I wrapped the pot in a heavy blanket and proudly set it in the draft-free spot she used in the kitchen. The next day, when we lifted the blanket, only a little bit of yogurt had formed in one corner surrounded by a pool of milk! She smiled and said, "This is your first lesson in cooking: make mistakes and learn."

IT IS OUR DAIRY FOODS THAT CUT ACROSS RURAL AND URBAN ECONOMIC DIVISIONS.

During the first year of introducing a new audience to Iranian food traditions at Sofreh, I twisted arms to make people fall in love with freshly made yogurt—its richness and tang a world away from sugary, store-bought brands. Even with the selection of some delicious Greek yogurts on the market, I noticed that among my guests unfamiliar with Persian cooking, yogurt either was a breakfast food to be consumed with granola or, worse, a frozen dessert. Waiters tried to persuade people to include a side of *maast* as an essential accompaniment to the rice and meatballs that they were ordering. But early on, I realized I needed to take matters into my own hands. I'd offer my yogurt to these resistant guests on the house. Then once I delivered it, I'd remain by their table, gently guiding them, saying, "Put a little bit of yogurt in your rice, and taste it now." Once they did as I told them, I'd see a look of shock come across their faces. "Yes, now you understand," I'd say. And then I would turn up the volume on Googoosh, my favorite pop star from the pre-revolution 1970s, before moving on to the next table and the next. If you come to Sofreh to dine, I want to make sure that yogurt is invited to the party!

During these tableside visits, I'd spare my guests a dairy history lesson, preferring instead to let the immediacy of yogurt's pleasures do the talking. Still, it's incredible to think that for thousands of years, nomads in Iran have raised sheep, goats, and cows in cool mountain highlands and used their milk for drinking, cheese making, and later, for making yogurt. Historians believe yogurt making was, most likely, an accidental discovery that emerged from the practice of storing milk in flasks made of animal stomachs. The natural enzymes that remained in the flasks fermented the milk and yogurt was born. Later, long before refrigeration and industrial farming practices, when the natural cycles of animal lactation occurred in the spring and summer, the practice of fermenting whey to make a richly creamy, umami-flavored product called *kashk* became a method for preserving every drop of milk.

For centuries, most of the population of Iran lived in rural mountain areas; modern industrialization, however, led to population growth in cities. And it's our dairy foods that cut across rural and urban economic divisions, making them the second-most important pillar of our culinary canon. Today, regardless of income, every Iranian starts their day with the fundamental trio of bread, a simple white brined cheese *(paneer)* that resembles feta, and glasses of black tea.

HOMEMADE YOGURT

MAAST | *makes 6 cups yogurt, plus 1 quart whey*

In Iran, we exalt yogurt for the way it balances sweet and sour flavors, how it cools and adds texture, and for its nutritional value. And we have so many uses for it. We add yogurt to cooked vegetables called *borani* (see page 39). We drizzle yogurt over warm *Koofteh Ghelgheli* (page 147)—just one of so many soft, tender meatball dishes in our culture. And there is no better textural counterpart to a wedge of herby green frittata called *Kuku Sabzi* (page 214). We eat hot *kababs* with warm bread, raw onions, fresh herbs, and cold yogurt. And if being an essential condiment isn't enough, yogurt is integrated into food preparation, taking advantage of its lactic acid to tenderize proteins.

Before beginning, gather a thermometer for measuring the temperature of your milk and a large towel or blanket to wrap your pot with during the incubation process. Also, do not discard the "yogurt water" or whey, which I also call liquid gold. It's full of natural probiotics, calcium, and protein and is naturally fat-free. You'll be left with about 1 quart of it, and you can refrigerate it for up to 2 weeks. Use it as a stock for soups or make the Persian savory yogurt drink with dried mint and rose petals called *Doogh* on page 34. You can also use it to dilute your yogurt if you prefer it to be a bit runny or for making my version of *paneer Tabrizi* (see page 42).

And finally, while you can substitute low-fat milk for making yogurt, if you are going to go to all this effort, you may as well use whole milk to yield the creamiest result.

Note You can use any starter culture for your yogurt, including homemade yogurt or a store-bought brand. I like Fage 5%. Just know that the flavor of your yogurt will vary depending on the starter. To achieve a tangier yogurt, select a tangy culture, or increase the incubation period in step 5. I've kept mine for up to 16 hours.

1 Prepare an ice water bath by filling your kitchen sink one-quarter of the way full with cold water and plenty of ice cubes. Adjust the rack in your oven to accommodate a large pot.

2 Put the milk in a large, deep stainless-steel pot with a tight-fitting lid, set over medium-high heat. Bring the milk to a rapid boil, stirring continuously, so that the milk doesn't scorch on the bottom. Lower the heat, so that the milk doesn't spill over, and continue cooking until the temperature of the milk reaches 185°F, about 5 minutes.

1 gallon (3.7 liters) whole milk
⅓ cup (95 grams) Homemade Yogurt or store-bought Greek yogurt as a starter

3 Transfer the pot to the prepared ice water bath and, stirring occasionally, cool the milk to 110°F.

4 Add the starter yogurt to a mixing bowl and slowly whisk in about 1 cup (235 ml) of the warmed milk to temper it. Next, add the yogurt mixture to the pot and stir well to incorporate (don't just place it in one part of the pot!).

5 Cover with the lid, then wrap the pot in a large, clean kitchen towel (or blanket). I prefer to place the pot in the oven, with the light on, for a minimum of 9 hours or overnight, but you may also place the pot out of the way on your countertop, or in a cabinet.

6 The next day, unwrap the pot and transfer to the refrigerator for a minimum of 8 to 9 hours (for a thicker yogurt, refrigerate for 24 hours). At this point, the yogurt will have a thick consistency, but it will seep water, so before using it, I like to strain the yogurt. (Because I enjoy some unstrained, runny yogurt to eat, I reserve some at this point, before straining the rest in the next step.)

7 Transfer the yogurt to a piece of cheesecloth and quickly gather the corners and tie them together to create a cheesecloth bag. Next, tie the cheesecloth bag to the handle of a wooden spoon. Lay the spoon across the top of an empty pot, making sure it is suspended with about 1 inch of room to spare, so that as the whey drains, it will collect in the bottom of the pot. Alternatively, you can suspend the cheesecloth bag by tying it to your kitchen faucet. Place a container beneath it to catch the whey. For a very thick yogurt, drain for 3½ hours, or for a looser yogurt, drain for less time.

8 Transfer the yogurt and whey into separate airtight containers and refrigerate for up to 2 weeks (see headnote for uses).

DOOGH

SAVORY YOGURT DRINK | *makes 4 servings*

Doogh, derived from the Farsi word for "milking"—*dooshidan*—is a salty, minty, savory yogurt drink that dates back to ancient Persia. We drink it for wonderful refreshment on hot summer days and as a cooling beverage to wash down a heavier meal, especially *kababs,* and *Abgousht* (page 138). The authentic way of making *doogh* is to combine highly fermented yogurt with some of the drained whey. But you can easily create *doogh* with store-bought yogurt and sparkling water. The amount of sparkling water you add depends on personal taste, so feel free to adjust the ratio to your liking, making the *doogh* as watery or thick as you wish. Although you can use flat water, I prefer to drink my *doogh* with sparkling, because the whole point of this drink is its refreshing, fizzy bubbles.

1 Combine the yogurt, salt, and dried mint in a blender.

2 Pour the yogurt mixture into a large pitcher, add the sparkling water, and stir, adjusting the consistency to your preference.

3 Divide among tall, ice-filled glasses and garnish with fresh mint, if using.

2 cups (570 grams) Homemade Yogurt (page 32) or store-bought Greek yogurt

½ teaspoon kosher salt

2 teaspoons dried mint

2 cups (470 ml) sparkling water

Fresh mint leaves for garnish (optional)

SHALLOT YOGURT

MAAST-O-MUSIR | *makes 4 to 6 servings*

Musir is a wild Persian shallot that grows in the foothills of the Zagros Mountains. It differs from an American shallot, offering a more delicate garlic flavor. *Musirs* look like round, large garlic chips and are sold dried (see Resources, page 317). Once rehydrated, they are combined with yogurt and a bit of salt for this traditional dip or side dish. Dips in general always taste better stored overnight and enjoyed the next day. I store mine in a quart container to use throughout the week or, for a party, I serve it in a pretty bowl. If you wish, use this dip to accompany Sofreh Roasted Cauliflower (page 280).

Note You will need to soak the *musir* for 2 to 3 days before using it.

1 Soak the *musir* in 2 cups (470 ml) cold water and store in the refrigerator for 2 to 3 days until fully hydrated.

2 Drain and dry each chip of softened *musir*, cutting away any dry spots or stems that remain. Next, finely chop the *musir* by hand, as I prefer, or you may use a garlic press.

3 Combine the yogurt, salt, and *musir* in a mixing bowl, tasting and adjusting for seasoning. Refrigerate a few hours to let the flavors meld before serving.

1 ounce (28 grams) dried *musir*

2 cups (570 grams) Homemade Yogurt (page 32) or store-bought Greek yogurt

1½ teaspoons kosher salt

CUCUMBER and YOGURT

MAAST-O-KHIAR | *makes 4 to 6 servings*

Traditionally, sweet, crisp, tender Persian cucumbers are grated and combined with seasoned yogurt for this dip. I cut my cucumber into tiny, square pieces called *brunoise,* because they release less water than when grated, but I do use more grated cucumber as my garnish. If you like, you can also add garlic, as well as walnuts, to further enhance the texture and make the dip more special.

Note Of course, you can grate all of your cucumbers instead of dicing, but be sure to drain any excess water they release before combining them with the yogurt.

1 Combine the cucumber, salt, pepper, mint, and yogurt in a mixing bowl and mix well to combine.

2 Refrigerate for a few hours. Before serving, garnish with the garlic and walnuts, if using, and grated cucumber.

4 ounces (112 grams) good-quality small (about 4 ounces/112 grams) cucumber, such as Persian, English, or Japanese, skin on, finely chopped into square shapes, plus more for grating (see headnote)

1 tablespoon kosher salt

1 teaspoon freshly ground black pepper

2 teaspoons dried mint

2 cups (570 grams) Homemade Yogurt (page 32) or store-bought Greek yogurt

1 garlic clove, finely grated (optional)

¼ cup (28 grams) finely chopped walnuts (optional)

COLD YOGURT SOUP

A'AB DOOGH KHIAR | *makes 4 to 6 servings*

Similar to Spanish gazpacho, *a'ab doogh khiar* is a cold, blended, summer soup that uses yogurt and cucumber as a base instead of tomato. You can combine the cucumber-yogurt base with the mix-ins, as I have done here, or you can use my alternative method, which gives your guests the option of choosing those they like best. Either way, serve it with toasted bread or crackers for a snack or light lunch. See the photograph on page 28.

1 Preheat the oven to 375°F.

2 Brush the bread with olive oil, place in a single layer on a baking sheet, and toast in the oven until crispy, about 10 minutes.

3 Add the yogurt, salt, and garlic to a mixing bowl and whisk well, adding a bit of water to loosen it (but don't make it watery), then add the cucumbers, walnuts, raisins, dill, tarragon, basil, and mint leaves. Taste and adjust the seasoning.

4 Fill an 8-ounce (240-ml) glass with equal parts water and ice. Slowly add enough of the ice water to the yogurt mixture until it is the consistency of a thick soup.

5 Divide the mixture among 4 to 6 bowls, set some of the bread in each bowl, and garnish with dried mint and rose petals before serving.

Alternatively Combine the yogurt, salt, garlic, and cucumbers in a large bowl. Place a large, square ice cube in each of 4 to 6 bowls, as needed, and divide the yogurt mixture among the bowls. Garnish with the dried mint and rose petals, and set the walnuts, raisins, dill, tarragon, basil, and mint leaves on the table for your guests to add in as they wish.

---

4 to 6 pieces homemade or store-bought pita or *naan* bread, toasted

Light olive oil for brushing

4 cups (907 grams) Homemade Yogurt (page 32) or store-bought Greek yogurt

Kosher salt to taste

2 garlic cloves, finely pureed

2 large good-quality cucumbers, such as Persian, English, or Japanese, skin on, finely diced

2 cups (214 grams) chopped walnuts

1 cup (160 grams) golden raisins or small red raisins

3 ounces (85 grams) fresh dill, leaves and tender stems, finely chopped

2 ounces (56 grams) fresh tarragon, leaves and tender stems, finely chopped

2 ounces (56 grams) fresh basil, leaves and tender stems, finely chopped

½ cup fresh mint leaves

2 tablespoons dried mint for garnish

Rose petals for garnish

BORANI BADEMJOON

EGGPLANT YOGURT DIP | *makes 4 to 6 servings*

The name *borani* is often credited to the yogurt-loving Sassanian Queen Boran, who ruled ancient Persia for a short time in the seventh century. Through the centuries, *borani* evolved from a category of stews containing yogurt to the *borani* that we know today, which is a cooked vegetable blended with yogurt to make a dip. *Borani* are the perfect make-ahead bite for entertaining, and whenever I have guests at home, I always have a big bowl of my favorite seasonal *borani* (eggplants in the summer and spinach in the winter) with crackers for dipping, surrounded by a platter of seasonal fresh and dried fruit and bowls of salted nuts.

At Sofreh, I make a garlicky kale *borani* topped with toasted walnuts and barberries that my guests love. The trick is to sauté the kale with salt until it releases its water, then add the garlic and go for it—don't be afraid to get both the garlic and the kale charred, edges darkened and smelling intense. Then mix the garlic into your kale to stop the cooking process and cool it down in your refrigerator before mixing in the yogurt. The beauty of *borani* is that the sky is the limit for the number of variations that you can dream up. The idea is the same for all of them. The secret to a simple *borani* is to use thick yogurt; otherwise you will have a soup, not a dip. And, your *borani* will be all the more remarkable when you garnish it—even the simplicity of good-quality walnuts can elevate it.

1 Working with one eggplant at a time, trim the ends, peel the skin, then cut each eggplant into ½-inch-thick disks. Sprinkle liberally with salt and place the eggplants in a colander to release their water for about 1 to 3 hours. Meanwhile, if you haven't done so already, now is a good time to prepare the garnishes.

2 Pat the eggplants dry with paper towels to remove excess moisture and salt. Coat the bottom of a large skillet with a tight-fitting lid with ¼ cup (60 ml) neutral oil, or more as needed, and warm over medium-high heat. Place the eggplant rounds in the skillet, working in batches if necessary; gently fry until dark golden on each side, about 10 minutes per side. Remove the eggplants and set aside.

3 To the now-empty skillet, add the onions and 4 tablespoons olive oil and sauté over medium heat, adding more oil if needed, so that the onions turn golden, their edges darken, and they soften, about 5 to 7 minutes. Add the turmeric, a bit more oil, and stir, allowing the turmeric to bloom and release its fragrance, about 30 seconds. Next, add the garlic and a bit more oil →

4 Italian eggplants
(about 1 pound/454 grams)

Kosher salt

Neutral oil, such as vegetable or canola oil, for frying

1 large yellow onion, medium diced

Light olive oil

1 tablespoon ground turmeric

8 garlic cloves, finely diced

½ cup (112 grams) tomato paste

¼ cup (60 ml) bottled lemon juice

1 tablespoon freshly ground black pepper

1 teaspoon ground cinnamon

½ cup (56 grams) chopped walnuts →

(so the garlic doesn't burn), and stir. Add the tomato paste and sauté, stirring occasionally, until the tomato paste takes on a shiny color, about 1 minute more (the mixture will pull away from the bottom of the skillet).

4 Add the reserved eggplants to the onion mixture, along with ½ cup (235 ml) water, the lemon juice, 1 tablespoon salt, the pepper, and cinnamon. Cover with the lid and allow to cook, mixing occasionally and pressing down on the eggplants with the back of a wooden spoon so that they break up, become very soft, and can be easily blended into a dip, about 35 minutes.

5 Remove from the heat, add the chopped walnuts, stir to combine, and set aside to cool.

6 Once the mixture is cool, add the yogurt and mix to combine. Serve this dip warm or at room temperature garnished with saffron water, mint oil, and crispy garlic chips. Or, do as I prefer and refrigerate the cooked eggplant mixture for a few hours, then add the yogurt, mix to combine, garnish, and serve cold.

½ cup (143 grams) or more Homemade Yogurt (page 32) or store-bought Greek yogurt

Saffron Water (page xxxiv) for garnish

Mint Oil (page 196) for garnish

Crispy Garlic Chips (page 195) for garnish

PERSIAN CLOTTED CREAM

KHANEH | *makes 6 to 8 servings*

My first experience of tasting dreamy, soft, homemade *khameh* (clotted cream), along with warm bread and honey, was as a young child at my grandmother Khanoom's farm in Dehagh; it will be etched into my brain until the day I die. This highly prized breakfast item is sold everywhere in Iran, and as an adult, I became obsessed with it over long breakfast rituals at my parents' home. Over the years, I tried various methods to replicate the taste of *khameh* in New York. Finally, I settled on an English clotted cream recipe that may not look exactly like Iranian *khameh,* but it is close in taste—lightly nutty, barely sweet, and so rich it cuts like butter.

1 Fill an 8-quart (7.6-liter) pot with water (up to about 2 inches below the top) and bring to a boil.

2 In a medium bowl, gently whisk the flour and milk to combine. Place the cream in a medium pot, add the milk mixture, and set the pot over medium heat. Cook, stirring constantly, until very hot but not boiling.

3 Transfer the mixture to a 9 x 13-inch Pyrex dish and place it on top of the pot with the boiling water and reduce the temperature to a gentle boil. Cover any open areas on the sides of the pot with aluminum foil to trap the steam, and slowly cook the mixture, about 5 to 6 hours, until a yellow film begins to form on top. Throughout the cooking time, add enough water to the pot to consistently maintain a water level that reaches about 3 to 4 inches below the top. Be careful not to disturb the Pyrex dish, taking care to add the water to the sides, removing and replacing the foil if necessary.

4 Once the mixture is cooked, gently transfer the Pyrex dish to the countertop and allow to cool completely. Cover it with plastic wrap and place in the refrigerator for a minimum of 12 hours and up to 24 hours.

5 Run a knife around the edges of the dish to release the crust. Pour off any liquid that has collected underneath the crust into a container and reserve for baking or adding to soups. Fold the cream into a jar and refrigerate for up to 1 week. Enjoy with honey and marmalade.

1 tablespoon all-purpose flour

½ cup (60 ml) whole milk

2½ cups (600 ml) pasteurized heavy cream (not ultra-pasteurized)

FRESH CHEESE with CUMIN

PANEER TABRIZI | *makes 6 to 8 servings*

Near Tabriz, in the northwest Azerbaijan province, you'll find a highly prized regional *paneer* (cheese) called *Lighvan* that is difficult to find in other parts of Iran. It's a pressed curd cheese with an intensely sour taste and a distinct saltiness and aroma that is typically made on small farms with raw ewe milk, then brine ripened. I took inspiration for my fresh cheese from this *paneer Tabrizi,* adding the zesty warmth of toasted cumin seeds. My kids weren't fans of it. Later, when I brought my *paneer Tabrizi* to Sofreh for Ali to taste, he loved it, and we agreed that it's a great, "grown-up" cheese. And an easy one to make, too. Drizzle date syrup over the top, if you like, to take it to another level. Or enjoy cubes of it with Sofreh Bread (page 271) for breakfast.

Note Making this *paneer Tabrizi* is the same concept as making fresh ricotta cheese. My kids, Soshy and Noony, liked it better when I skipped the cumin seeds, and after draining the whey, I resisted pressing the curds so hard, leaving them softer, with a ricotta-like consistency. The kids enjoyed this spreadable version over toasted pita with drizzles of honey.

1 Lightly toast the cumin seeds in a small skillet set over medium heat, gently tossing for 1 to 2 minutes, until fragrant. Set aside.

2 Line a colander with a piece of cheesecloth and set over an empty bowl.

3 Bring the milk to a boil in a large stainless-steel pot over medium-low heat, stirring constantly. Once the milk boils, add 1 tablespoon of the salt and all the cumin seeds, and lower the heat to a gentle simmer for about 3 minutes.

4 Next, add the garlic, yogurt, and yogurt water, and mix gently. The curds will separate from the whey. Turn off the heat and allow to rest for 5 minutes.

5 Transfer the mixture to the cheesecloth and strain. Fold the cheesecloth over and place a weight on top to squeeze out excess whey and let stand for about 10 to 15 minutes. Reserve the whey for other uses, if you like.

6 Cut the pressed cheese to your desired shape—my default is always a rectangle because that's the shape of my storage containers. But you can shape it into a circle, if you like.

Note To store, add the remaining 1 tablespoon salt to enough cold, filtered water to submerge the cheese in an airtight container. Cover and refrigerate for up to 2 weeks.

2 tablespoons cumin seeds

8 cups (2 liters) whole milk

2 tablespoons kosher salt

3 garlic cloves, crushed

¼ cup (70 grams) Homemade Yogurt (page 32) or store-bought Greek yogurt

⅓ cup (80 ml) yogurt water (acid whey), or substitute ¼ cup (60 ml) bottled lemon juice

Kashk (Whey)

Kashk is a rich, salty, tangy, fermented dairy product with a terrific depth of umami flavor that is an Iranian pantry staple—it's also commonly used in Egypt, Uzbekistan, Turkey, and Pakistan.

It is a by-product of the yogurt-making process that evolved for milk preservation. Yogurt is slowly cooked until the liquid evaporates, and the resulting curds are used as a nutrient-rich thickener for soups or stews. In the past, the curds would be rolled into balls for further preservation, dried in the sun, and rehydrated for later use. Today, store-bought *kashk* is sold jarred as a thick, creamy liquid or in a powdered form (see Resources, page 317) that can be rehydrated. I prefer using liquid *kashk* in my kitchen, loosening its texture with a bit of water, when necessary, and always tempering it first before adding it to a hot dish. *Kashk* is used throughout this book as a garnish and as a base for Warm Eggplant Dip with Whey (page 117) and the quick, satisfyingly creamy Whey Soup that you'll find on page 44. I also use *kashk* to add a deeper flavor dimension to other dishes, especially pasta dishes or soups—the same way one would use Parmesan cheese rinds. And it brings homemade hummus to another level. Once opened, a jar will last you about 5 days, but you can freeze it in smaller portions for later use.

WHEY SOUP

KALÉ JOUSH | *makes 2 servings*

Kalé joush is a classic "pantry soup" that is made in variations all over Iran—think of it as a Persian version of French onion soup. The creamy *kashk* base and the addition of humble ingredients that everyone has on hand make it a comforting, quick meal served along with day-old bread or, if you'd like to make it fancy, top it with homemade croutons. Elevate this simple soup even further by garnishing it with mint oil, too, if you like.

Note Cook your onions slowly, allowing their natural sugars to be released.

1 Combine the *kashk* with 1 cup (235 ml) water in a medium bowl and set aside.

2 Add the onions and 4 tablespoons olive oil to a medium, heavy-bottomed pot with a tight-fitting lid and sauté over medium heat, adding more oil if needed, so that the onions turn golden, their edges darken, and they soften, about 5 to 7 minutes. Add the turmeric, a bit more oil, and stir, allowing the turmeric to bloom and release its fragrance. Add the pepper and walnuts and sauté for a few minutes. Add the mint and sauté for a few minutes more.

3 Add 2 cups (470 ml) water to the onion mixture, cover with the lid, and cook for 5 minutes.

4 Finally, add the reserved diluted *kashk* to the pot, mix well to combine, return the lid, and cook for 5 minutes more. Taste and adjust the seasoning before serving. Garnish with mint oil, if you like.

1 cup (235 ml) *kashk,* store-bought

2 medium yellow onions, thinly sliced

Light olive oil

1 tablespoon ground turmeric

1 tablespoon freshly ground black pepper

¾ cup (80 grams) chopped walnuts

1 tablespoon dried mint

Mint Oil (page 196) for garnish (optional)

RICE BERENJ

I found a tiny apartment in New Jersey within weeks of arriving in America. After a long day of school and work commuting to Queens, I'd come home to a single gas burner and one pot and pan. At times, I felt lonely and exhausted from working long hours. And the most accessible, delicious reminder of home that I could afford was rice.

The first time I went to buy rice at the supermarket in my new neighborhood, I thought I was losing my mind. The shelf of tiny boxes baffled me. They were totally at odds with the great sacks of Iranian long-grain, aromatic rice varietals I was used to—among them the intensely fragrant *Champa;* the long, slender, firm, and highly prized *sadri;* the short-grained *gerdeh;* and the smoked rice called *berenj doodi.* These were just the most popular of a dozen or more basmati varietals predominantly produced in the rice-growing regions of Gilan and Mazandaran and sold by the canvas bagful. Home cooks carefully inspected and respected the properties of each type of rice, knowing which to use to yield the delicate, perfectly separated grains for *chelo* and which would give up its starches for Saffron Rice Pudding (page 228) or *a'ash* (see pages 189–209). And there I was purchasing a small box of parboiled brown rice named after somebody's uncle.

What the hell is happening? I asked myself as I stood over my pot, watching the brown grains dance around in the water, unchanged in appearance and texture after what seemed like a lifetime of boiling. I was horrified. Although you can find comforting, luscious rice at the center of European and Asian cultures—from pilaf to risotto to paella and the endlessly accommodating fried rice from China—in Iran, we had for centuries raised rice cooking to an art form. And this Uncle Ben was failing me big time. It wasn't until many months later, when an Iranian woman I babysat for directed me to a Persian grocery store—and later to Pakistani and Indian markets in New York—that finally, gratefully, I got my hands on good-quality Indian basmati rice. Ah! So that's what they call it here. Basmati.

Iran's most basic rice preparation is called *chelo*. And its bounce-off-the-spoon grain separation and fluffy texture are one of our most important culinary gifts to world cuisine and an ever-present essential on the *sofreh*. The basics of Persian *chelo* involve a two-step method. First, good-quality long basmati rice grains are traditionally soaked, rinsed, and then parboiled in a large, roomy pot with plenty of water and salt until al dente—similar to the way Italians prepare pasta. Once drained, the parboiled rice, now arranged into a pyramid-shaped pile, goes back into the pot to steam. What emerges are fragrant, elegantly long rice grains with an airy texture that is unparalleled. *Chelo* traditionally accompanies our stews and *kababs* (see pages 151–157) and is topped with a bit of clarified butter to enhance its flavor. While you can further garnish *chelo* with Crispy Fried Onions (page 194) or Candied Barberries (page 52), it's commonly adorned with a portion of steamed rice removed from the pot and tinged with the earthy flavor of saffron for a burst of color before serving.

CHELO'S BOUNCE-OFF-THE-SPOON GRAIN SEPARATION AND FLUFFY TEXTURE ARE ONE OF OUR MOST IMPORTANT GIFTS TO WORLD CUISINE.

If you are well practiced in your *chelo* making, you'll render a perfectly compact, crispy *tahdig*, which translates as "bottom of the pot." It's a saffron- or turmeric-colored, crunchy rice layer that forms during steaming. The rice pot is either inverted to showcase the *tahdig*, or the *chelo* is separated for serving, and the oily rich *tahdig* is doled out in shards for sharing or fighting over. Although *chelo* has now become the iconic symbol of Persian cuisine, and the coveted *tahdig* has gone mainstream, the majority of rice production—and rice consumption—in Iran for hundreds of years had been largely limited to those northern wet lowlands near the Caspian Sea whose abundant annual rainfall made them suitable for rice growing. Instead, wheat was the staple crop in the drier, inland areas of the country, and bread was the food that sustained the average Iranian.

During the wealthy Safavid dynasty that ruled Iran from 1501 to 1736, a new category of rice emerged called *polo*. Royal court chefs began by taking the parboiled *chelo* a step further to reflect wealth and access to spices such as cinnamon and fresh and dried herbs; candied fruits, nuts, and vegetables; and fish and lamb that were prepared separately and added in layers to the pot during the steaming process. Two volumes of the earliest known cookbooks of Persian food have survived from the Safavid period. One of these, translated as *Manual on Cooking and Its Craft*, dates to 1521 and contains six chapters dedicated to the preparation of *polo* rice dishes. Over the course of two centuries, these festive and expensive perfumed fruit- and meat-studded *polo* creations, including Jeweled Rice (page 81), became the subject of travelogues from European traders and travelers who sought out the beauty of Iran's then-capital of Isfahan. But back in New Jersey, it was the no-fuss *kateh* that became the object of my obsession.

Instead of the more time-consuming rinsing, parboiling, and *then* steaming to make *chelo*, the rice for a *kateh* goes directly into a pot for an easy water absorption method followed by a short steaming process. I'd make an epic pot of *kateh*-style lentil rice about once a week, adding a few long, dark raisins called *maviz* that I had brought from Iran. A huge pot of lentil rice could feed me for days—I'd eat it with *torshi* (see pages 247–256) one day, spoonfuls of Homemade Yogurt (page 32) the next. Once I had access to good-quality basmati, the comforting goodness of home-cooked *kateh* in under thirty minutes was always at my fingertips. And with a whole host of affordable mix-ins available, such as black-eyed peas and mung beans, as well as a bit of beef or turmeric-scented chicken on the side, I soon felt happy and rich.

ALTHOUGH *TAHDIG* HAS GONE MAINSTREAM, FOR HUNDREDS OF YEARS, WHEAT WAS THE STAPLE CROP AND BREAD WAS THE FOOD THAT SUSTAINED THE AVERAGE IRANIAN.

During my second year in the States, a classmate from school invited me to her parents' home for a family and friends potluck Thanksgiving. It was my first, and I had my heart set on bringing something wonderful to the table. A quick look in my humble pantry and I was able to make *tachin* (see Saffron Yogurt "Cake" with Chicken, page 71), a baked rice bound with saffron, yogurt, and egg with a cake-like texture. Once inverted, the gorgeous crispy, golden-brown crust that forms on the bottom gets flipped to the top and garnished with a field of ruby-red barberries. And so I set off on a bitter-cold morning, a container of candied barberries tucked into my winter coat pocket and my heavy Pyrex dish pulled close, guarding it with my life. I schlepped my *tachin* through the New Jersey and New York transit systems to the Bronx.

When I arrived, my friend introduced me to a crowd of mingling guests. "Hello, I'm Nasim. Nasim. Na-seem." When I made my way to the kitchen to ask for a tray to invert my *tachin*, I noticed my friend's mom was overwhelmed, so I ended up hanging out in the kitchen to help her until dinner. Now and then, guests would pop their heads in: "Do you know where the forks are? The napkins?"

Once we finally sat down to the giant turkey, the likes of which I had never seen before, and the strange-looking dark, thick gravy beside it, I felt so out of place. But then I saw my *tachin* and was comforted. When my friend's mom stood to say "grace" and mentioned her gratitude for my helping hands, I watched as it dawned on everyone that I, too, was a guest at the party. And as swiftly as the conversation turned to Iran and my culture, each square of the *tachin* that I had cut into wedges was passed around and devoured.

I will leave you with this for now; no matter how fancy or simple a spread is in Iran, the last bite we reach for with our spoons is rice.

"Before You Begin Your *Berenj*"

Before you begin, consider the size of your rice pot and the colander you will use to drain it. I recommend an 8-quart (7.6-liter) good-quality nonstick rice pot with a tight-fitting lid. Because rice expands to about three times its volume when soaked and cooked, it needs ample space for parboiling. In Iran, we make big pots, so expect leftovers with these recipes.

While a nonstick pot will help you achieve a crispy *tahdig*, if you do not use one, line your rice pot with aluminum foil to make sure that the *tahdig* doesn't get stuck and burn on the bottom. Then, once you transfer the rice, you may lift out the *tahdig* by the edges of the foil. While traditionally rice forms the *tahdig* layer, in these recipes, you'll discover *tahdig*s made from potato rounds and leafy greens, such as kale, as well as bread, such as store-bought pita, *naan*, or homemade *Naan-e Taftoon* (page 6). While potato rounds are easy to dole out, I recommend cutting bread into portions before placing it on the bottom of the pot. I've learned that it reduces the risk of fighting over who gets the biggest piece of *tahdig*.

You may be familiar with the decorative fabric pot lid cover called a *damkoni* that covers your lid when you steam your rice. For some, *damkoni* have sentimental value and are often passed down for generations, with the steam stains to prove it. Save your money and wrap your lid in a clean cotton kitchen towel, and if one isn't handy, paper towels layered between the top of the pot and the lid work just fine.

Rice Selection and Preparation

Except for *tachin* (see Saffron Yogurt "Cake" with Chicken, page 71), each of these rice recipes calls for good-quality basmati rice. I use shorter-grain jasmine rice to yield the cake-like *tachin* texture, and for Saffron Rice Pudding (page 228) and in my recipes for *a'ash* (see pages 189–209). Often people ask what basmati rice I use, and I am not a brand pusher.

Instead, whatever brand you choose, smell your rice and make sure it has a pleasant, fresh aroma. Middle Eastern and Indian markets carry excellent basmati rice. Still, these days, you can find very good quality basmati rice for everyday *chelo* or weeknight layered-rice dishes, such as String Bean, Tomato, Beef Rice (page 62), at most supermarkets and Costco.

I recommend a more expensive, top-quality brand for rice dishes where you want each separate grain to express its most elongated, firm, and fluffy texture, such as Jeweled Rice (page 81) as a centerpiece of your Thanksgiving feast. Or when you want to impress someone with your mastery of Persian rice making. It may sound counterintuitive, but I tend to use a lesser-quality basmati rice brand for some layered, celebratory rice dishes, such as Herbed "Nowruz" Rice (page 74). I need the grain to relax a bit in the pot and give in to the moisture of the herbs layered between the rice. I've learned that excellent and expensive basmati rice grains tend to be very firm and won't yield the texture I want. Also, I always reduce my parboiling time by one to two minutes in those layered rice dishes whose components have a lot of moisture—such as Kohlrabi Herb Rice (page 76) and Sour Cherry Rice (page 67)—ensuring that my rice doesn't overcook while steaming. So keep that tip in mind should you explore other *polo* rice dishes on your culinary journey, outside of the ones you find here.

In a pinch, if you open your pantry one day to find that you have only jasmine rice or perhaps a short-grain Spanish rice on hand, you can still yield a decent Saffron Basmati Rice (page 56); just note that the cooking time will be shorter than recommended, and those grains will yield stickier rice.

I do not soak my rice. But I do wash it and then rinse it once before cooking. There is a great deal of controversy surrounding the method of washing and soaking rice for a prolonged period before parboiling, and many cooks in Iran swear by washing your rice until the water runs clear. I depart from tradition here, partly because I think the type of basmati rice available to us in the United States does not need soaking. But mostly because the prolonged soaking, rinsing, and boiling strips the rice of all of its starches.

I use kosher salt throughout these recipes to season my water before parboiling. As a rule of thumb, your rice water should be salty enough to season the rice but not as "salty as the sea" as when making pasta. With regard to checking that you have the correct al dente texture, pull a grain out of the water and bite into it. If you see a white dot in the middle, it is sufficiently parboiled.

And finally, if you are new to rice cooking, I recommend practicing. If your rice goes south, don't be miserable. You can, of course, cook it again—it takes under an hour. Or you can turn any overcooked rice into stuffed and fried rice balls or use it as a starch to thicken your soups. And, of course, you can always store cooled, cooked rice in a ziplock bag in the freezer for later.

Rice Garnishes

When I was growing up, preparing *polo* was still considered a luxury and rice dishes were made only for guests or on special occasions. Today, a quick online search for jeweled rice, carrot rice, and sweet rice (*shirin polo*) yields recipes and photos that are all, unfortunately, interchangeable. Each rice may have two types of nuts, barberries, candied zest, or even chicken added! Sometimes the ratio of rice to garnishes is almost equal. And it's not just a Western understanding of Persian rice; I have also experienced this sensory overload on return trips to Iran. Rice has, for centuries, been a mirror of sorts, reflecting the state of the Iranian people. And when I dig a little deeper, I wonder if current embargoes affect the price of rice in Iran to the point where home cooks and restaurants compensate for lesser-quality rice by overloading it with a ton of garnishes. Not to be preachy, but as a restaurateur who represents my culture simultaneously to both Iranian and Western guests, I feel responsible for reinstating the integrity of my culture's rice. Should you like to add any of these garnishes to your *chelo,* use them thoughtfully to enhance rather than overpower. Following are the master recipes for rice garnishes for candied barberries, candied orange peels, golden raisins, and cinnamon raisins, referenced in recipes throughout this chapter. In addition to these garnishes, I also recommend Crispy Fried Onions (page 194) for your rice. Just not everything all at once.

CANDIED BARBERRIES

makes 1 cup

Dried barberries must be soaked in cold water before using. Depending on the age of your barberries, increase the soaking time accordingly, anywhere from 10 to 25 minutes. But do not soak them longer than 30 minutes or they will get mushy. When you strain them, allow them to retain a bit of water. I like to have some moisture cling to them when they go into the pan (they will splash a little bit). Do not allow the barberries to come into contact with the heat in the pan for longer than 10 seconds or so; otherwise they will turn black or brown. And that would destroy their beauty.

1 Add the barberries to a medium bowl and cover with cold water. Soak for at least 10 minutes if they are very fresh, and up to 25 minutes if older. Strain, gently shaking, allowing for a bit of excess moisture to cling to the barberries.

2 Warm a medium skillet over medium-high heat. Add the olive oil, quickly followed by the barberries, and lower the temperature to medium. Give the pan a shake, add 2 tablespoons of the sugar, gently stir once to incorporate, and turn off the heat.

3 Scatter the remaining 1 tablespoon sugar across the barberries and set aside to rest. Just before ready to use, mix to incorporate all of the sugar.

Note Candied barberries can be stored in an airtight container in the refrigerator for up to 1 week.

1 cup (112 grams) dried barberries
2 tablespoons light olive oil
3 tablespoons granulated sugar

CANDIED ORANGE PEELS

makes 1 cup

In Iran, grandmas sit late at night making little strips of orange peel by hand. They remove the bitterness of the peels by soaking them in frequent changes of cold water. However, you can simplify the process by purchasing dried orange peels (see Resources, page 317).

1 Bring two small pots of water to a boil. Add the orange peels to one and boil for 5 minutes. Drain. Return them to the second pot and repeat, boiling for another 5 minutes.

2 Drain and taste a peel. If it is too bitter, bring more water to a boil and repeat the process a third time.

3 Return the peels to a pot. Add ⅛ cup (30 ml) water and the sugar and bring to a boil, thoroughly combining and stirring constantly, so that the sugar doesn't burn, about 5 to 7 minutes, until the peels are translucent and have a syrup-like consistency.

Note Candied orange peels can be stored in an airtight container in the refrigerator for 1 week or more.

½ cup (48 grams) dried orange peels

¾ cup (150 grams) granulated sugar

GOLDEN RAISINS

makes 1 cup

In addition to garnishing rice, these golden raisins are great to have on hand to add to your favorite salads.

1 Combine 2 cups (470 ml) water, the lemon juice, and salt in a small saucepan and bring to a boil. Turn off the heat and add the golden raisins. Cover the pot with a lid and allow the raisins to sit for 20 minutes.

2 Transfer the mixture to a container, allow to cool before covering with a lid, and refrigerate until ready to use.

Note Once cooled, golden raisins can be stored in an airtight container in the refrigerator for 1 week or more.

½ cup (120 ml) bottled lemon juice
1 teaspoon kosher salt
1 cup (160 grams) golden raisins

CINNAMON RAISINS

makes 1 cup

1 Warm the olive oil in a medium skillet over medium heat, until shimmering. Add the golden raisins and stir, coating them in the oil. Raise the heat to high, continuously stirring, until the raisins plump and begin to change color, going from light to darker golden, about 1 minute.

2 Remove from the skillet to a bowl, add the cinnamon, and mix to combine. Set aside until ready to use.

Note Cinnamon raisins can be stored in an airtight container in the refrigerator for 1 week or more.

2 tablespoons light olive oil
1 cup (160 grams) golden raisins
1 tablespoon ground cinnamon

Barberries *(Zereshk)*

Barberries are long, red, sour berries that grow on a bush plant *(Berberis vulgaris)* native to Iran, the Middle East, and North Africa. In Iran, the season for fresh barberries is very short, so in the United States you will find only dried barberries. Once barberries are dried, they are tiny, and they have a delicate, tangy flavor and dazzling ruby-red color that I adore. It's necessary to soak dried barberries for a bit to clean and plump them before using—they are picked from a bush that grows low to the ground and will inevitably contain a little bit of earthy dust. They are best when sold by a purveyor who keeps them refrigerated. You may keep dried barberries in the freezer, as I do, to extend their life and keep them fresh. When purchasing dried barberries, give the bag a gentle press to make sure that the berries are soft. Candied Barberries (page 52) are used as a garnish for Jeweled Rice (page 81), but can also be used to elevate Saffron Basmati Rice (page 56).

SAFFRON BASMATI RICE

CHELO | *makes 4 to 6 servings*

At Sofreh, if a guest neglects to order a side of *chelo* with their *Ghormeh Sabzi* (page 103) or Sofreh Rib-Eye *"Kabab"* (page 291) to soak up all the juices, you can bet that Amir or I will send one flying out of the kitchen, on the house, just so our non-Iranian guests can experience the incomparable taste of authentic Persian rice with their meal. I offer this saffron basmati rice for you to enjoy with every dish in this book where I recommend *chelo* for serving. Or, if you want to enjoy *chelo* as a meal in itself, add a fried egg, a swirl of yogurt, or pickles to it! Also, to help you create an excellent layer of *tahdig,* I've given a direction to mix yogurt into the rice, because it helps bind it, making it easier to get a crispy, compact layer. To flavor my *tahdig,* I use turmeric rather than saffron, because blooming saffron over heat causes it to lose so much of its beautiful aroma. Turmeric will give you a burst of color and a slightly nutty flavor. I save my precious and expensive saffron for making Saffron Water (page xxxiv). I combine the saffron water with a portion of steamed rice that I remove from the pot and use as a saffron-colored rice garnish, as is tradition, before serving the *chelo.* I take it a step further, adding a few drops of rosewater to my saffron water for enhanced aroma. I leave it up to you whether to separate the *tahdig* and serve it alongside the rice or invert the rice pot over a serving platter to show off the *tahdig* layer on the bottom. And if you are making *chelo* to show off your Persian cooking skills, why not garnish the rice with Candied Barberries (page 52)?

1 Place the rice in a large bowl, cover with cool water, and using your fingers, gently swish the rice around to wash it. Drain the rice in a large colander, rinse once under cold water, allow to drain, and set aside.

2 Parboil the rice: Add 5 quarts (4.7 liters) water and the salt to an 8-quart (7.6-liter) nonstick pot set over high heat and bring to a boil. Add the rinsed rice, give it a stir so that it doesn't stick, and parboil, uncovered, until al dente, about 8 to 10 minutes. (If you bite into a grain, you'll see a white dot in the center.) Next, drain the rice in the colander and rinse quickly with cold water to stop the cooking process. Shake the colander to remove excess water and set the parboiled rice aside.

3 Rinse the now-empty rice pot of any starch remnants clinging to the sides, and thoroughly dry. Pour the olive oil into the pot and warm over medium-low heat. Add the turmeric, give it a stir, allowing it to bloom and release its fragrance, about 30 seconds. Remove the pot from the heat. Add the yogurt

4 cups (740 grams) basmati rice

½ cup (144 grams) kosher salt

3 tablespoons light olive oil

1 teaspoon ground turmeric

1 cup (285 grams) Homemade Yogurt (page 32) or store-bought Greek yogurt

3 tablespoons Saffron Water (page xxxiv)

1 tablespoon rosewater (optional)

⅓ cup (80 ml) clarified butter or 4 tablespoons (½ stick/56 grams) salted butter, melted

½ cup (56 grams) Candied Barberries (page 52) for garnish (optional)

and 1 cup of the parboiled rice to the turmeric mixture, quickly stir until well combined, and press gently to the bottom of the pot for the *tahdig* layer.

4 Layer the rice: Using a large spoon, layer the remaining parboiled rice into the center of the pot, allowing it to land in a loose mound and forming a pyramid shape inside the pot. Do not press it down.

5 Steam the rice: Place a lid on the pot and set over medium heat for about 8 minutes, then lower the heat to low and remove the lid. Wrap the bottom side of the lid in a clean kitchen towel and place it back on the top of the pot. Cook over low heat for about 45 to 50 minutes. Meanwhile, prepare the candied barberries, if using.

6 Turn off the heat, partially remove the lid, leaving it ajar, and allow the rice to rest for about 2 to 3 minutes. Remove 1 cup of rice from the pot and mix it with the saffron water and rosewater, if using, and set the saffron rice aside.

7 To serve, gently remove the rice from the pot and transfer it to a serving platter. Pour the clarified butter or melted butter over the rice and garnish with the reserved saffron rice and candied barberries, if using. Remove the *tahdig* from the bottom of the pot and serve either on top of the rice or on the side.

Alternatively Place a 12-inch or larger serving platter upside down on top of the pot, hold the pot handles and the platter on both sides, and in one motion, invert the rice onto the platter so that the crispy golden *tahdig* is on top. Garnish the rice with the reserved saffron rice and candied barberries, if you wish, and serve.

LENTIL RICE with DATES

ADAS POLO BA KHORMA | *makes 4 servings*

Nine out of ten times that I make rice at home, it is *kateh* style. It's a style of rice cooking that originated in the Caspian rice-growing regions, where rice has been eaten for centuries at all three meals due to its widespread availability. While the wider Iranian palate appreciates the separated, fluffy rice grains of the *chelo* method, I love the comfort of the slightly sticky texture of *kateh*-style rice. And it has been for decades my one-pot, no-fuss meal to feed myself and, later, my family. As a working mom, I didn't have the time to go through the two-step method of making *chelo* every day. Instead, I would send the kids into the shower after soccer practice and within thirty minutes have a *kateh* rice with salad and yogurt on the table and call it a delicious and, more important, nutritious dinner. Because rice prepared in this way doesn't require the parboiling and rinsing of *chelo,* the grains naturally retain more of their starch.

The recipe that follows is based on one I made myself for years when I first came to the United States and later made for my kids. You can use golden raisins, if you prefer. Add them to the rice pot in step 3, around the midway point of cooking, before the rice has absorbed all of the water. Make a well in the center of the rice, bury the raisins, then cover with the rice and continue cooking. You can also create your own *kateh* rice variations by pairing it with your favorite legume or bean, such as black-eyed peas, or dried or fresh fava beans or sweet peas, along with fresh herbs, such as tarragon and dill, and a dried fruit, such as dried apricots or plums. Just adjust the cooking time accordingly for each legume. Add nuts, such as toasted almonds and pistachios, for a textural interplay with sticky, sweet fruit and your soft, delicate rice. Divine.

1 Bring 4 cups (1 liter) water to a boil in a 5-quart (4.7-liter) saucepan with a tight-fitting lid. Add the lentils, cinnamon, turmeric, and salt, and stir well to combine, breaking up any clumps of cinnamon. Cover with the lid, lower the heat to medium, and simmer until the lentils are cooked but still have a bite, about 7 to 8 minutes.

2 Meanwhile, in a separate saucepan, bring 2 cups (470 ml) water to a boil. Add the rice, cooked lentils, and enough hot water to cover the rice by 1 inch. Raise the heat to high and continue cooking, uncovered, until all the water is absorbed, about 13 to 14 minutes.

3 Reduce the heat to low, wrap the bottom side of the lid in a clean kitchen towel, place the lid back on the top of the pot, and steam for 10 minutes. Meanwhile, while the rice is cooking, prepare the onion and date mixture.

For the rice

1 cup (200 grams) green lentils, rinsed

2 tablespoons ground cinnamon

½ teaspoon ground turmeric

3 tablespoons kosher salt

2½ cups (300 grams) basmati rice, rinsed and drained

Drizzles of extra-virgin olive oil, ⅓ cup (80 ml) clarified butter, or 4 tablespoons (½ stick/56 grams) salted butter, melted, for garnish

1 cup (285 grams) Homemade Yogurt (page 32) or store-bought Greek yogurt for serving

4 Add the onions and 4 tablespoons olive oil to a medium skillet and sauté over medium heat, adding more oil if needed to cook the onions to your liking, making them as soft and golden, or dark and crispy, as you like. Or prepare Crispy Fried Onions (page 194) as a garnish. Remove from the skillet and set aside.

5 Return the skillet to the heat and melt the butter. Add the dates and cook until warmed through, about 1 to 2 minutes. Transfer the dates to the bowl with the onions and mix to combine.

6 As you are serving, spoon the onion-date mixture over the rice, in layers. Garnish with extra-virgin olive oil, clarified butter, or melted butter, and serve with yogurt.

Alternatively My kids, like everyone else, love a crispy *tahdig*. *Kateh*-style rice cooking will give a *tahdig* layer, though it may not satisfy that crispy craving due to all of the starches that collect on the bottom of the pot. So, try this: Just before the water is at the point of being fully absorbed, remove the pot from the heat and transfer the rice and everything you have added to it to a bowl. Give the pot a quick rinse and, to the same pot, add a generous amount of oil. Place the pot back on the heat, add a bit of turmeric to bloom, and then layer pieces of thin lavash on the bottom. Transfer the semi-cooked *kateh* rice mixture back to the pot, increase the heat slightly, and cover with the lid. Within this final steaming time of about 10 to 15 minutes, you will achieve an excellent rice *tahdig*. Do *not* use potatoes or pita bread, as they are too thick to cook in the window of time allotted.

For the onion and date mixture

2 medium yellow onions, finely diced

Light olive oil

2 tablespoons (¼ stick/28 grams) salted butter

12 fresh Medjool dates, pitted and diced

Dates *(Khorma)*

Dates, the sweet fruit of the date palm trees *derakht-e khorma,* have been cultivated and have flourished in the warm and dry southern provinces of Iran for five thousand years and are among its most prized fruits. More than four hundred varieties exist in Iran, but the most widely consumed and beloved are the fresh, soft and plump, dark Mazafati dates from Bam, in the largest province, Kerman, and the widely exported semi-dried Sayer date. Iranian dates are among the best dates you can find in the world, and they are perfect on their own when served as a snack with tea or made into Walnut and Date Cake (page 224). In addition to adding dates to rice dishes, smoothies, and eggs, they are reduced to make the thick date molasses (*shireh khorma*) used in baking, and can be made into a syrup for *sharbat* (see pages 295–301).

SOFREH CANDIED ORANGE and CARROT RICE

HAVIJ POLO | *makes 4 to 6 servings*

This sweet and colorful carrot rice is among the many celebratory rice dishes served at weddings. When we first introduced this rice to our guests at Sofreh, I wanted it to be really festive. So, I added both golden raisins and candied orange peels. But, I noticed that the raisins tended to get flattened and mushy. To solve this, I plump my raisins separately in lemon juice and add them to my rice after cooking.

Note Prepare the golden raisins and homemade candied orange peels up to 1 day in advance.

1 Prepare the carrots: Set a large skillet over medium heat and warm. Add the carrots and salt, and stir until the carrots release their water, about 3 to 5 minutes.

2 Add the sugar and stir; raise the heat to medium-high, add the butter or olive oil, and stir to coat the carrots. Continue cooking until the carrots are slightly limp but still retain a bite, about 3 to 5 minutes. Remove from the heat, add the rosewater, and set aside. Allow the mixture to cool at room temperature, then add ¼ cup (20 grams) of the candied orange peels (reserving the remaining orange peels for garnish).

3 Place the rice in a large bowl, cover with cool water, and using your fingers, gently swish it around to wash it. Use a large colander to drain, then rinse the rice once under cold water, drain, and set aside.

4 Parboil the rice: Add 5 quarts (4.7 liters) water and the salt to an 8-quart (7.6-liter) nonstick pot set over high heat and bring to a boil. Add the rinsed rice, give it a stir so that it doesn't stick, and parboil, uncovered, until al dente, about 8 to 10 minutes. (If you bite into a grain, you'll see a white dot in the center.) Next, drain the rice in the colander and rinse quickly with cold water to stop the cooking process. Shake the colander to remove excess water and set the parboiled rice aside.

5 Rinse the now-empty rice pot of any starch remnants clinging to the sides and thoroughly dry. Add the olive oil to the pot and layer the pita bread pieces or carrot coins on the bottom of the pot for the *tahdig*.

6 Layer the rice: Using a large spoon, layer about 2 cups of the rice over the *tahdig* layer to make a small mound in the center of the pot. Next, add a generous spoonful of the carrot mixture over the rice. Continue the process

For the carrots

1 pound (454 grams) carrots, cut into matchsticks or shredded on a box grater

Pinch of kosher salt

½ cup (100 grams) granulated sugar

4 tablespoons (½ stick/56 grams) salted butter or ¼ cup (60 ml) light olive oil

1 tablespoon rosewater

½ cup (40 grams) Candied Orange Peels (page 53), homemade or store-bought

For the rice and *tahdig*

4 cups (740 grams) basmati rice

½ cup (144 grams) kosher salt

¼ cup (60 ml) light olive oil

1 large store-bought pita bread, cut into wedges, or store-bought carrot coins

3 tablespoons Saffron Water (page xxxiv)

⅓ cup (80 ml) clarified butter or 4 tablespoons (½ stick/56 grams) salted butter, melted

1 cup (160 grams) Golden Raisins (page 54)

of layering, alternating the rice and the carrot mixture, building a pyramid-shaped mound in the pot as you layer.

7 Steam the rice: Place a lid on the pot and set over medium heat for about 8 minutes, then lower the heat to low and remove the lid. Wrap the bottom side of the lid in a clean kitchen towel and place the lid back on the top of the pot. Cook on low heat for 30 minutes.

8 Turn off the heat, partially remove the lid, leaving it ajar, and allow the rice to rest for about 2 to 3 minutes. Remove 1 cup of rice from the pot and combine it in a small bowl with the saffron water. Set the saffron rice aside.

9 To serve, remove the lid and pour the clarified butter or melted butter over the remaining rice in the pot. Gently transfer the rice to a serving platter, garnish with the remaining candied orange peels and the golden raisins, and top with the reserved cup of saffron rice. Remove the *tahdig* from the bottom of the pot and serve either on top of the rice or on the side.

STRING BEAN, TOMATO, BEEF RICE

LOOBIA POLO | *makes 6 to 8 servings*

Because this rice dish is layered with a thick, aromatic, cinnamon-infused tomato, meat, and vegetable sauce, it's a complete meal—and a satisfying family favorite in my house. I often make *loobia polo* when string beans are summer-fresh, preferring the thick, farmers' market varieties to the longer, thinner French beans for this dish. Like any layered rice with tomato in it, the sugars in the tomatoey rice *tahdig* on the bottom of the pot can quickly burn. I like that overcaramelized browned part in my rice, but to be practical, when I make layered rice that incorporates a tomato-based sauce, I use a layer of potato rounds on the bottom to create a crunchy potato *tahdig* instead. Plus, potato rounds are easy to dole out because you can allocate the number of potatoes everyone gets! You may prepare *loobia polo* with delicious cubes of lamb shoulder instead of beef, if you like.

1 Prepare the sauce: Add the onions and 4 tablespoons olive oil to a large, heavy-bottomed pot with a tight-fitting lid and sauté over medium heat, adding more oil if needed, so that the onions turn golden, their edges darken, and they soften, about 5 to 7 minutes. Add the turmeric, a bit more oil, and stir, allowing the turmeric to bloom and release its fragrance, about 1 minute more.

2 Add the beef, a generous pinch of salt, and the pepper, and then lower the heat to medium. Continue simmering until the meat releases its juices and the liquid starts to evaporate, about 5 minutes.

3 Next, add the tomato paste and stir until it is incorporated, then deglaze the pan with the lemon juice, scraping up any stuck bits of meat on the bottom. Add 1 cup (235 ml) water, the sugar, and cinnamon stick, and stir. Cover the pot with the lid and bring to a boil, then lower the heat to low and cook until the meat is almost cooked but is still a little tough, about 45 minutes.

4 Taste and adjust the sauce for seasoning, add the green beans, cover, and continue cooking until the green beans and beef are tender, and the sauce thickens, about 15 to 20 minutes. Turn off the heat, fish out the cinnamon stick, and set the mixture aside.

For the sauce

1 large yellow onion, finely diced

Light olive oil

2 tablespoons ground turmeric

1 pound (454 grams) beef chuck, cut into about 1-inch cubes

Kosher salt as needed

1 tablespoon freshly ground black pepper, plus more as needed

¾ cup (170 grams) tomato paste

⅓ cup (80 ml) bottled lemon juice

2 teaspoons granulated sugar

1 cinnamon stick (2 inches long)

1 pound (454 grams) fresh green beans, ends trimmed, cut into ¾-inch pieces

5 Meanwhile, while the sauce is cooking, prepare the rice: Combine 4 cups (1 liter) water and ¼ cup (72 grams) of the salt in a medium bowl. Peel and slice the potatoes into ¼-inch-thick rounds. Don't slice them too thin or they may stick to the bottom of the pot. Soak the potatoes for 30 minutes.

6 Place the rice in a large bowl, cover with cool water, and using your fingers, gently swish it around to wash it. Use a large colander to drain, then rinse the rice once under cold water, drain, and set aside.

7 Parboil the rice: Add 5 quarts (4.7 liters) water and ½ cup (144 grams) of the remaining salt to an 8-quart (7.6-liter) nonstick pot set over high heat and bring to a boil. Add the rinsed rice, give it a stir so that it doesn't stick, and parboil, uncovered, until al dente, about 6 to 8 minutes. (If you bite into a grain, you'll see a white dot in the center.) Next, drain the rice in the colander and rinse quickly with cold water to stop the cooking process. Shake the colander to remove excess water and set the parboiled rice aside.

8 Rinse the now-empty rice pot of any starch remnants clinging to the sides, and thoroughly dry. Drain the reserved potatoes, pat them dry, and season generously on both sides with the remaining 1½ teaspoons salt. Add the olive oil to your now-empty rice pot and place it over medium heat. Place the potato rounds in a single layer on the bottom of the pot, without overlapping or touching, and allow them to warm and sizzle for 1 minute. Remove the pot from the heat.

9 Layer the rice: Using a large spoon, layer about 2 cups of the parboiled rice over the potato layer, adding enough to make a small mound in the center of the pot. Using the same spoon, add a generous spoonful of the cooked green bean and beef sauce over the rice, focusing on the center of the mound, and sprinkle with the 1 tablespoon cinnamon. Continue the process of layering the rice, the sauce, and more large pinches of cinnamon, building a pyramid-shaped mound in the pot as you layer.

10 Steam the rice: Place a lid on the pot and set over medium heat for about 8 minutes, then lower the heat to low and remove the lid. Wrap the bottom side of the lid in a clean kitchen towel and place it back on the top of the pot. Cook on medium-low heat for 50 minutes.

11 Turn off the heat and allow the rice to sit for about 2 to 3 minutes with the lid ajar. Do not allow the rice to sit longer, as this will cause the potato *tahdig* to get soggy. Gently remove the rice from the pot and transfer to a serving platter. Remove the *tahdig* from the bottom of the pot and serve either on top of the rice or on the side. To enhance flavor, prior to serving, pour the clarified butter or melted butter over the rice.

For the rice

¾ cup (216 grams) plus 1½ teaspoons kosher salt

2 medium russet potatoes

4 cups (740 grams) basmati rice

3 tablespoons light olive oil

1 tablespoon freshly ground cinnamon, plus more as needed

⅓ cup (80 ml) clarified butter or 4 tablespoons (½ stick/56 grams) salted butter, melted

SPICY SHRIMP RICE

MAYGOU POLO | *makes 4 to 6 servings*

Maygou polo originates in the province of Bushehr, near the Persian Gulf, where the almost six-hundred-mile coastline is home to ten surrounding port cities that all claim that their version of this shrimp rice is best. Some cooks use more tomato and less tamarind, others add saffron and turmeric; some use more herbs or fewer herbs; others add potato; and some layer their large prawns (*maygou*) into the rice. I don't like the strong smell of shrimp to permeate the rice and compete with the fenugreek and tamarind sauce flavors, so I serve large (22/25) shrimp alongside the rice.

Note When purchasing shrimp, their size is determined by the number of shrimp it takes to compose about 1 pound.

For the tamarind sauce

1 large yellow onion, medium diced

Light olive oil

10 garlic cloves, roughly chopped

1 tablespoon ground turmeric

½ teaspoon red chili flakes

10 ounces (283 grams) fresh cilantro, leaves and tender stems, finely chopped

5 ounces (142 grams) fresh flat-leaf parsley, leaves and tender stems, finely chopped

4 ounces (112 grams) fresh fenugreek leaves, finely chopped, or ¼ cup dried fenugreek

1 cup thick Tamarind Paste (page 181), homemade or store-bought

2 tablespoons tomato paste

1 tablespoon kosher salt, or more to taste

2 to 3 tablespoons granulated sugar, or more to taste $\longrightarrow$

1 Make the tamarind sauce: Add the onions and 4 tablespoons olive oil to a large, heavy-bottomed skillet and sauté over medium-high heat, adding more oil if needed, so that the onions turn golden, their edges darken, and they soften, about 5 to 7 minutes. Make a well in the center of the skillet, add the garlic and a bit more oil (so that the garlic doesn't burn), and sauté until fragrant, about 3 minutes more. Add the turmeric, a bit more oil, and stir, allowing the turmeric to bloom and release its fragrance, about 1 minute more. Add the chili flakes and sauté for another minute. Remove the onion mixture from the skillet and set aside.

2 Using the same skillet, add 4 more tablespoons olive oil over medium heat. Next, add the cilantro, parsley, and fenugreek and sauté, stirring continuously until the herbs wilt and some of them begin to brown, about 5 minutes. Next, return the onion mixture to the skillet with the herbs, followed by the tamarind paste, tomato paste, salt, and sugar, starting with the 2 to 3 tablespoons and adding more to taste. Stir until well incorporated.

3 Raise the heat to high and continue sautéing and stirring continuously until the sauce reduces and thickens, about 5 minutes. Reserve ½ cup (120 ml) of the tamarind sauce for preparing the shrimp. The remaining tamarind sauce is to layer the rice.

4 Place the rice in a large bowl, cover with cool water, and using your fingers, gently swish it around to wash it. Use a large colander to drain, then rinse the rice once under cold water, drain, and set aside. $\longrightarrow$

5 Parboil the rice: Add 5 quarts (4.7 liters) water and the salt to an 8-quart (7.6-liter) nonstick pot with a tight-fitting lid set over high heat and bring to a boil. Add the rinsed rice, give it a stir so that it doesn't stick, and parboil, uncovered, until al dente, about 6 to 8 minutes. (If you bite into a grain, you'll see a white dot in the center.) Next, drain the rice in the colander and rinse quickly with cold water to stop the cooking process. Shake the colander to remove excess water and set the parboiled rice aside.

6 Rinse the now-empty rice pot of any starch remnants clinging to the sides, and thoroughly dry. Add the olive oil to the pot and warm over medium-low heat. Add the turmeric and stir, allowing the turmeric to bloom and release its fragrance, about 30 seconds. Remove from the heat.

7 Layer the rice: Using a large spoon, layer about 2 cups of the parboiled rice on the bottom of the pot for the rice *tahdig,* adding enough to make a small mound in the center of the pot. Sprinkle a bit of the dried herb mix, if using, over the rice, followed by some of the reserved tamarind sauce, and continue the layering process by alternating the rice, dried herbs, and sauce, building a pyramid-shaped mound in the pot as you layer.

8 Steam the rice: Place a lid on the pot and set over medium heat for about 8 minutes, then lower the heat to low and remove the lid. Wrap the bottom side of the lid in a clean kitchen towel and place the lid back on the top of the pot. Cook on low heat for 30 minutes. Meanwhile, prepare the shrimp.

9 Season the shrimp with the salt. Melt 3 tablespoons (1½ ounces/43 grams) of the butter in a large skillet over medium heat. Add the shrimp and sauté, stirring occasionally, until slightly firm and opaque, about 2 minutes. Lower the heat, add the reserved ½ cup tamarind sauce and the remaining 1 tablespoon (½ ounce/14 grams) butter, and continue to baste the shrimp with the sauce for about 1 minute more (being careful not to overcook it).

10 Turn off the heat and allow the rice to rest for about 2 to 3 minutes with the lid ajar. Do not allow the rice to sit longer or the *tahdig* will get mushy. Gently remove the rice from the pot and transfer to a serving platter. To serve, arrange the shrimp over the rice, along with the *tahdig* on the side. To enhance the flavor, prior to serving, pour the clarified butter or melted butter over the rice.

For the rice

4 cups (740 grams) basmati rice

½ cup (144 grams) kosher salt

2 tablespoons light olive oil

1 tablespoon ground turmeric

½ cup (45 grams) *sabzi polo* dried herb mix (optional; see Resources, page 317)

⅓ cup (80 ml) clarified butter or 4 tablespoons (½ stick/56 grams) salted butter, melted

For the shrimp

1½ to 2 pounds (670 to 906 grams) 22/25 shrimp, peeled and deveined, tail on

1 teaspoon kosher salt

4 tablespoons (½ stick/56 grams) salted butter

½ cup (120 ml) tamarind sauce (reserved from above)

SOUR CHERRY RICE

ALBALOO POLO | *makes 4 to 6 servings*

In Iran, the sour cherry season lasts much longer than it does in New York, so my mom would store a ton of the fruit in her freezer year-round. Each time we'd visit, she made sure that (1) we enjoyed at least one sour cherry rice and (2) no one else was coming to her house so that she could ration her supply just for us! I like my sour cherries very sour, so when you make this recipe, use as much or as little of the bottled lemon juice as you like and add more sugar if you want yours sweeter. I do not like extremely syrupy sour cherries for my rice, so I start with ½ cup, but some families add more. And as far as the cinnamon goes, stick your head in the pot as you are layering the rice and take a deep smell. As the rice steams, it will lose some of the cinnamon aroma, so don't be afraid to use a heavy hand. My family enjoys this dish with the tiny beef meatballs that you'll find with the Kohlrabi Herb Rice recipe on page 76, but for summer parties or a special occasion, I also love to serve it with Saffron-Marinated Cornish Hens (page 173).

My ideal way to prepare a sour cherry rice is by letting the sugars in the cherry juice caramelize. So, if you have thirty minutes, as well as the patience and expertise to nurse your rice, watching and listening for the crackle of caramelization on the bottom layer before it burns, then that is the way to go. But because cherry rice *tahdig* can go from caramelization to burned rather quickly, or if perhaps you don't have the experience yet, you can create a delicious bread *tahdig* with store-bought pita bread, lavash, or homemade *Naan-e Taftoon* (page 6).

1 Make the sour cherry sauce: Place the reserved sour cherry syrup in a nonreactive saucepan over high heat and cook until reduced to one-third of its original quantity, ending up with about 1 cup (235 ml) syrup. Add the sugar, lemon juice, vanilla, and salt, and continue cooking until the mixture reaches a temperature of 245°F, or until it coats the back of a spoon.

2 Add the sour cherries to the mixture. They will release their liquid and thin the sauce out. Continue to cook the cherries and syrup on medium-high until the sauce has thickened slightly and reaches a temperature of 225°F, about 10 to 12 minutes. Remove from the heat and set aside.

3 Place the rice in a large bowl, cover with cool water, and using your fingers, gently swish it around to wash it. Use a large colander to drain, then rinse the rice once under cold water, drain, and set aside. $\rightarrow$

For the sour cherries

Two 24-ounce (680-gram) jars of sour cherries in light syrup, drained, syrup reserved

1 cup (200 grams) granulated sugar, or to taste

⅓ cup (80 ml) bottled lemon juice

1 teaspoon pure vanilla extract

Pinch of kosher salt $\rightarrow$

4 Parboil the rice: Add 5 quarts (4.7 liters) water and the salt to an 8-quart (7.6-liter) nonstick pot set over high heat and bring to a boil. Add the rinsed rice, give it a stir so that it doesn't stick, and parboil, uncovered, until al dente, about 6 to 8 minutes. (If you bite into a grain, you'll see a white dot in the center.) Next, drain the rice in the colander and rinse quickly with cold water to stop the cooking process. Shake the colander to remove excess water and set the parboiled rice aside.

5 Rinse the now-empty rice pot of any starch remnants clinging to the sides, and thoroughly dry. Add the olive oil to your pot and place the bread pieces on the bottom for the *tahdig*.

6 Layer the rice: Using a large, slotted spoon, layer a generous 2 cups of the parboiled rice over the bread to make a small mound in the center of the pot. Using the same spoon, layer the sour cherries from the sour cherry sauce over the rice. (Reserve the liquid during this process; it will be poured over the rice in step 7.) Next, sprinkle a pinch of cinnamon over the cherries and the rice. Continue the process of layering rice, cherries, and pinches of cinnamon, building a pyramid-shaped mound in the pot as you layer.

7 Once you have completed the layering process, gently pour the reserved sour cherry syrup all over the top of the rice mixture, allowing it to permeate the layered rice.

8 Steam the rice: Place a lid on the pot and set over medium heat for about 8 minutes, then lower the heat to low and remove the lid. Wrap the bottom side of the lid in a clean kitchen towel and place the lid back on the top of the pot. Cook on low heat for 20 minutes.

9 Turn off the heat and allow the mixture to cool for about 2 to 3 minutes with the lid ajar. Do not allow the rice to sit longer or the *tahdig* will get soggy. Gently remove the rice from the pot and transfer to a serving platter. Remove the *tahdig* from the bottom of the pot and serve either on top of the rice or on the side. To enhance the flavor, prior to serving, pour the clarified butter or melted butter over the rice.

Alternatively For a fresh sour cherry variation, if excellent-quality fresh sour cherries are available to use, pit them with a cherry pitter or push the pit out through the stem end by using the end of a chopstick, ensuring the integrity of the fruit. Add 1 pound (454 grams) fresh sour cherries to a large saucepan with ½ cup (100 grams) granulated sugar, or to taste, and bring to a boil over medium-low heat. Lower the heat to very low and allow the cherries to macerate in their juices, undisturbed, for about 15 minutes. Add more sugar, or lemon juice to taste, if you like, depending on your desire for sourness.

For the rice and bread *tahdig*

5 cups (925 grams) basmati rice

½ cup (144 grams) kosher salt

3 tablespoons light olive oil

1 large pita bread, *naan,* or lavash bread, homemade or store-bought, sliced into equal portions

2 tablespoons ground cinnamon, or more to taste

⅓ cup (80 ml) clarified butter or 4 tablespoons (½ stick/56 grams) salted butter, melted

Sour
Cherries

I know a Greek produce guy in Astoria, Queens.
"Nasim, I got a case of top-quality sour cherries!"
I rushed to pick up two cases,
plump with the ruby-red color of Isfahan summer memories.
Back home I yelled: "Soshy! Noony! Akis!"
and the four of us sat among the mess of leaves
stemming and pitting the fruit, as if we were handling gems.
Once I "bagged" and "dated"—spring 2012—
I placed my packs of sour cherries in the freezer,
a mother-chef tucking her precious cherries into bed for the winter.
I am always just a couple cases of sour cherries away
from a rice that touches the depth of love for
my mother, my neighbors, my country, my Isfahan.
Fast forward to fall 2012.
Superstorm Sandy hit, my electricity went out, and
my twenty pounds of glorious sour cherries perished.
Since then, I have not gotten my hands on another case
that could compare.
"The snow is killing the blossoms, Nasim. No cherries this year."
But each spring, his phone I ring.

SAFFRON YOGURT "CAKE"
with CHICKEN

TACHIN BA MORGH | *makes 4 to 6 servings*

Tachin translates as "arranged on the bottom" and refers to the layer of crunchy baked saffron and yogurt rice that forms on the bottom of this layered rice cake. Traditionally, this rich and celebratory rice is baked in a dome-shaped glass baking dish. I layer my *tachin* with cinnamon-scented chicken and tart barberries. But you'll find many variations that also include tender lamb. Although the dome baking dish is pretty, I recommend using a deep 11 x 13-inch casserole dish for this recipe because it provides the most surface area and ensures a better ratio of saffron yogurt crust to meaty rice cake with every slice. If you don't have a casserole dish, you may use a 12- to 14-inch nonstick skillet. The skillet also offers a large surface area, and more important, it's deep enough for the rice to expand. Because you're looking for that beautiful cake texture in *tachin,* use jasmine rice; its shorter, rounder grain yields more starch. You may also omit the meat and offer *tachin* as a vegetarian dish or as a side.

Note Bloom the saffron in the yogurt at least 4 to 6 hours in advance, and up to overnight. Soak the ½ cup barberries in water for 10 minutes and drain before using.

1 Four to 6 hours in advance, or the night before making this recipe, place the yogurt in large mixing bowl, sprinkle the saffron over the top, and stir gently. Place the bowl, uncovered, in the refrigerator to allow the saffron to bloom. Stir occasionally to combine.

2 Prepare the chicken: Generously season the chicken with salt and pepper and set aside. Add the onions and 4 tablespoons olive oil to a large, heavy-bottomed pot with a tight-fitting lid and sauté over medium heat, adding more oil if needed, so that the onions turn golden, their edges darken, and they soften, about 5 to 7 minutes. Add the turmeric and a bit more oil and stir, allowing the turmeric to bloom and release its fragrance, about 1 minute more. Add the chicken and cook for a few minutes to coat the chicken with the onion and turmeric mixture.

3 Pour ½ cup (120 ml) water over the chicken, raise the heat to high, and bring to a boil. Continue to boil for 5 minutes, then lower the heat to low and cover the pot with the lid. Simmer for about 30 minutes, stirring occasionally. After 30 minutes, the chicken should be cooked through, and the cooking liquid should have reduced and slightly thickened. $\rightarrow$

For the saffron yogurt mixture

3 cups (735 grams) good-quality, store-bought full-fat plain yogurt (a runny variety is best)

⅛ to ¼ teaspoon saffron powder

3 tablespoons kosher salt

3 tablespoons bottled lemon juice

2 large egg yolks

For the chicken

1 small whole chicken (less than 2 pounds/907 grams), skin removed, quartered, *or* 1½ pounds (680 grams) skinless, bone-in chicken breasts

Kosher salt

Freshly ground black pepper

1 large yellow onion, medium diced $\rightarrow$

4 While the chicken is cooking, prepare the rice. Add 5 quarts (4.7 liters) water and the salt to an 8-quart (7.6-liter) nonstick pot set over high heat and bring to a boil. Add the rinsed rice, give it a stir so that it doesn't stick, and parboil for about 3 to 4 minutes. The rice should remain a bit crunchy because it will continue to cook in the oven. Drain the rice in a large colander and rinse quickly with cold water to stop the cooking process. Shake the colander to remove excess water and set aside to cool for a bit before you mix with the cold yogurt in step 7.

5 Remove the chicken from the pot, reserve the cooking liquid, and when the chicken is cool enough to handle, break it into smaller chunks, discarding the bones. In a large bowl, combine the chicken chunks with the reserved cooking liquid, the cinnamon, and soaked barberries and set aside.

6 Set a rack in the center of the oven and preheat the oven to 450°F.

7 Remove the saffron yogurt mixture from the refrigerator and season with the salt and lemon juice, tasting and adjusting as needed. Add the egg yolks and stir well to thoroughly combine. In a large mixing bowl, gently combine the parboiled rice and saffron yogurt mixture until the rice is well coated.

8 Coat the bottom of a deep 11 x 13-inch casserole dish with the extra-virgin olive oil. Using a large spoon, place half of the rice mixture into the baking dish to form an even layer that reaches about halfway up the dish. Gently place the chicken mixture over the rice (do not press the chicken chunks into the rice), leaving a ½-inch border around the edges. Lightly spread the remaining rice mixture across the chicken.

9 To bake, cover the dish tightly with aluminum foil and bake for 30 minutes. Then lower the heat to 350°F and bake for 45 minutes, rotating the dish halfway through the baking. Starting with a very high temperature and then lowering it allows the rice to quickly bind with the yogurt, which creates the fabulous crust on the bottom.

10 Remove the dish from the oven, uncover, and allow to rest on a cooling rack for 10 minutes. After the "cake" has rested, place a serving platter on top of the casserole dish and, carefully, invert the "cake" onto the platter to showcase the sunset-orange crispy top. Garnish with the candied barberries and cut into wedges to serve.

Light olive oil

1 tablespoon ground turmeric

1 tablespoon ground cinnamon

½ cup (56 grams) barberries, soaked and drained (see headnote)

For the rice

½ cup (144 grams) kosher salt

4 cups (740 grams) jasmine rice, washed and rinsed once

½ cup (120 ml) extra-virgin olive oil

1 cup (112 grams) Candied Barberries (page 52) for garnish

HERBED "NOWRUZ" RICE

SABZI POLO | *makes 4 to 6 servings*

This aromatic rice is full of a profusion of herbs that symbolize spring, which is why it's traditionally enjoyed during Nowruz, our Persian New Year that begins on the spring equinox (see Nowruz: Persian New Year, page 236). Growing up in the landlocked province of Isfahan, we would eat *sabzi polo* alongside salted and smoked Caspian *mahi sefid* whitefish—the only fish available to us back then—with plenty of lime segments. Fish symbolizes good fortune and prosperity, and Nowruz was one of the few times Giti Joon tolerated it in our house.

Note If you do not use the dried herb mix, increase the fresh herbs by 2 ounces (56 grams) each.

1 Preheat the oven to 350°F.

2 Place the garlic cloves on a sheet of aluminum foil, drizzle with a generous amount of olive oil, and wrap and place on the middle rack of the oven to roast, until the garlic softens and turns a nutty light brown, signaling its sweetness, about 30 minutes. Set aside.

3 Place the rice in a large bowl, cover with cool water, and using your fingers, gently swish it around to wash it. Use a large colander to drain, then rinse the rice once under cold water, drain, and set aside.

4 Parboil the rice: Add 5 quarts (4.7 liters) water and the salt to an 8-quart (7.6-liter) nonstick pot set over high heat and bring to a boil. Add the rinsed rice, give it a stir so that it doesn't stick, and parboil, uncovered, until al dente, about 8 to 10 minutes. (If you bite into a grain, you'll see a white dot in the center.) Next, drain the rice in the colander and rinse quickly with cold water to stop the cooking process. Shake the colander to remove excess water and set the parboiled rice aside.

5 Rinse the now-empty rice pot of any starch remnants clinging to the sides, and thoroughly dry. Add 3 tablespoons olive oil to the pot and add the kale to cover the surface of the bottom of the pot for the *tahdig*.

6 Layer the rice: Using a large spoon, layer about 2 cups of the parboiled rice on top of the kale, adding enough to make a small mound in the center of the pot. Sprinkle a bit of the dried herb mix over the rice, followed by some of the chives or scallions, parsley, cilantro, and dill, and then more rice. Continue the layering process by alternating the rice, dried herb mix, chives or scallions, and other fresh herbs, building a pyramid-shaped mound in the pot as you layer.

30 garlic cloves
(about 1 cup/90 grams)

Light olive oil

4 cups (740 grams) basmati rice

½ cup (144 grams) kosher salt

4 to 5 kale leaves, stemmed, tough middle part of the leaf removed

½ cup (45 grams) *sabzi polo* dried herb mix (see Resources, page 317)

6 ounces (170 grams) fresh chives or scallions, both white and green parts, finely chopped

6 ounces (170 grams) fresh flat-leaf parsley, leaves and tender stems, finely chopped

6 ounces (170 grams) fresh cilantro, leaves and tender stems, finely chopped

6 ounces (170 grams) fresh dill, leaves and tender stems, finely chopped

⅓ cup (80 ml) clarified butter or 4 tablespoons (½ stick/56 grams) salted butter, melted

7 Steam the rice: Place a lid on the pot and set over medium heat for about 8 minutes, then lower the heat to low and remove the lid. Wrap the bottom side of the lid in a clean kitchen towel and place the lid back on the top of the pot. Cook on low heat for 35 minutes.

8 Turn off the heat and allow the rice to rest with the lid ajar for about 2 to 3 minutes. Gently transfer the rice to a serving platter. Remove the kale *tahdig* from the bottom of the pot and serve either on top of the rice or on the side. To enhance flavor, prior to serving, pour the clarified butter or melted butter over the rice.

KOHLRABI HERB RICE with KALE TAHDIG and TINY MEATBALLS

KALAM POLO | *makes 4 to 6 servings*

This dish, which originates from the city of Shiraz in southwestern Iran, is a perfect marriage of lemon citrus, a bounty of herbs, and sweet-peppery kohlrabi. I cherish this dish because it feels like a link to a grandmother whom I never had a chance to meet. My mother lost her mom when my mom was six years old, and her Shirazi aunt Khale Borzogeh raised her. According to the accounts of my family, her aunt was a terrible cook. "Her food is salty," they'd say, or "She burns whatever she makes," I'd hear. But I experienced her food so differently. In my opinion, this aunt, who was just a little absentminded and impatient, actually had an extraordinary sensibility about how to develop flavor from food when she put her mind to it. And I tell you, she would nail *kalam polo Shirazi* every time. I also owe my Meatballs with Mint and Vinegar Sauce (page 144) recipe to her as well. Using kohlrabi in this recipe is the authentic Shirazi expression. At Sofreh, we can't possibly dedicate the amount of time to preparing so many kohlrabi matchsticks to keep up with the demand for this rice, so we mix the kohlrabi with cabbage instead because it's in the same family. You can use either, or both, to make this dish.

Note These meatballs differ from the Western way of frying meatballs in that they cook slowly, without any added oil, over very low heat so that they release their juices, keeping them moist and tender. Chickpea flour makes the texture of the meatballs softer, but it is not essential, and you may omit it. However, keep the size of the meatballs consistent so they cook evenly. You can mix and roll them up to 1 day in advance, chilling them until ready to cook. You should get about 20 meatballs.

1 Warm a large stainless-steel or heavy skillet over medium heat. Add the kohlrabi and 3 tablespoons of the salt, and cook, stirring occasionally, to allow the kohlrabi to release some of its water, giving it some char, about 3 to 5 minutes. Next, add the lemon juice and raise the heat to high while stirring, allowing all of the liquid in the pan to evaporate, about 2 to 3 minutes. Remove from the heat, add the tarragon, stir to combine, and set aside.

2 Place the rice in a large bowl, cover with cool water, and using your fingers, gently swish it around to wash it. Use a large colander to drain, then rinse the rice once under cold water, drain, and set aside.

For the rice

1 pound (454 grams) kohlrabi, cut into matchsticks

3 tablespoons plus ½ cup (144 grams) kosher salt

½ cup (120 ml) bottled lemon juice

1 cup (about 3 ounces/85 grams) dried tarragon

4 cups (740 grams) basmati rice

¼ cup (60 ml) light olive oil

3 Parboil the rice: Add 5 quarts (4.7 liters) water and ½ cup (144 grams) of the salt to an 8-quart (7.6-liter) nonstick pot set over high heat and bring to a boil. Add the rinsed rice, give it a stir so that it doesn't stick, and parboil, uncovered, until al dente, about 6 to 8 minutes. (If you bite into a grain, you'll see a white dot in the center.) Next, drain the rice in the colander and rinse quickly with cold water to stop the cooking process. Shake the colander to remove excess water and set the parboiled rice aside.

4 Rinse the now-empty rice pot of any starch remnants clinging to the sides, and thoroughly dry. Add the olive oil to the rice pot and add the kale to cover the surface of the bottom of the pot for the *tahdig*.

5 Layer the rice: Using a large spoon, layer about 2 cups of the parboiled rice into the pot, adding enough to make a small mound in the center of the pot. Using the same spoon, add a generous pinch of each of the cilantro, parsley, and chives or scallions over the rice, followed by a spoonful of kohlrabi and large pinches of the dried herbs. Continue the process of layering the rice, the fresh herbs, kohlrabi, and dried herbs, building a pyramid-shaped mound in the pot as you layer.

6 Steam the rice: Place a lid on the pot and set over medium heat for about 8 minutes, then lower the heat to low and remove the lid. Wrap the bottom side of the lid in a clean kitchen towel and place the lid back on the top of the pot. Cook on low heat for 30 minutes. Meanwhile, prepare the meatballs.

7 Set out a large plate or tray. In a large bowl, combine the meat, onions, salt, pepper, turmeric, and chickpea flour, if using. Using your clean hands, mix well and shape the meat mixture into tiny meatballs, about the size of a small kumquat. As you roll, set them on the plate. Place them in the refrigerator to chill.

8 To cook the meatballs, add the meatballs, all at once, to a large skillet set over medium heat, spreading them out so that they are not overlapping. After 1 to 2 minutes, lower the heat to low and cook until they release themselves from the bottom of the pan. Gently rotate them, or give the pan a shake now and then, so that they brown on all sides, about 8 minutes. Remove from the heat and set aside.

9 Once the rice has steamed for 30 minutes, add the cooked meatballs to the pot, scattering them across the top of the rice. Return the lid to the pot and continue cooking, about 10 minutes more.

10 Gently transfer the rice and meatballs to a serving platter. Remove the kale *tahdig* from the bottom of the pot and serve either on top of the rice or on the side. To enhance flavor, prior to serving, pour the clarified butter or melted butter over the rice.

3 or 4 large Tuscan kale leaves, stems removed

3 ounces (85 grams) fresh cilantro, leaves and tender stems, finely chopped

3 ounces (85 grams) fresh flat-leaf parsley, leaves and tender stems, finely chopped

3 ounces (85 grams) fresh chives or scallions, both white and green parts, finely chopped

½ cup (45 grams) *sabzi polo* dried herb mix (see Resources, page 317)

⅓ cup (80 ml) clarified butter or 4 tablespoons (½ stick/56 grams) salted butter, melted

For the meatballs

1½ pounds (680 grams) ground beef (80% fat, 20% lean) or ground lamb

1 medium yellow onion, grated

2 teaspoons kosher salt

1 teaspoon freshly ground black pepper

2 teaspoons ground turmeric

2 tablespoons chickpea flour (optional)

NOODLE RICE with RAISINS and TOASTED ALMONDS

RESHTEH POLO | *makes 4 to 6 servings*

The word for noodle in Farsi is *reshteh*—which translates as "threads." *Reshteh polo* is a Nowruz rice and noodle *polo* that is more commonly enjoyed in Tehran than in the rest of Iran. When you offer *reshteh polo* on Nowruz, you are saying, "We hope you get a handle on your *reshteh* for the New Year," as if life's threads are to be woven into a larger tapestry of meaning. Age has afforded me the ability to examine my life in reverse, and often when I find myself alone, or taking a run along the Hudson River, I trace my life's *reshteh,* which in the past led to Sofreh and now, of course, has led to you. On a more practical note, because I always host our Nowruz celebration at my house, I like to include *reshteh polo* alongside Herbed "Nowruz" Rice (page 74). Better yet, it's a lovely complementary rice dish to my slow-cooked Roasted Leg of Lamb "Gigot" (page 141).

Note A little trick to bring the toasted almonds to the same temperature as the rice is to wrap them in aluminum foil and tuck them into the pot of rice while it's resting for a few minutes before serving. You may substitute ramen noodles for *reshteh* wheat noodles.

1 Place the rice in a large bowl, cover with cool water, and using your fingers, gently swish it around to wash it. Use a large colander to drain, then rinse the rice once under cold water, drain, and set aside.

2 Add 5 quarts (4.7 liters) water and the salt to an 8-quart (7.6-liter) nonstick pot set over high heat and bring to a boil. Add the rinsed rice, give it a stir so that it doesn't stick, and parboil. After about 4 minutes, add the noodles and continue cooking both, uncovered, until the rice is al dente, about 4 to 6 minutes more. (If you bite into a grain, you'll see a white dot in the center.) Next, drain the rice and noodles in the colander and rinse quickly with cold water to stop the cooking process. Shake the colander to remove excess water and set the rice and noodles aside.

3 Rinse the now-empty rice pot of any starch remnants clinging to the sides, and thoroughly dry. Add the olive oil to the pot and place the bread pieces on the bottom for the *tahdig.*

4 Using a large spoon, layer about 2 cups of the parboiled rice and noodles over the bread, adding enough to make a small mound in the center of the pot, followed by a sprinkle of the cinnamon and cinnamon raisins. Continue layering, alternating spoons of rice and noodles with pinches of cinnamon

4 cups (740 grams) basmati rice

½ cup (144 grams) kosher salt

4 ounces *reshteh* wheat noodles, broken into quarters (see Resources, page 317)

2 tablespoons light olive oil

1 large store-bought pita bread, *naan,* or *Naan-e Taftoon* (page 6), sliced into equal portions

3 tablespoons ground cinnamon

1 cup (160 grams) Cinnamon Raisins (page 54)

4 tablespoons Saffron Water (page xxxiv)

⅓ cup (80 ml) clarified butter or 4 tablespoons (½ stick/56 grams) salted butter, melted

¾ cup (52 grams) sliced almonds, lightly toasted, for garnish

1 cup Crispy Fried Onions (page 194) for garnish

and cinnamon raisins, building a pyramid-shaped mound in the pot as you layer.

5 Place a lid on the pot and set over medium heat for about 8 minutes, then lower the heat to low and remove the lid. Wrap the bottom side of the lid in a clean kitchen towel and place the lid back on the top of the pot. Cook on low heat for 30 minutes.

6 Turn off the heat and allow the noodle rice to rest with the lid ajar for about 2 to 3 minutes. Remove some rice (about 1 cup) from the pot and combine it in a small bowl with the saffron water. Set the saffron rice aside, then gently transfer the noodle rice to a serving platter. Pour the clarified butter or melted butter over the top and garnish with the saffron rice, toasted almonds, and crispy fried onions, and serve the *tahdig* on the side.

JEWELED RICE

MORASA POLO | *makes 4 to 6 servings*

Jeweled rice is named for the colors and beauty of its jewel-like garnishes. It's a feast for the senses that has, for centuries, been Iran's most treasured celebratory wedding rice. The rice preparation is as easy as preparing a basic *chelo,* but what makes an amazing jeweled rice is the attention to detail and the love that you give to each of its garnishes. Over the years, I've given excessive thought to them. You may prepare your garnishes first, as directed, or you will have time to prepare them while the rice is steaming. Here we go.

Years ago, I ignored the color of raisins. I treated dark-colored raisins and golden raisins interchangeably, reaching for whatever happened to be in my pantry. But each time I'd use dark raisins, I'd get so annoyed because I'd have to go out of my way to arrange them far apart on the rice, just so they wouldn't detract from the beauty of the candied red barberries. And then I landed on the solution: golden Cinnamon Raisins (page 54). Their golden color complements both the green pistachios and the sheen of red barberries, and the touch of cinnamon is so lovely. The master recipe for candied barberries is on page 52. They are not rocket science, but still, I obsess over them. The trick is to make sure not to overcook them or let them burn, and I give you some tips to ensure their success. You'll use ¾ cup (84 grams) candied barberries for this jeweled rice, but you can store any leftover barberries to use as a garnish for other rice dishes.

The most important thing to remember for the rosewater almonds is that the almonds need to be bright white and have a light fragrance, signaling their freshness. Taste one, and if it has any hint of bitterness, it's old, so don't use the almonds. I do as Iranian grandmas do and soak the almonds in rosewater. This method softens them, yet they retain a bite. And they take on the aroma of rosewater. How gorgeous. Still, for the temperature of the rice and nuts to be in balance, I drain the nuts from the rosewater, wrap them in aluminum foil, and set the package of almonds on top of my rice to warm while the rice rests for 5 minutes.

I'm used to making my jeweled rice with Iranian pistachios because they have an incomparable meaty texture, flavor, and aroma, but because that's not an option, given trade restrictions, see Resources (page 317) for recommendations on high-quality U.S. alternatives. Look for raw, bright green slivered pistachios with a slightly sweet aftertaste. Tossing them in warmed clarified butter or even olive oil provides a glimmer and shine to make them visually stunning. Lastly, I recommend saving jeweled rice for a momentous occasion, or a holiday table, as it was originally intended. →

1 Prepare the candied barberries if you have not done so already.

2 Prepare the cinnamon raisins if you have not done so already.

3 Prepare the rosewater almonds: Combine the almonds and rosewater in a medium bowl and soak for 15 minutes. Drain and wrap them in a sheet of aluminum foil to make a little package. When the rice is finished steaming, place the package on top of the rice to warm them for 5 minutes.

4 Prepare the pistachios: In a medium skillet over low heat, warm the clarified butter or olive oil, add the pistachios, and give them a gentle toss to coat them. Set aside until ready to use.

5 Place the rice in a large bowl, cover with cool water, and using your fingers, gently swish it around to wash it. Drain the rice in a large colander, rinse once under cold water, allow to drain, and set aside.

6 Parboil the rice: Add 5 quarts (4.7 liters) water and the salt to an 8-quart (7.6-liter) nonstick pot set over high heat and bring to a boil. Add the rinsed rice, give it a stir so that it doesn't stick, and parboil, uncovered, until al dente, about 8 to 10 minutes. (If you bite into a grain, you'll see a white dot in the center.) Next, drain the rice in a large colander and rinse quickly with cold water to stop the cooking process. Shake the colander to remove excess water and set the parboiled rice aside.

7 Rinse the now-empty rice pot of any starch remnants clinging to the sides, and thoroughly dry. Pour the olive oil into the pot and warm over medium-low heat. Add the turmeric, give it a stir, and allow the turmeric to bloom and release its fragrance, about 30 seconds. Remove the pot from the heat. Add the yogurt and 1 cup of the parboiled rice to the turmeric oil mixture, quickly stir until well combined, and press gently to the bottom for the *tahdig* layer.

8 Layer the rice: Using a large spoon, scoop the remaining parboiled rice into the center of the pot, allowing it to land in a loose mound, forming a pyramid shape inside the pot. Do not press it down.

9 Steam the rice: Place a lid on the pot and set over medium heat for about 8 minutes, then lower the heat to low and remove the lid. Wrap the bottom side of the lid in a clean kitchen towel and place the lid back on the top of the pot. Cook on low heat for about 45 to 50 minutes.

10 Turn off the heat, set the lid ajar, and allow the rice to rest for about 2 to 3 minutes. Do not allow the rice to sit longer or the *tahdig* will get soggy. Remove 1 cup of rice from the pot and mix it with the saffron water, and if you like, add the rosewater and set aside.

¾ cup (84 grams) Candied Barberries (page 52)

¾ cup (120 grams) Cinnamon Raisins (page 54)

For the rosewater almonds

¾ cup slivered almonds (skinless)

¼ cup rosewater

For the pistachios

1 tablespoon clarified butter or light olive oil

¾ cup shelled, thinly slivered pistachios

For the rice

4 cups (740 grams) basmati rice

½ cup (144 grams) kosher salt

3 tablespoons light olive oil

1 teaspoon ground turmeric

1 cup (285 grams) Homemade Yogurt (page 32) or store-bought Greek yogurt

3 tablespoons Saffron Water (page xxxiv)

1 tablespoon rosewater (optional)

⅓ cup (80 ml) clarified butter or 4 tablespoons (½ stick/56 grams) salted butter, melted

11 Gently remove the rice from the pot and transfer to a serving platter. Pour the clarified butter or melted butter over the rice, garnish with the reserved saffron rice, and, working with one garnish at a time, lay the candied barberries, cinnamon raisins, rosewater almonds, and pistachios in a row across the top. Lastly, remove the rice *tahdig* from the bottom of the pot and serve on the side.

HERBS SABZI

There are great heaps of bright, lemon-scented *gishniz* (cilantro) and sky-high piles of mildly peppery and clean-smelling *jafari* (parsley). Produce vendors stack thick, grassy, potent clusters of *shivid* (dill) among mounds of *tarreh*—a long, hollow Persian leek, redolent with an onion-garlic aroma. A dune of maple-scented fresh *shanbalileh* (fenugreek*)* leaves is layered among emerald-green swaths of earthy *esfenaj* (spinach), mildly peppery *shahi* (cress), and a hoard of *tarkhoon* (tarragon)—their coarse leaves offering a light licorice flavor. And it's here, at the produce bazaar, that you'll find both varieties of the strong, sweet flavor of Iranian basil called *rayhoon,* one type with purple veins running through its dark green leaves, the other entirely green.

PERSIAN COOKS USE FRESH HERBS FOR EATING RAW AND IN COOKING MORE THAN IN ANY OTHER CUISINE IN THE WORLD.

As steep as these mountains of fresh herbs are, against the wall are piles of canvas sacks, some three feet high and brimming with dried cilantro, parsley, dill, and fenugreek, as well as the scent of dried *na'na* (mint). Some herbs like *musir*—a small garlic-looking bulb with a hint of nuttiness and mild garlicky flavor—and *golpar* (hogweed)—a light brown, speckled dried herb that features prominently in pickling—are uniquely Iranian. And so, too, is our obsession with herbs. Persian cooks use fresh *sabzi* (the plural of *sabz,* which means "green" in Farsi) for eating raw and in cooking more than in any other cuisine in the world.

So, there's our guy, standing before me in his red work apron—a nice pop of color against all the hills of green behind him. He's reaching into the stacks to pull out bunches of scallions, parsley, and cilantro for my Celery Herb Stew (page 100).

Now he's gesturing to a huge industrial herb mincer. *(Eye roll.)* Quiet, Mom. I'll politely let him know that I'll carry my bushels of herbs home to chop by hand instead of watching them spin in the big silver barrel where the unseen blades will undoubtedly grind them into a pulp that is too fine for my liking. The shortcut of machine chopping herbs, whether done on site at the produce bazaar or with a food processor in your home kitchen, releases too much of the herbs' water, resulting in a stew that is runny or, worse, soupy. Iranians like their stews "tight," and I prefer to maintain some texture to my herbs. Old school, yes.

I've been carefully washing, picking, and finely chopping herbs by hand since I was a child, alongside my mom and aunts. And I continued the ritual of chopping herbs by hand, cooking, portioning, and freezing my herbs to save prep time for my Prune and Spinach Stew (page 92), a dish that I've been feeding my kids since before they could walk. It is no different at Sofreh, where vendors deliver cases to me in Brooklyn: chop, chop, chop. Can I convince you to do the same, when the sirens' call of modern equipment wants to take everything out of our hands for the sake of convenience? There are no shortcuts in love, my dear.

The vendor is looking at you now. Just say, *"Na kheili mamnoon,"* take your herbs, and grab my arm. We're leaving.

"Salads" in Persian cuisine take the form of an herb platter called *Sabzi Khordan* (page 88), which literally translates as "eating your greens." It provides a fresh, healthful counterpart to plentiful rice, slow-cooked stews, or beef and lamb *kababs*. And besides the acidity, tang, and diverse textures of our *torshi* (pickles; see pages 247–256), there is no more vital counterpart to our meals than herbs.

My theory for why we eat so many greens is rooted in our one-pot dishes, like herb-and-legume-based *a'ash* (see pages 189–209), as well as *khoresht* (stews). While these include copious amounts of herbs, we slow-cook them, resulting in the depletion of many of their vitamins and their nutritional value. Along the way, people figured out that clean-tasting, verdant produce on the table was a great way to make up for whatever nutrients they had cooked away.

During the First Persian Empire—in territory that encompasses modern-day Iran plus areas of Turkey, Afghanistan, and Iraq—engineers, led by Cyrus the Great, developed a series of underground tunnels and wells called *quanats* to pull water from the surrounding mountains into more arid and dry regions of Iran for drinking and irrigation. Herbs flourished and became widely available throughout the Persian empire. Even today, in neighboring countries, a platter of herbs is offered with meals.

The fresh herbs that you find herein, and their dried counterparts, are by no means a comprehensive list of what is available in Iran; the varieties of herbs foraged from the Alborz and Zagros Mountains are too obscure and too numerous to mention. Instead, I focus on the most readily accessible varietals. While it is not essential to incorporate dried herbs into these dishes, I like the extra kick of potent aromatics in my herb stews. You can find standard packs of dried herbs (see Resources, page 317) that are typically labeled as *sabzi a'ash, sabzi ghormeh*, for *Ghormeh Sabzi* (page 103), and other herb stews throughout this book, and *sabzi polo* for layered rice dishes (see pages 56–83).

The herb stew recipes that follow may be a grand departure if you are accustomed to using herbs in scant amounts: small bouquets dropped into a soup for flavor; snips, here and there, for garnishing. Instead, you'll source the best-looking and -smelling fresh herbs you can find and learn to treat them as treasured vegetables that are integral to your repertoire.

Sabzi Khordan (Fresh Herb Platter)

Sabzi khordan, which translates as "eating your greens," is a platter of fresh herbs that accompanies lunch and dinner. The herbs that compose this platter depend on personal preference, regionality, and seasonality. However, everyone seems to agree that when it comes to adding parsley, as my mother, Giti Joon, says, *(We feed our cows with that or cook it down, it's not for eating raw)*.

You can arrange these herbs on a platter, using them in whichever amounts you wish. Or instead, do as I do, and mix them up, much like a salad. This way, people are forced to eat all of them! My husband, Akis, hates dill, and so he removes it. Perhaps when we grow old, and he starts helping me prepare *sabzi khordan,* he will finally get his way and leave it out entirely. Following are just some of the fresh herbs included on herb platters in Iran, along with my stateside equivalent.

RAYHOON *(Persian Basil)* You have no idea how much basil I need if I am making *sabzi khordan* for Iranians. Unless, of course, you do! When it's in season in Iran, basil forms the base of our herb platter. Farmers plant both green and purple-veined types of this lemon-scented variety, but vendors dole out mostly green. When I am in Iran, I try to get the produce vendor to give me more of the purple, because I love it. But there's always a back-and-forth where they tell me that they have to save a balanced ratio for others. I grow my own *rayhoon* in New York, but your local farmers' market should offer dozens of varieties that you can substitute; use Thai basil for its lemon notes and spiciness, as well as sweeter, more common Italian basil. Purple basil is accessible at Asian markets and offers striking color as well as comparable flavor to Iranian *rayhoon*. And look for the spicy and savory small-leaved Greek dwarf basil. I use them all.

SHAHI *(Cress)* *Shahi*, in whose name you'll find the word *shah*, for "king," is an important part of our *sabzi khordan*. Native to Iran, *shahi* is a leafy green plant that is related to watercress and mustard plants. I substitute *shahi* with piquant baby arugula because it offers a similar flavor.

TARKHOON *(Tarragon)* Indigenous to Iran, the leaves and tender stems of *tarkhoon* offer a lovely, light anise flavor.

GISHNIZ *(Cilantro)* The tender leaves and stems of cilantro are a bright, citrus burst of flavor.

SHIVID *(Dill)* Iranian dill has a potent aroma that is incomparable. Look for the most intense-smelling, bright, and grassy dill to add.

TARREH *(Garlic Chives)* Native to Iran, *tarreh* are a delicate broad-leafed leek that we use in both the herb platter and in cooking. I use flat, dark green, and strong-smelling Chinese market chives called *jiu cai* because *tarreh* are not grown in the United States. Select the nonflowering kind.

TOROBCHE *(Radishes)* Deep pink radishes lend color, beauty, and peppery flavor.

PIYAZCHE *(Scallions)* *Piyazche* in Iran are milder in flavor than scallions grown in the United States. We use the white part only in our *sabzi khordan* and save the light and dark green parts for cooking.

EDIBLE FLOWER TIPS Traditionally, we don't add these in Iran, but I add them for beauty on occasion. Use as you wish.

Herbs for Cooking

Fresh herbs such as cilantro, chives, scallions, and dill are eaten raw in *sabzi khordan* and are also used copiously for cooking. Here are additional fresh herbs used in Persian cooking.

JAFARI *(Parsley)* Flat-leaf or Italian parsley is commonly used for cooking.

NA'NA *(Mint)* There exist numerous types of mint in Iran, but the one that we cultivate for cooking is the peppermint that you find in your supermarket. We also use dried peppermint in cooking as well as to make Mint Oil (page 196). In the Gilan province of Iran near the Caspian Sea, strong, sharp *chuchagh* mint grows wild and gives dishes a deeply minty kick that is characteristic of that region.

SHANBALILEH *(Fenugreek)* You can find fresh fenugreek on display everywhere in Iran when it is in season. It has an unmistakable sweet and nutty flavor and is essential to making our national stew, *Ghormeh Sabzi* (page 103). It's tricky to find fresh fenugreek outside of Iranian or Indian markets in the United States, but don't despair. Dried fenugreek leaves are wonderful and also widely used in Iran, so use those.

ESFENAJ *(Spinach)* Technically, spinach is not considered an herb in the United States. But the line between vegetable and herb is blurred in Iranian cuisine because we treat all herbs as vegetables. Fresh spinach leaves are used in herb mixes for stews because they add body and a silky texture.

Dried Herbs

Fresh herbs are so flavorful in Iran that I do not need to add dried herbs to my herb bases when I cook there, with the exception of dried fenugreek, which is seasonal. But over the years, cooking in New York, I began to incorporate the dried counterparts of our most commonly used herbs into my cooking for an increased potency of flavor. I am not one of those chefs who advocates that you can get delicious flavor only from importing your herbs. But my passion to improve on flavor is why I still bring dried herbs back with me from Iran. I have weighed my suitcases down with *musir* (dried shallots) as well as dried tarragon and dried dill. Recently, my son, Noony, brought back a huge suitcase of bulk herbs for me from Iran. The produce vendor repackaged the herbs into one-kilo bags. When Noony tried to pass by customs, no doubt smelling like weed, he was stopped by two customs' officers, where they made him open every single bag. They couldn't believe that this twenty-six-year-old guy was traveling with so many herbs! In short, dried herbs are not absolutely necessary for these recipes. You can still deliver great flavor by using only excellent-quality fresh herbs. If you omit the dried herbs, increase the fresh herb amounts in these recipes by 2 ounces (56 grams) each. See Resources (page 317) for sourcing excellent-quality dried herbs.

Ja-oftadeh: "The Stew Has Found Its Place"

The saying *ja-oftadeh* translates as "the stew has found its place" and is admittedly ambiguous. But in general, it is a point of exaltation, similar to "Ah, it's perfect!" We do not apply *ja-oftadeh* to solid food, such as *kuku* or *kababs*. Instead, we reserve it for those foods whose cooking process involves liquid, as well as layering of ingredients, such as *a'ash* (see pages 189–209*), haleem* (see page 122), and these herb stews.

After forty years of cooking, I've reached a point where I can tell by the look of an herb stew if it is *ja-oftadeh*. But that has come with years of practice, observation, and trial and error. And even as a working mom, when I didn't have the luxury of time, there were plenty of times that I didn't even follow my own steps for "helping my stews find their place."

The elements of ensuring *ja-oftadeh* are embedded in these recipes and include the selection of excellent ingredients, how you fry your onions, at what point you add turmeric, as well as how you cook the meat (see *Zohm,* page 128) and how you fry your herbs—slowly, coaxing out all of their earthy sweetness. *Ja-oftadeh* also encompasses the amount of water in the stew, as well as the proper cook time—long and gently. It includes a visual cue as well, which is how the stew's oil rises and settles at the top of the pot and how long you allow your stew to rest, covered, so that the flavors deepen and meld before serving. And finally, with the exception of Sofreh Butter Bean and Dill Stew (page 97), which should be brothy, I like my herb stews to have a tight consistency, rather than a loose or watery one. Or as we mockingly say in Farsi: *"Ab yevar, dun yevar,"* which translates as "Material in one place, water in the other."

Herb Stews

PRUNE and SPINACH STEW

ALOO ESFENAJ | *makes 4 to 6 servings*

My mother stayed with us in New York to help guide me through the early months of caring for our twins, Soshy and Noony. And from the time the twins were around three months old, I would watch her dip the tip of her finger into whatever stew, sauce, or yogurt that we had on the table—even a little bit of lime juice or lemon juice—and offer them a taste of the tart and savory flavors of our cuisine. My mom also brought with her from Iran many small, thick cheesecloth sacks. She would fill each with a bit of rice and drop it into the pot to cook, rendering the rice as soft as farina and allowing it to soak up all the nutrition from whatever meal we had been preparing for ourselves. I remember watching Noony, as young as five months old, bubbling with excitement and ready to pounce each time he saw me mixing the flavor-infused rice with some of my milk for him. Soshy, on the other hand, would take just the tiniest taste then close her mouth so tight her lips disappeared. From dishes full of legumes, like Sofreh Herb and Noodle *A'ash* (page 208) to the incredible, layered flavors of *Ghormeh Sabzi* (page 103), Soshy and Noony had their palates primed for Persian flavors. I laughed at our six-month pediatrician visit when our doctor told us that it was time to introduce them to baked pears!

But then, when they were nine months old, I brought my still-toothless babies back home to Isfahan with me for the first time, and my mom made *aloo esfenaj,* a silky spinach stew with small, dark, dried *aloo baraghani* plums. I hadn't tasted it in at least fifteen years, and I realized how much I was missing it in my life. From the time my children were babies to today, this comforting stew remains a staple in my home cooking repertoire.

Note If you'd like to use *aloo baraghani* dried plums (see Resources, page 317), be aware that they have pits and take longer to cook. American store-bought prunes do not need more than 15 minutes, or else they fall apart, so add them last.

1 Add the onions and 4 tablespoons olive oil to a large, heavy-bottomed pot with a tight-fitting lid and sauté over medium heat, adding more oil if needed, so that the onions turn golden, their edges darken, and they soften, about 5 to 7 minutes. Add the turmeric, a bit more oil, and stir, allowing the turmeric to bloom and release its fragrance, about 1 minute.

2 Pat the cubes of meat dry and add them to the pot. Season the meat with the salt and pepper, cover the pot with the lid, lower the heat to low, and cook, allowing the meat to release its juices, about 5 minutes. Remove the lid, give the mixture a stir, raise the heat to medium-high, and continue cooking, uncovered, until the meat is glossy and any remaining liquid in the pot evaporates, about 6 minutes more. Add 4 cups (1 liter) water, cover, raise the heat to high and bring to a boil, then lower the heat to a gentle boil and cook for about 25 minutes. While the meat is cooking, fry the herbs.

3 Place the spinach, chives or scallions, parsley, and cilantro in a large, dry sauté pan over high heat, and cook, stirring occasionally, about 2 to 3 minutes, until they release all of their liquid. Add ¼ cup (60 ml) olive oil and continue cooking, about 2 to 3 minutes, until the herbs cook down and take on a glossy shine.

4 Add the fried herbs, the lemon juice, sugar, and Persian plums, if using, to the meat pot. Taste and adjust the seasoning. If the stew looks dry, add 1 cup (235 ml) water. Cover and continue cooking at a gentle boil for 20 minutes more, then lower the heat to medium-low. If using American prunes, add them at this point, and continue cooking for about 15 minutes more. Allow to rest, partially covered at room temperature, for 1 hour.

5 Squeeze fresh lemon wedges over the dish for a bright, fresh garnish before serving.

1 large yellow onion, medium diced

Light olive oil

1½ tablespoons ground turmeric

1½ pounds (680 grams) beef chuck or boneless lamb shoulder, cut into 1-inch cubes

2 tablespoons kosher salt

2 teaspoons freshly ground black pepper

1 pound (454 grams) fresh spinach, leaves and tender stems, finely chopped

4 ounces (112 grams) fresh chives or scallions, both white and green parts, finely chopped

6 ounces (170 grams) fresh flat-leaf parsley, leaves and tender stems, finely chopped

6 ounces (170 grams) fresh cilantro, leaves and tender stems, finely chopped

⅔ cup (160 ml) bottled lemon juice

⅓ cup (66 grams) granulated sugar

16 to 18 *aloo baraghani* Persian dried plums or large American prunes (see headnote)

2 to 3 fresh lemons, cut into wedges

SOUR CHICKEN with POMEGRANATE, VERJUS, SPLIT PEAS, and HERBS

MORGH TORSH | *makes 4 to 6 servings*

Wild fruit trees and a profusion of herb varieties—including seven different varieties of mint—flourish in the forested areas of the northern region of Gilan. Locals use these wild herbs in abundance in their cooking, and for this *khoresht-e morgh torsh*—sour chicken stew—they grind them in a massive stone mortar, breaking their fibers, which gives them a loose, almost pureed texture. The herbs of this region are not accessible to me in New York or even to Iranians outside of Gilan, but I like to keep the tradition of the pureed texture that the herbs yield. So just for this stew, I use a food processor to chop my herbs versus my preference for hand-chopping my herbs.

Also, in Gilan, you'll find distinctively dark, rich, very tart pomegranate molasses made from a tiny wild pomegranate that lends the province's *morgh torsh* (and its *fesenjan, see* page 285) an intensely sour flavor profile, although the degree of sourness varies from home to home, based on personal preference. The addition of Iranian verjus, called *abgooreh,* gives my *morgh torsh* a beautiful tart edge that I look for in the stew. Also, in some homes, you'll find this stew served with eggs, as well as chicken. I think the eggs *and* chicken are overkill.

Note I call for cooking the split peas separately and discarding the cooking liquid because I don't want the flavor of the split peas to overpower the stew.

1 Bring a small pot of water to a boil, add the split peas, and parboil for 20 minutes. Set the split peas aside in their cooking liquid until ready to use.

2 Working in batches, place the fenugreek, mint, cilantro, parsley, and chives in the bowl of a food processor. Process with the steel blade until pureed. Repeat until all of the herbs have been processed. Set aside.

3 Add the onions and 4 tablespoons olive oil to a large, heavy-bottomed pot with a tight-fitting lid and sauté over medium-high heat, adding more oil if needed, so that the onions turn golden, their edges darken, and they soften, about 5 to 7 minutes. Make a well in the center of the pot, add the garlic and a bit more oil (so that the garlic doesn't burn), and sauté until fragrant, about 3 more minutes. Add the turmeric, a bit more oil, and stir, allowing the turmeric to bloom and release its fragrance, about 1 minute. →

½ cup (112 grams) dry split peas

2 ounces (56 grams) fresh fenugreek, leaves and tender stems, or ½ cup dried fenugreek

2 ounces (56 grams) fresh mint, leaves and tender stems

6 ounces (170 grams) fresh cilantro, leaves and tender stems

6 ounces (170 grams) fresh flat-leaf parsley, leaves and tender stems

6 ounces (170 grams) fresh chives

1 large yellow onion, medium diced

Light olive oil →

4 Add the chicken thighs, season with salt and pepper, and lower the heat. Cook the chicken until it is lightly browned and begins to release its juices, about 2 to 3 minutes per side. Remove from the heat and set aside. Meanwhile, fry the herbs.

5 Place the pureed herbs in a large, dry sauté pan over high heat, and stir continuously, allowing them to release all of their liquid. Add ¼ cup (60 ml) olive oil and continue stirring until the herbs begin to turn glossy and wilt, about 5 to 6 minutes. Turn off the heat and allow the stuck bits of herbs to release themselves from the bottom of the pan. After a few minutes, return the pan to high heat, add ¼ cup (60 ml) more olive oil, and stir continuously, about 5 minutes more.

6 Add the herbs to the chicken pot, along with 4 cups (1 liter) water, the pomegranate molasses, and verjus or lemon juice. Raise the heat and bring to a boil, then lower the heat to a gentle boil, cover with the lid, and cook for 30 minutes, or until the chicken is cooked through.

7 Drain the reserved split peas and add them to the pot, taste, and adjust the seasoning, adding more verjus, if you like. Cover, leaving the lid ajar, and cook for 10 minutes more. Allow to rest, partially covered, at room temperature for 1 hour before serving.

8 Squeeze fresh lemon wedges over the dish and serve.

1 large garlic head, cloves peeled and finely chopped

2 tablespoons ground turmeric

8 skinless, bone-in chicken thighs

3 tablespoons kosher salt

2 teaspoons freshly ground black pepper

¾ cup (180 ml) pomegranate molasses

1 cup (235 ml) verjus or 1 cup (235 ml) bottled lemon juice

2 to 3 fresh lemons, cut into wedges

Verjus *(Abgooreh)*

Whole, unripe green grapes (*gooreh*) are beloved for their sharp, tart flavor. Their season is a very short window in summer, so we preserve their juice in *abgooreh,* an Iranian verjus that is more delicate than lemon juice but still offers a bright edge to your stew. While you can freeze seasonal sour grapes, you can also purchase sour grapes in brine year-round to use in Eggplant Stew with Split Peas (page 111). Persian *abgooreh* is made exclusively from grapes, whereas European- and American-made verjus can be made with sour crab apples.

SOFREH BUTTER BEAN and DILL STEW

BAGHALI GATOGH | *makes 4 to 6 servings*

This robust vegetarian bean stew from northern Iran is traditionally full of speckled *pacha baghala*. They are from the pinto bean family, but because it's nearly impossible to find them outside of Iran, most cooks swap them out for fresh fava beans. But I prefer dried butter beans to deliver the texture and hearty consistency that I want. I love to use a mix of intensely fragrant fresh dill and additional dried dill. I have high standards for dill, so if your fresh dill isn't up to par, it's better to stick to a good-quality dried dill instead. *Baghali gatogh* should have a thick broth, so adding the bean liquid a little at a time also helps you achieve the desired body.

Poultry and eggs traditionally factor into many of the herb stews of northern Iran, like *baghali gatogh* and *morgh torsh* (see page 95), and sauces, such as *mirza ghasemi* (see page 114). Typically, cooks add the eggs directly to the dish and gently whisk them into the stew, but I never liked it that way because some parts of the egg get rubbery, while others are undercooked. When I came to the United States and ate poached eggs for the first time, I thought, Well, here's an answer to my prayers! At Sofreh, I poach the egg separately and sit it on top of the stew so that when you break it, all that gorgeous, soft yolk oozes to intermingle with the warm, intoxicating dill and butter beans beneath it. Omit the egg entirely for a fantastic vegan dish to add to your repertoire. If you like, you can substitute half the amount of water called for with stock of your choice.

Note You will need to soak the beans for a minimum of 4 hours and up to overnight before making this recipe.

---

1 Put the beans in a large bowl and cover with water by 2 inches. Soak for 4 to 6 hours.

2 Drain and rinse the beans, then place them in a large pot and cover with about 7 cups (1.6 liters) water, or until covered by 2 inches. Bring to a boil, then lower the heat to medium-low and cook gently, for about 30 minutes. Spoon off any foam that rises to the top and discard, then add the salt and continue cooking, covered, until the beans are soft but still toothsome, about 1 to 1½ hours more. Remove from the heat and set aside to rest in their liquid.

3 Meanwhile, add the onions and 4 tablespoons olive oil to a large, heavy-bottomed pot with a tight-fitting lid and sauté over medium heat, adding →

2 cups (368 grams) dry butter beans

1½ tablespoons kosher salt, plus more to taste

1 large yellow onion, finely diced

Light olive oil

1 large garlic head, cloves peeled and finely chopped

2 tablespoons ground turmeric

⅓ cup (80 ml) bottled lemon juice

1 tablespoon freshly ground black pepper, plus more to taste →

more oil if needed, so that the onions turn golden, their edges darken, and they soften, about 5 to 7 minutes. Make a well in the center of the pot, add the garlic and a bit more oil (so that the garlic doesn't burn), and raise the heat to medium-high for some quick browning action, about 1 to 2 minutes. Lower the heat and continue cooking until the garlic softens and the aroma is sweet, stirring occasionally, as the garlic will stick, about 1 minute more. Add the turmeric, a bit more oil, and stir, allowing the turmeric to bloom and release its fragrance, about 1 minute more. Add the lemon juice, and using a wooden spoon, deglaze the onion mixture, scraping up any browned bits from the bottom.

4 Next, drain the beans, reserving the liquid. Add the beans to the pot, along with the pepper and the dried dill, and sauté for 1 minute or so to incorporate the flavors. Raise the heat to high and slowly add the reserved bean water, adding as much or as little as you wish to reach your desired consistency. Cook, uncovered, stirring occasionally, until the flavors meld, about 2 minutes. Add the fresh dill (I like my fresh dill to remain bright, fresh, and green, so add it at the last minute) and turn off the heat. Garnish with drizzles of extra-virgin olive oil.

5 Before serving, divide the stew among serving bowls and top each bowl with a poached egg, if using. Squeeze the fresh lemon wedges over the dish, add more drizzles of the extra-virgin olive oil, if it's to your liking, and more freshly ground pepper, and serve immediately.

½ cup dried dill

2 ounces (56 grams) fresh dill, leaves and tender stems, finely chopped

Extra-virgin olive oil for drizzling

4 to 6 poached large eggs (optional)

2 to 3 fresh lemons, halved

CELERY HERB STEW

KHORESHT-E KARAFS | *makes 4 to 6 servings*

One night, shortly after Akis and I had started dating, I passed through the bustling, makeshift produce stands in Chinatown en route to Akis's South Street Seaport apartment. From long beans and squash to varietals of Chinese lettuces and choy, a rainbow of fruits and vegetables overflowed from newspaper-lined cardboard boxes and tubs set off the ground on plastic milk crates. Each box had its own hand-scribbled sign, but of all the offerings, I was smitten with the most beautiful, emerald-green whole bunches of celery. I love celery in all forms—raw, roasted, stewed—and I was so excited to introduce Akis to *khoresht-e karafs,* a celery and herb stew whose minty fragrance makes your home smell heavenly. As he was eating it enthusiastically, he said, "I hate celery. Are you sure it's celery?" Baffled, I thought, Wow, this guy just ate *a lot* of celery for someone who hates celery—big, gulping spoonfuls of it. By the end of our dinner, his new disclaimer became, "I guess I hate raw celery." I can understand that perhaps, like Akis, you, too, may not have the enthusiasm I have for celery. But celery shines in this herb stew, its raw bitterness giving way to a sweeter, more complex flavor as it cooks. And when you use the aromatic celery leaves, they fortify the flavor. For the record, over the years, Akis has also claimed to dislike cauliflower and cilantro, among other things, and my kids and I have learned not to take him too seriously.

1 Add the onions and 4 tablespoons olive oil to a large, heavy-bottomed pot with a tight-fitting lid and sauté over medium heat, adding more oil if needed, so that the onions turn golden, their edges darken, and they soften, about 5 to 7 minutes. Add the turmeric, a bit more oil, and stir, allowing the turmeric to bloom and release its fragrance, about 1 minute.

2 Pat the meat cubes dry and add them to the pot. Season the meat with the salt and pepper, cover with the lid, lower the heat to low, and cook, allowing the meat to release its juices, about 5 minutes. Remove the lid, give the mixture a stir, raise the heat to medium-high, and continue cooking, uncovered, until the meat is glossy and any remaining liquid in the pot evaporates, about 6 minutes more. Add 8 cups (2 liters) water, cover, and bring to a boil, then lower the heat to a gentle boil and cook for about 1 hour. While the meat is cooking, fry the herbs.

1 large yellow onion, medium diced

Light olive oil

2 tablespoons ground turmeric

1½ pounds (680 grams) beef chuck or boneless lamb shoulder, cut into 1-inch cubes

2 tablespoons kosher salt, plus more to taste

2 teaspoons freshly ground black pepper

8 ounces (226 grams) fresh chives or scallions, both white and green parts, finely chopped

3 Place the chives or scallions, parsley, and cilantro in a large, dry sauté pan over high heat, and cook, stirring occasionally, for about 2 minutes, until they release all of their liquid. Add ¼ cup (60 ml) olive oil, then continue cooking, about 3 to 4 minutes, until the herbs cook down and take on a glossy shine. Turn off the heat, then add the dried mint and mix to combine.

4 Add the fried herbs, celery, and lemon juice to the pot. Cover and lower the heat to medium-low, and continue cooking for 1 hour more. Allow to rest, partially covered at room temperature, for 1 hour before serving.

5 Squeeze fresh lemon wedges over the dish and serve.

8 ounces (226 grams) fresh flat-leaf parsley, leaves and tender stems, finely chopped

8 ounces (226 grams) fresh cilantro, leaves and tender stems, finely chopped

¼ cup dried mint

1 pound (454 grams) celery, white ends trimmed, leaves separated and finely chopped, stalks cut into 1-inch pieces

½ cup (120 ml) bottled lemon juice

2 to 3 fresh lemons, cut into wedges

GHORMEH SABZI

HERB, KIDNEY BEAN, AND BEEF STEW | *makes 4 to 6 servings*

Fried herbs, earthy kidney beans, tender pieces of beef or lamb, and the powerful kick of earth and citrus from sun-dried limes. The components of *ghormeh sabzi,* Iran's most iconic herb stew, are the same throughout the whole country, albeit with slight variations. On one trip home, I observed my mother adding fresh spinach to hers. When I questioned her about it, she replied, in typical Iranian fashion—which is to answer a question with a question—*(And you don't?)*. I began to add it to my mix from that point forward, too, the fresh spinach lending a silky texture.

Ghormeh sabzi is synonymous with celebration, and it's why I offer it at Sofreh, where I want my guests to feel like they are at a Persian party in my home. I fry the hell out of the herbs, adding oil in stages, allowing them to burn along the edges and stick to the bottom of the pan. Then I turn off the heat, which allows any stuck herbs to release themselves, and with a wooden spoon, I gently scrape them before starting all over again, frying, adding a bit more oil, and intensifying their flavor. I undertake this process three or four times to chase that deep, lavish herbal flavor that is the base of this stew. What follows is my *ghormeh sabzi* recipe that I make for my family, which entails less oil and less frying time.

I call for six sun-dried limes for this recipe. But if you don't have them, use dried lime powder. We love sun-dried lime so much in my house that we need two limes each in our pot. Before serving, press the limes with the back of your spoon to release their juices into the pot. Or squeeze them over your accompanying rice. At Sofreh, I can't keep up with the demand for sun-dried limes, so I break them into pieces and add more lemon juice to capture the sourness. I like a strong lemon flavor in my *ghormeh sabzi,* so if ⅔ cup (157 ml) seems too much for you, add ½ cup (120 ml) and taste. You can always add more.

Note You need to soak the kidney beans for a minimum of 4 hours and up to overnight before making this recipe. If you do not add the dried herb mix, increase each fresh herb by 2 ounces (56 grams) more. →

1 Place the beans in a large bowl and cover with water by 2 inches. Soak for a minimum of 4 hours and up to overnight.

2 Add the onions and 4 tablespoons olive oil to a large, heavy-bottomed pot with a tight-fitting lid and sauté over medium heat, adding more oil if needed, so that the onions turn golden, their edges darken, and they soften, about 5 to 7 minutes. Add the turmeric, a bit more oil, and stir, allowing the turmeric to bloom and release its fragrance, about 1 minute more.

3 Pat the meat cubes dry and add them to the pot. Season the meat with salt and pepper, cover with the lid, lower the heat to low, and cook, allowing the meat to release its juices, about 5 minutes. Remove the lid, give the mixture a stir, raise the heat to medium-high, and continue cooking, uncovered, until the meat is glossy and any remaining liquid in the pot evaporates, a few minutes more. Add 10 cups (2.4 liters) water to the pot, cover, and cook, on medium-high for 30 minutes.

4 Drain the beans and add them to the pot, along with the dried limes or lime powder, and raise the heat to high and bring to a boil. Then lower the heat to a gentle boil and cook, covered, for about 1 hour. While the meat and beans are cooking, fry the herbs.

5 Place the cilantro, parsley, chives or scallions, spinach, and fresh fenugreek, if using, in a large, dry sauté pan over high heat, and stir continuously, until they release all of their liquid and start sticking to the bottom of the pan. Next, add the dried herb mix (and dried fenugreek, if using) and slowly add ¼ cup (60 ml) olive oil, in batches, and continue frying, until the herbs are dark and you have used up all the olive oil. Remove the pan from the heat and allow to rest, until the herbs release easily from the bottom of the pan, about 10 minutes. Add the fried herbs to the meat and bean pot, and using a wooden spoon, deglaze any herbs still stuck to the pan with the lemon juice and add them to the pot, too. Cover with the lid, lower the heat to medium-low, and continue cooking until the meat is fork-tender, about 30 to 45 minutes. Taste for seasoning.

6 Lift the lid, and using the back of a spoon, press the dried limes while they are in the pot to allow them to release more of their juices. Leave the lid slightly ajar and allow to rest at room temperature for 1 hour.

7 Squeeze the fresh lemon wedges over the dish before serving.

½ cup (92 grams) dry kidney beans

1 large yellow onion, medium diced

Light olive oil

1 tablespoon ground turmeric

1 pound (454 grams) beef chuck or boneless lamb shoulder, cut into 1-inch cubes

2 tablespoons kosher salt

1 tablespoon freshly ground black pepper

6 whole sun-dried limes, halved, or 1½ tablespoons dried lime powder

8 ounces (226 grams) fresh cilantro, leaves and tender stems, finely chopped

8 ounces (226 grams) fresh flat-leaf parsley, leaves and tender stems, finely chopped

8 ounces (226 grams) fresh chives or scallions, both white and green parts, finely chopped

6 ounces (170 grams) fresh spinach, leaves and tender stems, finely chopped

3 ounces (85 grams) fresh fenugreek, leaves and tender stems, finely chopped, or ½ ounce dried fenugreek

½ cup *sabzi ghormeh* dried herb mix (see Resources, page 317)

⅓ cup (80 ml) bottled lemon juice

2 to 3 fresh lemons, cut into wedges

EGGPLANT BADEMJOON

I'm nine years old. And the voices of the fruit and vegetable vendors enchant me. They lumber down our street in Isfahan, leading donkeys that carry their wares in sacks, announcing their produce with a signature intonation, as specific as a bird's song. *"Chaghaleh badam!"* *"Chaghaleh badam!"* This one is promoting fuzzy-skinned, green spring almonds. Another one booms *"Goje sabz!"* A short pause. And then louder: *"Sour PLUMS."* Soon, April spring rains will give way to the produce of summer, and the lyrics will change: *"Khiar, khiar, khiar,"* a staccato rhythm cutting through the air as crisp as the tiny cucumbers he's selling. And then, *"Kadoo! Kadoo!"* Tender zucchini, like a love song. But it's the steady beat of *"Bademjoon, bademjoon, bademjoon"* that has my mother heading straight to the door today, because the eggplant vendor has arrived. And I bolt to her side.

My schoolteacher mother is home during summers. We are all home; kids, moms, neighbors. And even though she can go to the grocery store for many of her fruits and vegetables, I am glad she doesn't. Even at nine years old, I relish this ritual. On our way, we'll give the vendor one of the plastic bags hanging on the side of our house. It's full of watermelon rinds for his donkey. And another has dried bread for his chickens, and still another is heavy with the excessive amount of lemon skins. Goats love lemons!

The eggplants of my childhood are deep purple, one and a half to two inches in size, and extremely narrow. In the kitchen, I watch my mother dig out a little chunk with the tip of her finger and taste it, assessing it for bitterness. She's teaching me how to select produce. Each purchase is a lesson, as she guides me to rely on my senses to ascertain the worthiness of the goods. These moments (as well as the fact that she lets me use a knife at nine years old) are a wellspring of happiness. She has a little step made for me to give me some height when I cook with her. Today I notice that she is buying a lot of eggplants, way more than the zucchini she purchases for our lunch or dinner. "Why?" I ask her. *(Eggplants are tricky, many will wind up too bitter to eat, and so I'll save those for pickling.)*

My affection for eggplants is an extension of my mother's love for them. And it comingles with my love of cooking with her. Eggplants also capture my heart because they are the most versatile of all the vegetables—and they are the most work to prepare.

And then, of course, I adored their taste. In the late 1960s and '70s, Isfahan's produce—especially cucumbers and eggplants—were grown on small farms whose rich soil was irrigated by the then-still-flowing waters of Iran's largest river, the Zayandeh Rud, which runs east to west through the city of Isfahan. Along with our seasonal weather, this convergence of nature yielded eggplants with a creamy texture and pleasingly sweet flavor that were superior to all others. And I never tired of eating them two or three times a week, as we did then.

As I grew up and away from Isfahan, eggplants and all they represented followed me. During my second year at the University of Tehran, I was in the thick of the revolution. I remember joining my friends on a hike into the Alborz Mountains for a week's stay. The elevation provided safety, privacy, and space to process all the chaos that was happening around us. For this hike, we were responsible for bringing rations because there was no food or water available where we would be camping. I knew my friends would bring feta and bread, along with hard-boiled eggs and enough nuts and dates to last through the week. So, naturally, I thought I should bring a lot of fried eggplant! After our eight-hour hike up the mountainside, I started emptying my backpack, pulling out containers of eggplant layered with fried onions, tomatoes, and cheese that I had premade in my tiny dorm room. And it didn't take long for me to realize from their sideways looks that my friends thought I was an oddball. But no matter, along with the bread and herbs on hand, I had set us up for a feast. And in the process of cooking, I had dipped into a well of childhood comfort that I had so desperately needed.

The recipes in this chapter are dedicated to offering possibilities for capitalizing on the flavor and texture that eggplants offer. Sometimes, eggplant is a canvas for intoxicating layers of flavor—such as the caramelized tomato, onion, and salty feta of my Sofreh Roasted Eggplant with Tomato Sauce and Feta (page 109), which tastes just like the one my great-grandmother would fry for us for lunch. And as much as my passion for eggplant began in Isfahan, I take you to the north, with a smoked eggplant and tomato sauce called *mirza ghasemi* (see page 114). It's included here as an homage to my dear aunt Mihan, my mother's sister. You'll find it on my menu at Sofreh, too, even though making it for a restaurant setting makes little economic sense. Sourcing eggplants year-round is expensive, and smoking large quantities of eggplant is a senseless labor cost. But that's the thing about my passion for eggplants. Sometimes it blinds me to the practicalities of business.

Bademjoon!
Bademjoon!

Bademjoon Basics

At Sofreh, I have a reputation for "doing eggplants right," turning naysayers into eggplant lovers. So, what does it mean to raise this oft-polarizing vegetable to new heights? Just as my mother taught me, each eggplant dish depends on the quality of the eggplant. Look for very firm, dark eggplants— if they are soft or bruised in some areas, put them back. I recommend smaller, teardrop-shaped Italian eggplants for many of these recipes. Or a larger varietal, like globe eggplants, for the eggplant dip *kashk-o-bademjoon* (see page 117) and for Smoked Eggplant (page 114). A larger eggplant lends itself well to the creamy, mashed texture of both dishes. To this day, if Akis comes through the door after purchasing eggplants, he wonders if he has passed or failed my eggplant test.

Today, farmers genetically breed eggplants to remove much of their bitterness. But sufficiently salting them is still essential. While I salt them to remove any possibility of bitterness, more important, I salt them before cooking because they are like sponges; salting draws out their water, which helps reduce oil absorption. One to three hours of salting is enough for these recipes, but depending on the volume of eggplants you are working with, you may want to increase the salting time to overnight. I leave that up to you. Also, for whatever purpose you are preparing an eggplant, don't undertake the process with haste. Medium, gentle heat and less oil are best in most cases. If you crank the heat too high, the eggplant will absorb the oil all at once, and you'll find that you have to keep flipping it and adding more oil, resulting in sodden, heavy eggplant.

Whenever possible, I advocate buying eggplants in season from your local farmer. I know that the lines of seasonality are blurred these days, and the desire for year-round produce supersedes even the best of intentions to eat locally. In that case, if you come across a greenhouse varietal at your grocer it will work well in these recipes, too. However, when cooking with eggplants in winter, keep these two tips in mind: (1) allow for a longer frying time on each side (when in doubt, use a cake tester to make sure your eggplant is cooked through) and (2) increase the amount of oil you use from the ⅓ cup (80 ml) called for in these recipes to ½ cup (120 ml) or more as needed.

Finally, in many of these recipes, unless I am cutting the eggplants into rounds, I leave the stems intact because not only does it make for good-looking eggplants, it also holds the eggplants together while frying.

SOFREH ROASTED EGGPLANT
with TOMATO SAUCE and FETA

makes 4 to 6 servings

I offered this eggplant dish at Sofreh the first summer we opened, and all night in my dining room, I heard, "My goodness, what did you put in this?" The secret is in the layered flavors of caramelized onion, rich tomato paste, sour grapes, and salty feta on top. Instead of feta, you can also enjoy this dish with a dollop of thick yogurt, or if you like, glorify and elevate this eggplant, as we do at Sofreh, with Mint Oil (page 196) and Saffron Water (page xxxiv) for an added layer of color and aroma. Also, this eggplant is great to make ahead of time for a party. Make it in the morning, cover it, and serve at room temperature.

Note I like to roast the eggplant in the same dish I plan on serving it in. When you lay your eggplant beautifully on the bottom of the roasting dish, and then add the garnishes over it, it's ready to be served right out of the oven without overhandling.

1 Working with one eggplant at a time, use a sharp knife to trim any spines along the stem, but leave the stems intact. Peel 4 narrow stripes lengthwise on each eggplant, then halve lengthwise. Sprinkle liberally with salt and stand the eggplants upright in a colander to drain for 1 to 3 hours.

2 Preheat the oven to 375°F.

3 Pat the eggplants dry with paper towels to remove excess moisture and salt. Coat the bottom of a large skillet with the neutral oil and warm over medium-high heat. Place the cut side of the eggplant halves facedown in the skillet, lower the heat to medium, and gently fry until dark golden, about 25 minutes. Turn and fry the other side, until you can see the oil bubble up through the tops of the eggplants, about 10 minutes more. Remove from the pan and set aside.

4 Add the onions and 4 tablespoons olive oil to a medium pan and sauté over medium heat, adding more oil if needed, so that the onions turn golden, their edges darken, and they soften, about 5 to 7 minutes. Make a well in the center of the pan, add the garlic and a bit more oil (so that the garlic doesn't burn), and sauté until fragrant, about 3 minutes more. Add the turmeric, a bit more oil, and stir, allowing the turmeric to bloom and release its fragrance, about 1 minute more. Next, add the tomato paste and sauté, stirring occasionally, until the tomato paste takes on a shiny color, about 1 minute more (the mixture will pull away from the bottom of the skillet). →

5 to 6 small Italian eggplants (about 2½ pounds/1.1 kilograms)

Kosher salt

⅓ cup (80 ml) neutral oil, such as vegetable or canola oil, for frying

1 large yellow onion, halved and thinly sliced into half-moons

Light olive oil

6 garlic cloves, thinly sliced on a mandoline

1 tablespoon ground turmeric

¾ cup (170 grams) tomato paste

2 tablespoons granulated sugar

1 tablespoon freshly ground black pepper

¼ cup (60 ml) bottled lemon juice

½ cup (114 grams) pickled sour grapes in brine *(gooreh)*, store-bought, drained (see Resources, page 317; optional)

⅔ cup (100 grams) crumbled feta cheese or dollops of thick yogurt

Mint Oil (page 196) for garnish (optional)

Saffron Water (page xxxiv) for garnish (optional)

5 Add the sugar, 1 tablespoon salt, and the pepper. Deglaze the pan with the lemon juice and ¼ cup (60 ml) water. Remove from the heat and set aside.

6 Pour ¼ cup (60 ml) water in the bottom of a medium roasting pan and place the eggplants in the pan, cut side up. Spread some of the onion mixture on the top of each one, followed by a few sour grapes, if using. Cover the pan with aluminum foil and bake for 30 to 45 minutes.

7 Remove the pan from the oven and spread the feta on top of the eggplants. Cover and rest at room temperature for a few minutes, or until the feta softens. Before serving, garnish with the mint oil and saffron water, if desired.

EGGPLANT STEW
with SPLIT PEAS

GHAYME BADEMJOON | *makes 4 to 6 servings*

My daughter, Soshy's, favorite stew is *khoresht-e ghayme*—a fulfilling split pea stew flavored with sun-dried limes that is popular throughout Iran, and eaten year-round, regardless of the season. The ingredients are inexpensive (as with every traditional stew, the ratio of meat to vegetables or legumes is low), and it's often served for religious ceremonies, because a big pot goes far when feeding large groups of people.

Traditionally, the eggplants simmer in the pot and fall apart, leaving you with a pile of mush. In general, I am against getting a lot of dishes dirty, but for this stew, it pays to go the extra mile, cooking the eggplants separately and then gently layering the sauce over them and serving the stew in a lovely serving or Pyrex dish.

1 Working with one eggplant at a time, use a sharp knife to trim any spines along the stem, but leave the stems intact. Peel 4 narrow stripes lengthwise on each eggplant, then halve lengthwise. Sprinkle liberally with salt and stand the eggplants upright in a colander to drain for 1 to 3 hours.

2 Pat the eggplants dry with paper towels to remove excess moisture and salt. Coat the bottom of a large skillet with the neutral oil and warm over medium-high heat. Place the cut side of the eggplant halves facedown in the skillet, lower the heat to medium, and fry gently until dark golden, about 20 minutes. Turn and fry the other side, until you can see the oil bubble up through the tops of the eggplants, about 10 minutes more. Remove from the pan and set aside.

3 Add the onions and 4 tablespoons olive oil to a large, heavy-bottomed pot with a tight-fitting lid and sauté over medium heat, adding more olive oil if needed, so that the onions turn golden, their edges darken, and they soften, about 5 to 7 minutes. Add the turmeric, a bit more oil, and stir, allowing the turmeric to bloom and release its fragrance, about 1 minute more.

4 Pat the meat cubes dry and add them to the pot. Season the meat with 1½ tablespoons salt and the pepper, cover with the lid, lower the heat to low, and cook, allowing the meat to release its juices, about 5 minutes. Remove the lid, give the mixture a stir, raise the heat to medium-high, and continue cooking, uncovered, until the meat is glossy and any remaining liquid in the pot evaporates, about 6 minutes more. Add the tomato paste, mix well, then add the cinnamon sticks, sun-dried limes, and 8 cups (2 liters) water. $\rightarrow$

2½ to 3 pounds (1.1 to 1.4 kilograms) small Italian eggplants (the smaller, the better)

Kosher salt

⅓ cup (80 ml) neutral oil, such as vegetable or canola oil, for frying

1 large yellow onion, medium diced

Light olive oil

2 tablespoons ground turmeric

1½ pounds (680 grams) beef chuck, cut into 1-inch cubes

1 tablespoon freshly ground black pepper

½ cup (112 grams) tomato paste

2 cinnamon sticks (about 2 inches long)

4 sun-dried limes, halved, or 1 tablespoon dried lime powder

½ cup (112 grams) split peas

½ cup (114 grams) pickled sour grapes in brine (*gooreh*), store-bought, drained (see Resources, page 317)

4 small tomatoes, such as grape, Campari, or large cherry tomatoes, halved

Cover with the lid and bring to a boil, then lower the heat to a gentle boil for about 1½ hours.

5 Add the split peas to the pot and continue cooking, covered, until they are soft but still have a bite, about 15 minutes more. Remove the sauce from the pot to a bowl, place the reserved eggplants on the bottom of the pot, and transfer the sauce back into the pot. Place the sour grapes and tomatoes on top and return to a gentle boil for an additional 20 minutes.

Alternatively Preheat the oven to 350°F. Place the reserved fried eggplants in an ovenproof serving dish and top with the meat and split pea sauce. Cover with aluminum foil and continue cooking for 20 minutes. Taste and adjust the seasoning, then top with the sour grapes and tomatoes, and cook for 25 minutes more.

SMOKED EGGPLANT

MIRZA GHASEMI | *makes 4 to 6 servings*

I owe my penchant for bold flavors and obsessive attention to detail to my mother's sister Khale Mihan. (*Khale* denotes an aunt on your mother's side.) Even today, when I go to my aunt Mihan's home in Iran for one of her glorious spreads, I can see the wheels in her head turning. I'll interrupt her daydream to ask, "Dear Auntie, what are you thinking?" And she'll answer, "I'm thinking about what I can make for *tomorrow's* lunch."

Aunt Mihan's husband is from the north of Iran, and many of my aunt's specialties, such as this smoked eggplant and tomato sauce with runny poached eggs, called *mirza ghasemi,* come from that part of the country. This eggplant sauce is made in the provinces of both Gilan and Mazandaran, with one of them adding fresh tomatoes, while the other omits tomatoes altogether and uses lots of garlic. Also because of the proximity to the Caspian Sea, you can find variations of this dish topped with caviar.

I was on my first visit home, after nine years away, when Khale Mihan went out of her way to impress my then-new husband, Akis, by going all out and preparing a whole tableful of northern specialties and reintroducing me to this dish. As is typical of home cooks in Iran, she never gave me a recipe. I just watched her intently and copied her technique of finely chopping the charred skin and adding it for smoky depth of flavor, along with any liquid the charred eggplant may release.

Note Nothing beats *mirza ghasemi* in the summer when eggplants are at their most flavorful, and you can take advantage of late-summer tomatoes (I love New Jersey tomatoes). Swap out the peeled tomatoes for 6 whole tomatoes (about 1½ pounds/680 kilograms) skinned, seeded, and chopped into medium pieces. Also, you can omit the eggs, if you like. If using them, however, you can poach the eggs separately or in the sauce.

1 Cover a stove-top range with a layer of aluminum foil for easy cleanup, making sure to keep the burner exposed. Pierce the eggplants with a fork and place them directly on the grate, over a medium flame, and roast, giving a quarter turn now and then, for about 1 to 2 minutes on all sides, until the skin is uniformly charred, and the flesh is soft. Remove from the heat and set aside on a baking sheet to cool, reserving any liquid that weeps from the eggplant.

2 When the eggplants are cool enough to handle, peel the charred skin (discarding any skin that feels leathery to the touch) and finely chop—really running your knife through it. Set the skin aside. Roughly chop the eggplants, then set them aside, too.

2 to 3 large globe eggplants (about 3 pounds/1.3 kilograms)

1 large yellow onion, finely chopped

Light olive oil

10 large garlic cloves, finely chopped

1½ tablespoons ground turmeric

½ cup (112 grams) tomato paste

1 cup diced, peeled, canned tomatoes

2 tablespoons kosher salt

3 Meanwhile, add the onions and ⅓ cup (80 ml) olive oil to a large, heavy-bottomed pot with a tight-fitting lid and sauté over medium heat, adding more oil if needed, so that the onions turn golden, their edges darken, and they soften, about 5 to 7 minutes. Add the garlic and a bit more oil (so that the garlic doesn't burn), and stir. Then, add the turmeric, a bit more oil, and stir, allowing the turmeric to bloom and release its fragrance, about 30 seconds. Next, add the tomato paste and sauté, stirring occasionally until the tomato paste takes on a shiny color, about 1 minute more (the mixture will pull away from the bottom of the pot).

4 Add the diced tomatoes, salt, pepper, sugar, the chopped eggplant, and 1 tablespoon of the chopped skin, and stir to incorporate, using the back of a spoon to break up the eggplant. Add the lemon juice and ¼ cup (60 ml) water. Stir well to combine. Cover with the lid, raise the heat, and bring to a boil until it steams, about 2 to 3 minutes. Lower the heat to low and cook for 30 minutes, covered, stirring now and then so the bottom doesn't scorch. Taste and adjust the seasoning, adding more of the eggplant skin, if you like, and ¼ cup (60 ml) more water, if the mixture seems dry.

5 Uncover, add the extra-virgin olive oil, and stir. The sauce is ready.

6 To serve *mirza ghasemi* with eggs, poach 2 eggs per person and set them on top before serving. Or alternatively, create a well for each egg and crack them directly into the pan. Season each egg with more salt and pepper, cover with the lid, and cook over low heat for 3 to 4 minutes more for runny yolks, or longer for a firmer yolk.

Alternatively For step 1, prepare a hardwood-charcoal fire in a grill. Let the coals cool to medium heat, then place the eggplants directly on the coals and cook, using tongs to turn them occasionally, until their skins are blackened and their flesh collapses, about 10 minutes. Transfer to a rimmed baking sheet to cool. Save any liquid that weeps from the eggplants.

1 tablespoon freshly ground black pepper

2 tablespoons granulated sugar

¼ cup (60 ml) bottled lemon juice

½ cup (120 ml) extra-virgin olive oil for finishing

2 large eggs per person (optional)

WARM EGGPLANT DIP
with WHEY

KASHK-O-BADEMJOON | *makes 4 to 6 servings*

We cannot keep up with the demand for this dip at Sofreh. Guests from every walk of life come through our doors and tell me that they heard from someone that our eggplant dip is a must-have. As is the case with so many of our traditional recipes, many versions of *kashk-o-bademjoon* exist throughout Iran. But for those newcomers to Persian cooking at Sofreh, I realize that this eggplant dip is often their first entry point into understanding the depth of flavor and feast for the senses that our food offers.

I cover the silky eggplant with Saffron Water (page xxxiv), herby Mint Oil (page 196), Crispy Fried Onions (page 194), Crispy Garlic Chips (page 195), and good-quality store-bought *kashk*. We serve it with our warm Sofreh Bread (page 271) for dipping, and I never tire of watching people swipe their plate clean. I always make *kashk-o-bademjoon* for parties, too. It keeps in the refrigerator, ungarnished, for up to 1 week.

1 Peel the eggplants, trim off the ends, and slice the eggplants into ½-inch-thick disks. Sprinkle liberally on both sides with salt and set aside to drain on a wire rack set on a baking sheet for about 1 to 3 hours.

2 Pat the eggplant rounds dry with paper towels to remove excess moisture and salt. Coat the bottom of a large skillet with the neutral oil and warm over medium-high heat. Lower the heat to medium and, working in batches if necessary, gently sauté the eggplant rounds on both sides, until golden, about 3 to 5 minutes per side. Avoid rendering the eggplants fully browned. This way, you will guarantee that they will not overcook, preventing them from soaking up the flavors of the onion when you add it. Set them aside.

3 Add the onions and 4 tablespoons olive oil to a large, heavy-bottomed pot with a tight-fitting lid and sauté over medium heat, adding more oil if needed, so that the onions turn golden, their edges darken, and they soften, about 5 to 7 minutes. Make a well in the center of the pot, add the garlic and a bit more oil (so that the garlic doesn't burn), and sauté until fragrant, about 3 minutes more. Add the turmeric, a bit more oil, and stir, allowing the turmeric to bloom and release its fragrance, about 1 minute.

4 Add the fried eggplant rounds to the pot, and using the back of a spoon, break up any hard pieces to achieve a mashed, but evenly chunky consistency. Taste for salt, adding 1 teaspoon, or a pinch more if necessary, then add the pepper and ½ cup (120 ml) water. Stir to combine. $\longrightarrow$

2 large globe eggplants (about 2 pounds/907 grams)

Kosher salt

⅓ cup (80 ml) neutral oil, such as vegetable or canola oil, for frying

1 large yellow onion, medium diced

Light olive oil

7 large garlic cloves, finely chopped

1½ tablespoons ground turmeric

1 tablespoon freshly ground black pepper

½ cup (120 ml) *kashk*, store-bought, plus 1 to 2 tablespoons for garnish

½ cup (56 grams) chopped walnuts for garnish

Saffron Water (page xxxiv) for garnish

Mint Oil (page 196) for garnish

Crispy Fried Onions (page 194) for garnish

Crispy Garlic Chips (page 195) for garnish

5 Cover with a lid, set over medium-low heat, and cook for about 30 minutes. Meanwhile, prepare the saffron water, mint oil, fried onions, and garlic chips.

6 Remove the pot from the heat. Stir in the *kashk* and thoroughly combine.

7 Transfer the mixture to a serving bowl. Dilute 1 to 2 more tablespoons *kashk* with water and drizzle over the top. Garnish with the walnuts, saffron water, mint oil, fried onions, and garlic chips.

STUFFED EGGPLANT
with MINCED BEEF

DOLMEH BADEMJOON | *makes 4 to 6 servings*

Dolmeh, meaning "stuffed," is an entire category of food in Iran, with traditions for stuffed grape leaves such as *dolmeh barg mo* (see page 133), as well as zucchini, bell peppers, and tomatoes. Each *dolmeh* variation in Iran brims with herby fragrances, stuffings of cracked wheat or chickpeas, and varying levels of our favorite sweet and sour flavors, depending on what is available in the region. But this version of *dolmeh bademjoon* came about years ago while I was away for the summer in Mykonos, Greece, when each trip I'd take advantage of the beauty of Greek eggplants in summer.

Hot city summers with two small kids can be challenging. And because I don't believe in summer camps, I would pack up Soshy and Noony and head to Greece for six or eight weeks. My parents or my brother Amir would sometimes join us, and we'd visit Akis's mom, "Yaya," until Akis could get away and join us for two weeks of family vacation. One night, I was invited to an elaborate party in a sprawling private villa. I didn't know a soul other than the host. But I was desperate for adult company. And I was determined to bring something unique to the party besides a boring box of sweets, and stuffed eggplant on vacation just felt right. Apart from the container of turmeric that I always take with me when I travel, it was just a matter of gathering meat from the butcher and whatever additional spices I could find along the way. When the hostess greeted me, she offered me a beautiful silver tray and some fresh oregano from her garden to garnish. "What is that?" "Who made it?" the other guests said, and my eggplant became an icebreaker.

Note If using large eggplants, after frying, you can use a knife to make an incision down the center of the eggplant halves to stuff the meat mixture inside because they will have more depth. For smaller eggplants, you can use your hands to gently make a pocket in the eggplants to spoon the eggplant mixture into.

1 Working with one eggplant at a time, use a sharp knife to trim any spines along the stem, but leave the stems intact. Peel 4 narrow stripes lengthwise on each eggplant, then halve lengthwise. Sprinkle liberally with salt and stand the eggplants upright in a colander to drain for 1 to 3 hours.

2 Preheat the oven to 350°F.

3 Pat the eggplants dry with paper towels to remove excess moisture and salt. Coat the bottom of a large skillet with a tight-fitting lid with the neutral oil and warm over medium-high heat. Place the cut side of the eggplant →

5 to 6 small Italian eggplants (about 4 pounds/1.8 kilograms) or 3 large eggplants (see headnote)

Kosher salt

⅓ cup (80 ml) neutral oil, such as vegetable or canola oil, for frying

1 large yellow onion, medium diced

Light olive oil →

halves facedown in the skillet, and fry until the underside is golden, about 5 to 7 minutes. Remove from the pan and set aside.

4 Using the same skillet, add the onions and 4 tablespoons olive oil and sauté over medium heat, adding more oil if needed, so that the onions turn golden, their edges darken, and they soften, about 10 minutes. Add the garlic and a bit more oil (so that the garlic doesn't burn), and stir. Then, add the turmeric, a bit more oil, and stir, allowing the turmeric to bloom and release its fragrance, about 30 seconds. Next, add the tomato paste and sauté, stirring occasionally until the tomato paste takes on a shiny color, about 2 to 3 minutes.

5 Add the meat, cinnamon, cumin, sugar, pepper, and 1½ tablespoons salt and cook, breaking up the meat as you go, until well browned and cooked through, about 5 minutes (the mixture will caramelize and stick to the bottom of the pan). Next, raise the heat to high and deglaze the pan with the lemon juice and ¼ cup (60 ml) water. Lower the heat to low, cover, and cook for about 5 minutes.

6 Uncover, add the green peas and ½ cup of the parsley, mix well to incorporate, and turn off the heat.

7 Pour ¼ cup (60 ml) water into the bottom of a roasting pan and place the eggplants in the pan, cut side up. Stuff the eggplants with the meat sauce (see headnote), cover the pan with aluminum foil, and bake until they are well cooked but not falling apart, about 20 to 30 minutes.

8 Remove the pan from the oven and uncover, allowing the eggplants to come to room temperature. Garnish with the remaining ½ cup parsley and the crumbled feta, if you like, before serving.

4 to 6 garlic cloves, chopped

1 tablespoon ground turmeric

⅓ cup (75 grams) tomato paste

¾ pound (340 grams) ground beef or lamb

1 tablespoon ground cinnamon

1 tablespoon ground cumin

1 tablespoon granulated sugar

1 tablespoon freshly ground black pepper

½ cup (120 ml) bottled lemon juice

¼ cup (72 grams) fresh or frozen green peas

1 cup finely chopped fresh flat-leaf parsley (about 2 ounces/56 grams)

¼ cup (38 grams) crumbled feta cheese for garnish (optional)

ISFAHANI EGGPLANT HALEEM

HALEEM BADEMJOON | *makes 6 servings*

Hearty and thick and similar to *a'ash* (see pages 189–209), *haleem* is made throughout Iran. Both are prepared in large quantities for special occasions or to enjoy in a group setting and for religious ceremonies and offerings. I've had Tehrani variations and southern Iranian versions that include wheat pearls, cracked wheat, or walnuts. Still, I prefer this Isfahani summer version that uses rice as the starch, giving it a lighter texture. Each summer, when I return to Isfahan, older generations of friends and neighbors bring *haleem* as a gesture to say, "Welcome home!" The preparation of *haleem* involves pounding the lamb neck with a heavy, flat-bottomed wooden meat mallet called a *ghusht kub*. The connective tissue breaks down over low and slow cooking, yielding up tons of flavor and a gelatinous texture. Separately, you pound the eggplants and rice into a paste. When you slowly incorporate them, the result of all of this labor is *haleem*'s sticky, rich, and comforting texture. I've seen younger generations of cooks rely on a food processor to do the work for them, which turns the *haleem* to mush and, in my opinion, kills the dish—it should be very well beaten together but never pureed.

Note Use the bottom of a clean, empty wine bottle if you don't have a *ghusht kub*. I have reduced the amount of meat typically used in this dish.

1 Peel the eggplants, trim off the ends, and slice the eggplants into ½-inch-thick disks. Sprinkle liberally on both sides with salt and drain on a wire rack set on a baking sheet for about 1 to 3 hours.

2 Add half of the onions and 4 tablespoons olive oil to a large, heavy-bottomed pot with a tight-fitting lid and sauté, adding more oil if needed, so that the onions turn golden, their edges darken, and they soften, about 5 to 7 minutes. Add the turmeric, a bit more oil, and stir, allowing the turmeric to bloom and release its fragrance, about 1 minute more. Next, add the lamb or beef neck, 2 tablespoons salt, the pepper, and 8 cups (2 liters) water. Cover the pot, bring to a boil over high heat, then lower the heat to a gentle boil, and cook until the meat is tender and falls apart, about 1½ hours.

3 Remove the meat from the pot, reserving the cooking liquid, and allow the meat to cool. Once it is cool, separate the meat from the bones and ligaments and use two forks to shred it. Cover and set aside.

4 Meanwhile, prepare the eggplant. Coat the bottom of a large skillet with neutral oil and warm over low heat. Working in batches, and using more oil as needed, fry the eggplant on both sides, 3 to 4 minutes, or until golden.

4 large globe eggplants
(about 4 pounds/1.8 kilograms)

Kosher salt

1 large yellow onion,
medium diced

Light olive oil

3 tablespoons ground turmeric

2 pounds (906 grams) bone-in
lamb neck or beef neck

2 tablespoons freshly ground
black pepper, plus more as
needed

Neutral oil, such as vegetable
or canola oil, for frying

¾ cup (138 grams) jasmine rice,
rinsed

1½ cups (360 ml) *kashk,* store-
bought, plus more for garnish

Saffron Water (page xxxiv)
for garnish

5 Place the eggplant in a large pot and pour the reserved meat liquid over it. Add the rice to the pot along with 2 cups (470 ml) water, cover with a lid, and bring to a boil over high heat. Lower the heat to low and cook, stirring often so that the rice doesn't stick to the bottom, until the eggplant and rice are mushy, about 40 minutes.

6 While the eggplant is cooking, add the remaining onions and 4 tablespoons olive oil to a medium pan and sauté, adding more oil if needed, so that the onions turn golden, their edges darken, and they soften, about 5 to 7 minutes. Set aside.

7 Once the eggplant is fully cooked, add the shredded meat to the pot. Use a *ghusht kub* (see headnote) to break and mix the eggplant mixture and meat together, until they are thoroughly incorporated.

8 Temper the *kashk* before adding most of it to the pot. Add more water if needed, and taste and adjust the seasoning, adding more pepper, if you like. Add the reserved sautéed onions, cover the pot, and continue cooking until the texture of the *haleem* is thick and rich, about 10 minutes more.

9 Garnish with saffron water, mint oil, fried onions, and more *kashk*.

¼ cup (60 ml) Mint Oil (page 196) for garnish

Crispy Fried Onions (page 194) for garnish

LAMB AND BEEF
GHUSHT-E BAREH AND GHUSHT-E GHAV

New York City, 1994. My mom, Giti Joon, is using the power of her pointer finger to direct the Afghani butcher on Main Street in Flushing, Queens, on *exactly* how she'd like him to cut up the entire spring baby lamb she has instructed me to preorder. *(I want the legs separated from the shanks.)* My husband, Akis, acting as her assistant, stands close by, smiling sympathetically at the guy. I am sure, from the moment the butcher laid eyes on the dynamic, four-foot eight-inch fifty-six-year-old Iranian woman, striding through the shop toward his counter like a military dictator— no, more like a tank—he could tell that she was a powerful force.

I'm visualizing this scene in my mind's eye, alone in my apartment, lying pregnant and still on my doctor-ordered bedrest. Soon, they'll come through the door carrying lamb neck for *haleem* (see page 122) and lamb ribs for stuffing. Giti Joon will make use of every organ, meat, and muscle, right down to the collagen in the last lamb bone, believing that lamb, the most revered animal in Iranian culinary traditions, will provide the best source of protein and nourishment that her pregnant daughter needs.

During the early years of my marriage, I couldn't wait to become a mother. When I found out I was pregnant with twins, we were beyond thrilled. But seven months into my pregnancy, we lost them. As I began to come through the other side of my grief, I felt an urgency to live my life with a lighter approach. "I want to focus on opening a small Persian restaurant," I told Akis shortly after the loss, and his support was unwavering. But less than a year later, just when I decided to focus on my dream, I was pregnant, again with twins!

And so, there I lay, ordered to cease all physical activity—which included cooking—for the duration of my pregnancy. I turned my kitchen over to Giti Joon, who had rushed to New York from Isfahan to take care of me. As soon as she arrived, she took one look at the cuts of beef I had on hand in my refrigerator and proclaimed *(I am not cooking with that)*. And then *(Why is it so red?)*. She promptly rid my home of beef and made me call several butchers, from my bed, to source instead whole, small, tender spring lamb. I finally landed on the Afghani butcher in Queens.

Layers of centuries-old nomadic traditions intimately tied to topography, region, climate, economy, and class culture drive the preference for and predominance of *ghusht-e bareh* (lamb) in Iranian cuisine. What sets Iran apart from surrounding countries in the Middle East, such as Saudi Arabia, which is more than 95 percent desert, is that more than 50 percent of the land in Iran is rangelands. These rangelands, which exist in the high-elevation mountain ranges, and the flat, grassy belts and shrubs called the Iranian steppe, are well suited to raising smaller, more nimble animals that can traverse high elevations for grazing. And for centuries in Iran, pastoralists—tribes of nomadic people—have bred herds of sheep and goats supplying people living in sedentary villages along the steppe with meat, as well as milk for yogurt and cheese, and wool for clothing.

MORE THAN 50 PERCENT OF THE LAND IN IRAN IS RANGELANDS.

While this is the case in central Iran, where the province of Isfahan is located, venture farther north and you will find a tradition of raising cattle and cooking with *ghusht-e ghav* (beef) in the rice-producing regions of Gilan, Mazandaran, and Golestan, where nomads have traditionally raised cows along the fertile crescent of land surrounding the Caspian Sea. But consider that it is only since the 1950s, the beginning of a period of industrialization in Iran, that cattle farms and pasteurization plants have been constructed near Tehran, Iran's largest city. And that eating beef and drinking cow's milk have become part of the diet of other provinces of the country. And so, for the majority of home cooks, such as my mother and aunts, who grew up surrounded by delectable chickens, goats, and sheep, the look of a brightly colored red meat, borne from a massive, hulking animal, could never compare with the petite, grass-grazing, tender and pink lamb of the Iranian steppe. And from the time I was a young girl, it was ingrained in me that *(beef is for those who can't afford lamb)*. And as far back as I can remember, cooking with beef was not common in our culture.

My culinary perspective changed when I arrived in New York in the early 1980s. Back then, it was difficult to find lamb in U.S. grocery stores, and even if I did find it, I couldn't afford it. By nature, I am not a big meat eater, so I quickly grew accustomed to using less costly cuts of beef chuck, or ground beef, in place of the lamb shoulder and ground lamb I ate in my childhood, rendering it agreeable to my palate by using loads of onions and turmeric. But all of that changed when my Giti Joon arrived, because by the time our fraternal twins, Noony and Soshy, were born, not only had I gained seventy-five pounds from her home cooking but my mother had renewed my taste for the lamb dishes of my culture.

Each of the lamb recipes in this section—from my Isfahani childhood to new motherhood in New York City and on to Sofreh—tells a story.

Older generations of Iranian home cooks, such as the women in my family, still will not cook with *ghusht-e ghav,* but I want to offer you the flexibility to use both meats interchangeably, as I do.

So, in the pages that follow, you'll also find my favorite comforting beef dishes, as well as techniques for making several of our most well-known beef *kababs.* On page 145, there's my brother Amir's favorite *Makaroni* with Potato *Tahdig,* a cumin- and cinnamon-scented sauce that has all the comfort of beef Bolognese but is prepared in the same two-step method as we prepare rice, including a crunchy *tahdig* on the bottom of the pot.

Finally, I can't underestimate the wealth of knowledge a great butcher can offer you in sourcing excellent cuts of lamb and beef for these recipes. By the time I was back on my feet and cooking again, satisfying the demanding palate of my daughter, Soshy (who we soon discovered has a strength ten times greater than mine and my mother's combined!), I had left the Afghani guy and found a Greek butcher to supply me with excellent cuts of lamb to add to my repertoire. And he has been my supplier ever since. For more than twenty-five years now! There is something special about growing gray with him. We have a history together, making the exchange feel like family.

And that, my dear, means everything to me.

Zohm

While Americans look for the grass-fed, bold flavor of beef and lamb to shine through, Iranians purposefully mitigate the natural, gamy flavor profile and smell of animal proteins, called *zohm,* through the use of marinades or cooking techniques. My theory is that a flavor preference emerged over thousands of years of cooking meat with spices, herbs, and onions. It's also common in Iran to marinate proteins for what might seem like an extended period, sometimes up to two days. But the most repeated application of "getting rid of the *zohm*" that I use when I cook is my treatment of lamb, poultry, and beef for my home-cooked stews. You'll notice a pattern in each recipe where I first sauté onions, then bloom turmeric, to create a base before adding the meat. Next, I'll season the protein with additional turmeric (often, but not always) plus salt and pepper, cover it, and lower the heat. Once the meat releases its liquid and is swimming in its juices, I remove the lid, crank up the heat, and cook the juices down until they are almost a thick paste. Only then will I move on to the next step in the cooking process and add the remaining ingredients. This way, the flavor of the meat is treated as a backdrop, allowing other components—legumes, sour fruits, herbs, and vegetables—to shine through.

Lamb *(Ghusht-e Bareh)*

SOUTHERN IRANIAN SPICY OKRA STEW

KHORESHT-E BAMIYEH | *makes 4 to 6 servings*

I love the mildly sweet flavor of *bamiyeh* (okra), but its slimy texture is a turnoff for some. Even when I order okra at fancy restaurants, no matter who prepares it, no one has ever nailed it like the owner of the taverna in Greece where we celebrated our twins' christening. He placed a huge platter of the tiniest finger-like okras that I had ever seen on every table for our party of more than a hundred people. Each okra was identical. And I couldn't keep my eyes off them as I was milling around to greet our family. Before I knew it, he held up a platter in front of me: "Did you try the okra?" "Eat the okra!" *"Efayes tis bamies!"* And he went on to proudly explain to Akis, who translated for me, that he had gone to a local farm and bought their entire crop. Before I started dancing, I asked him to show me exactly what he had done. *"Akolouthisé me,"* he said, and led me to the back of the taverna. There I saw massive baking sheets covered with even more baby okras that he had prepped for another feast the following day. He had salted them in the morning, sprinkled them with a bit of vinegar, and left them to sit in the sun. He then gently simmered them with onion, garlic, tomato, and oregano. Their texture was delicate and silky, and they had soaked up the beautiful flavor while remaining tender-crisp. Years later, I went to my Greek produce guy "Bobby" in the summertime, snatched up all of his baby okras, and used the method I had seen in Greece to make my southern Iranian version of *khoresht-e bamiyeh*. The addition of tamarind paste—a favorite souring agent in the south of Iran—and red chili flakes makes this stew tangy and spicy. And when I treat the okras separately, as I learned in Greece, and just let them simmer for a few minutes in the stew, their texture is divine.

Note Gently clean the tips of the okras if needed. When making slits in the okra's body, do not cut all the way through or the mucilage (slime) will come out. Reduce the amount of chili flakes for a less spicy stew. $\rightarrow$

1 Preheat the oven to 450°F.

2 Gently rinse the okras and pat them dry. The less you handle them, the better. Using a sharp knife, make 2 small incisions on each okra, near the tips. Place the okras in a large mixing bowl and pour the vinegar over them. Use your hands to gently toss to coat, then spread the okras on a baking sheet. Season with 1 tablespoon of the salt and roast for about 10 minutes, tossing them once. Set aside.

3 Meanwhile, add the onions and ⅓ cup (80 ml) olive oil to a medium, heavy-bottomed pot with a tight-fitting lid and sauté over medium heat, adding more oil if needed, so that the onions turn golden, their edges darken, and they soften, about 5 to 7 minutes. Add the garlic and a bit more oil (so that the garlic doesn't burn), and stir. Then, add the turmeric, a bit more oil, and stir, allowing the turmeric to bloom and release its fragrance, about 30 seconds. Next, add the chili flakes, a bit more oil, and stir. Add the tomato paste, a bit more oil, and sauté, stirring occasionally until the tomato paste takes on a shiny color, about 1 minute more (the mixture will pull away from the bottom of the pot).

4 Add the lamb, the remaining 1½ tablespoons of the salt, and the pepper and sauté in the pot for a few minutes. Next, add the tamarind paste and 5 cups (1¼ liters) water, cover, raise the heat, and bring to a boil. Lower the heat to medium-low and cook for 1 hour, or until the lamb is soft. Add the chopped tomatoes and continue cooking, 20 minutes more.

5 Add the reserved okras and cook for another 10 minutes (I don't like it too soft; I want it to still retain a bite). Turn off the heat, taste and adjust the seasoning, and allow to rest for 1 hour, partially covered, before serving.

2 pounds (906 grams) whole okras (about 2½ inches long)

1½ tablespoons distilled white vinegar

2½ tablespoons kosher salt, or more to taste

2 medium yellow onions, medium diced

Light olive oil

12 garlic cloves, finely chopped

1 tablespoon ground turmeric

1 teaspoon red chili flakes

3 tablespoons tomato paste

1 pound (454 grams) boneless lamb shoulder, cut into 1-inch cubes

1 tablespoon freshly ground black pepper

½ cup (120 ml) thick Tamarind Paste (page 181), homemade or store-bought

2 cups peeled, chopped tomatoes

LAMB PATTIES in POMEGRANATE SAUCE

KABAB SHAMI LORI | *makes 8 patties*

The name of these patties is derived from the Farsi word *shamm,* meaning "dinner." And while these doughnut-shaped patties are not technically *kababs,* because they're cooked on the stove top in a rich pomegranate and molasses sauce, they do make a terrific light dinner! You'll find some variation on this dish in India and throughout the Middle East. But in Iran, they are typical of the western province of Lorestan, where home cooks sometimes add shredded potatoes and chickpeas. Here, I use chickpea flour as the binding agent, along with plenty of herbs to make the patties fragrant. Add the touch of sugar, if you'd like a bit of sweetness.

1 Make the patties: Using a box grater, grate the onion into a large bowl. Add the lamb, egg, salt, pepper, turmeric, cilantro, parsley, mint, tarragon, if using, and chickpea flour, and using your hands, combine thoroughly until the mixture easily pulls away from the sides of the bowl. Shape into 8 flat, doughnut-shaped patties, about 2½ ounces (70 grams) each, and set aside.

2 Make the sauce: Add the onions and 4 tablespoons olive oil to a medium sauté pan with a tight-fitting lid and sauté over medium heat, adding more oil if needed, so that the onions turn golden, their edges darken, and they soften, about 5 to 7 minutes. Add the turmeric, a bit more oil, and stir, allowing the turmeric to bloom and release its fragrance, about 1 minute more. Add the walnut powder and sauté quickly. Add 1½ cups (360 ml) water, the pomegranate molasses, salt, and pepper, and bring to a boil. Cover, lower the heat to low, and cook until thickened, about 40 minutes. Uncover, taste, and adjust the seasoning, adding the sugar, if you wish.

3 Add the reserved patties to the sauce and cook, uncovered, until cooked through and they soak up the flavors, about 10 minutes. Serve with raw, thinly sliced red onions dusted with sumac, if you like.

For the lamb patties

1 medium yellow onion

1 pound (454 grams) ground lamb

1 large egg, lightly beaten

1 tablespoon kosher salt

1 teaspoon freshly ground black pepper

1 tablespoon ground turmeric

2 ounces (56 grams) fresh cilantro, leaves and tender stems, finely chopped

2 ounces (56 grams) fresh flat-leaf parsley, leaves and tender stems, finely chopped

1 tablespoon dried mint

2 tablespoons dried tarragon (optional)

1½ tablespoons chickpea flour

For the sauce

1 small onion, medium diced

Light olive oil

1 tablespoon ground turmeric

2 ounces (56 grams) walnuts, ground into a powder

½ cup (120 ml) pomegranate molasses

1½ teaspoons kosher salt, or more to taste

1 teaspoon freshly ground black pepper

1 tablespoon granulated sugar (optional)

Whole red onion, thinly sliced, for serving (optional)

Sumac for serving (optional)

STUFFED GRAPEVINE LEAVES

DOLMEH BARG MO | *makes about 40 to 50 grape leaves*

When spring arrived in Isfahan, and my father's grapevine leaves began to open up like hands waving at us from the vine, my mom would beg him to cut fresh leaves to make *dolmeh*. Over a couple of days, my father would take great care to trim the vines, sparing the leaves that were necessary to their survival, and my mother and I would wash, dry, and blanch the leaves he had cut, trimming the perfect ones for stuffing and pickling the not-so-perfect ones. Once the filling was ready, I would sit down next to my mother and begin to stuff and roll the *dolmeh* into hexagon-shaped packages, making sure not to overstuff them so that they didn't explode. And because *goje sabz* (sour plums) came into season at the same time as grape leaves, my mom would add them to the pot, too. They offer a wonderful tartness to the sweet grape molasses and lemon juice braise that infuses the *dolmeh* as they cook. The *dolmeh*'s filling of ground meat (I prefer a mix of lamb with beef), split peas, and the sublime aromas of a pound of savory herbs comes together quickly. A labor of love, *dolmeh* are perfect for sharing. And my parents always invited our aunts and uncles to join us on a Friday night to eat them with us.

The "cigar-style" rolls found across Turkey, Lebanon, and Israel, as well as the thick and creamy *avgolemono* lemon and egg sauce–covered *dolmeh* from Greece that I love, all use some variation of flavorful grain, rice, and herb filling. But my heart belongs to the *dolmeh* of my homeland. Iranian-style *dolmeh* are a bit finicky and take more patience and practice to roll, but I adore them because they offer just the right delicious filling–to–grape leaf ratio. I make these stuffed grapevine leaves for special occasions, or when I want to surprise someone with an outrageous display of love. You can make the filling and roll your *dolmeh* ahead of time, freezing them, if you like, so that when your friends arrive, all you have to do is layer them in the pot to braise. You'll start with 36 leaves, but some will break, and others you'll want to reserve for layering your pot, so count on a varying yield.

Note You can substitute for grape molasses by whisking ½ cup (120 ml) lemon juice, ½ cup (120 ml) white wine vinegar, and ½ cup (100 grams) granulated sugar together. If you omit the sour plums, try adding Candied Barberries (page 52) as a garnish. Soak the 1½ ounces barberries in water for 10 minutes and drain before using. $\rightarrow$

1 Line 2 large baking sheets or a large, flat work surface with a clean kitchen towel or paper towels.

2 If using fresh grape leaves: Prepare an ice water bath. Next, bring a large pot of lightly salted water to a gentle rolling boil. Rinse the fresh leaves several times under cold water, then, working in batches, gently blanch the leaves for about 30 seconds, or until softened. Do not let them stick together or get mushy. Use tongs to gently remove them from the water and dunk them in the water bath. Lay the leaves flat on the baking sheets or surface and pat dry. Use a sharp knife to trim the thick stem from the base of each leaf. Reserve several leaves, or any broken ones, for layering the pan.

3 If using jarred grape leaves: Gently rinse the leaves under cold running water to remove the flavor of the brine. Lay the leaves flat on the lined baking sheets or surface and pat dry. Reserve several leaves for layering the pan.

4 Bring 2 cups (470 ml) water to a boil, add the split peas and 1 teaspoon of the turmeric, lower the heat, and simmer, uncovered, for 15 minutes, or until the peas are tender but still firm. Add ½ teaspoon salt in the last few minutes of cooking. Drain, rinse under cold water, and set aside.

5 Meanwhile, bring a large pot of water to a boil. Place the rice in a colander, give it a quick rinse, then parboil until it is still firm but soft around the edges, about 4 to 6 minutes. Drain and rinse under cold water and set aside.

6 Add the onions and 4 tablespoons olive oil to a large skillet and sauté over medium heat, adding more oil if needed, so that the onions turn golden, their edges darken, and they soften, about 5 to 7 minutes. Add the remaining 1 tablespoon turmeric, a bit more oil, and stir, allowing the turmeric to bloom and release its fragrance, about 1 minute more. Next, add the lamb, beef, 1 tablespoon salt, and the pepper and stir, breaking the meat up, until the mixture is thoroughly combined. Cook, stirring continuously, until the meat is cooked through, about 5 to 7 minutes.

7 In a large bowl, combine the reserved split peas, reserved rice, the meat mixture, the cilantro, chives, tarragon, mint, basil, rosemary, and barberries.

8 To assemble the *dolmeh:* Working with one leaf at a time (or if they are small, put 2 leaves together), place the leaf with the ridged stem side facing upward on a flat surface, and spoon 2 to 3 teaspoons of the stuffing onto the bottom of each. Fold the lower part of the right side over the stuffing, followed by the lower part of the left side over the stuffing. Repeat with the top part of the right side of the leaf and the left side. Finish by folding the remaining top part of the leaf down. You should have a five-sided, firmly folded bundle. Continue filling the remaining leaves. $\rightarrow$

36 fresh grape leaves
(see Resources, page 317)
or one 16-ounce jar grape leaves
in brine

Kosher salt

1 cup (225 grams) split peas

1 teaspoon plus 1 tablespoon
ground turmeric

1 cup (185 grams) jasmine rice

1 medium yellow onion, small
diced

Light olive oil

½ pound (226 grams) ground lamb

½ pound (226 grams) ground beef

1 tablespoon freshly ground
black pepper

3 ounces (85 grams) fresh cilantro,
leaves and tender stems,
finely chopped

3 ounces (85 grams) fresh chives,
tender stems, finely chopped

3 ounces (85 grams) fresh
tarragon, leaves and tender stems,
finely chopped

3 ounces (85 grams) fresh mint,
leaves and tender stems,
finely chopped

3 ounces (85 grams) fresh basil,
leaves and tender stems,
finely chopped

2 to 3 sprigs fresh rosemary,
stemmed and finely chopped

1½ ounces (21 grams) dried
barberries, soaked and drained
(see headnote)

4 tablespoons (½ stick/56 grams)
salted butter, cut into small pieces

½ cup (120 ml) grape molasses
(see headnote)

⅓ cup (80 ml) bottled lemon juice

8 ounces (226 grams) sour plums
(*goje sabz*), pitted (optional)

½ cup (56 grams) Candied
Barberries (page 52) for garnish
(optional; see headnote)

9 Line the bottom of a large pot with a tight-fitting lid with the reserved or broken leaves (to prevent the *dolmeh* from sticking), and then arrange the stuffed leaves in the pot, building a dome shape as you layer them.

10 Scatter the butter pieces across the top, pour 2 cups (470 ml) water around the edges, and then place an inverted plate over the leaves to prevent them from moving. Cover with the lid and cook over medium heat for 30 minutes.

11 In a small bowl, combine the grape molasses and lemon juice and remove the plate before pouring the mixture over the leaves. If using sour plums, add them now, too. Cover with the plate, return the lid, and continue to cook for 30 minutes more.

12 The *dolmeh* can be served warm or at room temperature.

Goje Sabz

You know, by now, that I have a Greek produce guy
who goes by "Bobby." It's not very Greek, but that's his name. I digress.
On one trip to see him—perhaps my kids were in first or second grade
(as a mother-chef, time is measured by the seasons of school and produce),
I lost my mind over tiny, round *goje sabz* that I spotted in the corner.
Their unripened, thin green skin covering up
the burst of sour lip-puckering glory underneath.
"Why didn't you have them before?
"And why do you have them *now*?"
"Because people are asking me for them, Nasim."
("Bobby" rarely has patience for me.)
How could he know that even when tiny white flowers and cherry tree buds
show their welcome burst of color in New York,
for me, it isn't *really* spring because
I live it without *goje sabz*?
But that day, that little box of sour plums appeared around the corner,
giddy like a long-lost school friend who knew all my secrets, saying,
"If you had only asked to meet me here!"
And like spring itself, they made my head spin,
and struck renewal in my heart.

ABGOUSHT

LAMB AND BEAN STEW | *makes 4 to 6 servings*

The word *abgousht* translates as "meat water" and this dish is prepared in
a traditional stone or ceramic pot called a *dizi*. The roots of the stew are a
humble peasant dish that uses inexpensive but richly flavorful cuts of lamb.
Even today, people rise early for work on a winter's morning and get their
one pot of onions, lamb, and beans together to cook low and long while
they're out. The rich broth is separated from the tender meat and soft beans
and eaten separately with crumbled *sangak* bread (see page 4) to soak up its
goodness. Breaking the bread into the meat broth is called *tillit,* meaning "to
dunk and soak your bread." The remaining beef and beans are mashed with
a *ghusht kub*—a flat wooden mallet—into a pulpy, smooth, pâté-like paste
that you can spoon onto more bread and eat with pieces of cracked raw
onion, bites of pickles, *kashk,* and *Sabzi Khordan* (page 88).

In Iran, there are *dizi* restaurants that serve only *abgousht dizi* style, and
they are a wildly popular food adventure with a bunch of friends. These
restaurants are outfitted with massive ovens that hold dozens of individually
portioned *dizi* pots. Waiters bring everyone their own mini *dizi* container,
along with a tiny *ghusht kub*. You spoon out a layer of lamb fat from each
container and break it into your bowl. But when I make *abgousht* at home,
I skip the fat entirely, and I also use less meat and more beans than are
traditional. And for serving, I put lots of pickles into the bean and meat
mash, leaving some meat in whole pieces on top and separating the broth
and offering it in a large separate bowl. Among close friends and family, it's
typical for men to crack fresh onions with their hands and break off pieces to
pass around for everyone to enjoy with their *abgousht*. See the photograph
on page 124.

Note You will need to soak the chickpeas and red and white beans for a
minimum of 4 hours and up to overnight before making the recipe.

1 Put the chickpeas, red beans, and white beans in a large bowl and cover with water by 2 inches. Soak for a minimum of 4 hours and up to overnight.

2 Combine 3 cups (¾ liter) water and the potatoes in a medium bowl and set aside until ready to use.

3 Add the onions and 4 tablespoons (60 ml) olive oil to a large, heavy-bottomed pot with a tight-fitting lid and sauté over medium heat, adding more oil if needed, so that the onions turn golden, their edges darken, and they soften, about 10 minutes. Add the turmeric, a bit more oil, and stir, allowing the turmeric to bloom and release its fragrance, about 1 minute more.

4 Pat the lamb dry, season with the salt and pepper, and place it in the pot with the onion mixture (if using ribs, add them fat cap side up). Cover with the lid, lower the heat to low, and cook, allowing the meat to release its juices, about 10 minutes. Remove the lid, raise the heat to medium-high, and continue cooking, until any remaining liquid in the pot evaporates, about 10 minutes more.

5 Add the tomato paste, cinnamon sticks, paprika, sun-dried limes, and 4 cups (1 liter) water. Return the lid and bring to a boil, then lower the heat to low and cook for 30 minutes. Meanwhile, drain the chickpeas and beans.

6 Remove the lid and add the chickpeas and beans to the pot. Return the lid and continue cooking for 1½ hours more.

7 Drain and add the potatoes, and continue cooking for 20 minutes, or until the meat is fork-tender and the beans and potatoes are well cooked. Taste and adjust the seasoning.

8 To serve, separate the broth and offer it in a different large bowl. I also like to add pickles to the remaining beans and meat before mashing it and dividing it among separate *dizi* containers or bowls. Garnish each bowl with the tomatoes and saffron water and serve with bread, raw onions, and your choice of pickles.

⅓ cup (70 grams) dried chickpeas

⅓ cup (60 grams) dried red kidney beans

⅓ cup (60 grams) dried white beans

4 small Yukon Gold potatoes or 2 large russet potatoes, peeled and halved

2 large yellow onions, medium diced, plus 1 large yellow onion, cracked, for serving

Light olive oil

1 tablespoon ground turmeric

1 pound (454 grams) lamb neck or lamb rib meat, with fat cap

2 tablespoons kosher salt, or more to taste

1½ teaspoons freshly ground black pepper

¾ cup (170 grams) tomato paste

2 cinnamon sticks (about 1 inch long)

1 tablespoon paprika

2 to 3 sun-dried limes, halved

Sofreh House Pickles (page 253) or your choice of pickles for serving

4 small tomatoes on the vine, halved, for garnish

Saffron Water (page xxxiv) for garnish

Store-bought lavash or homemade *Naan-e Taftoon* (page 6) for serving

Raw onions, such as cipolline, for serving

SOFREH LAMB SHANK

makes 2 to 4 servings

Every night, there is one guest who orders this entire lamb shank, all for himself, and picks it down to the bone, morsel by glorious morsel. I've been serving it since we opened our doors, garnishing it with Crispy Fried Onions (page 194).

Note Use the leftover lamb bones to make lamb stock and freeze it in small batches to flavor simple rice dishes and soups.

1 Preheat the oven to 450°F.

2 Trim the lamb of any excess silver skin (fat deposits). Pat the shanks dry and season with the salt and pepper. In a large, wide ovenproof casserole with a lid, or a large Dutch oven, warm the oil over medium heat and brown the lamb shanks on all sides, about 15 minutes total. Transfer the lamb to a plate, reserving the juices in the pan, and set the lamb aside.

3 Add the onions to the same pan (to use the bits of lamb flavor) and sauté over medium heat so that the onions turn golden, their edges darken, and they soften, about 10 minutes. Add the turmeric, a bit more oil, and stir, allowing the turmeric to bloom and release its fragrance, about 1 minute more. Lower the heat, add 2½ cups (360 ml) water, and deglaze the pan, scraping up any browned bits.

4 Place the reserved shanks, the onion mixture, and juices into a deep roasting pan with a tight-fitting lid, and add the peppercorns, bay leaves, and cinnamon sticks. Cover and transfer to the oven. Cook for 30 minutes, then lower the heat to 350°F. and continue cooking until the lamb is fall-off-the-bone tender, about 2 hours more.

Alternatively You can continue cooking this dish on the stove top. Cover and bring to a boil, then lower the heat to low and simmer for 2 hours, stirring occasionally, until the meat is soft and tender.

2 lamb shanks
(about 1¼ pounds/566 grams each)

2 tablespoons kosher salt

1 tablespoon freshly ground black pepper

¼ cup (60 ml) neutral oil, such as vegetable or canola oil, for frying

1 large yellow onion, medium diced

1½ tablespoons ground turmeric

1 tablespoon black peppercorns

4 dried bay leaves

3 cinnamon sticks
(about 1 inch long)

Crispy Fried Onions (page 194) for garnish (optional)

ROASTED LEG of LAMB "GIGOT"

makes 10 to 12 servings

This whole roasted leg of lamb is a spoon-tender, crowd-pleasing holiday favorite that I make for American New Year's Day get-togethers and Thanksgiving (no one will even look at my turkey when I make it). The aroma of garlic and warm spices is intoxicating, as is the feeling of comfort and celebration that this dish evokes. While its origin is not Persian—*gigot* means "leg" in French—my mother would roast a whole lamb leg this way when she'd host parties. This lamb will yield 10 to 12 plentiful main-course servings, but when I was growing up I remember it as part of a spread, with other accompanying stews and rice dishes, and in that case, it fed a crowd of 20 people or so.

Note You will need a very large sauté pan to accommodate the entire leg. Use a mallet to crush the sun-dried limes.

1 Preheat the oven to 450°F.

2 Trim the leg of lamb of any thick visible fat, leaving a thin layer for flavor. Use a sharp knife to make ½-inch-deep incisions all over the lamb and stuff them with the garlic cloves.

3 Rub the lamb all over with 2 tablespoons of the salt, 2 tablespoons of the pepper, 2 tablespoons of the turmeric, and the paprika. Next, rub the flour all over the leg of lamb and pat well with paper towels to remove any excess.

4 In a large, wide, heavy-bottomed pan, warm the oil over medium heat and brown the lamb on all sides, about 15 minutes total. Remove the lamb from the pan and set aside.

5 Add the onions to the now-empty pan and sauté quickly, about 2 minutes, then add the remaining 1 tablespoon turmeric and stir, allowing it to bloom and release its fragrance, about 30 seconds. Next, add the tomato paste, remaining 2 tablespoons salt, and remaining 2 teaspoons pepper, and sauté, stirring occasionally, until the tomato paste takes on a shiny color, about 1 minute more.

6 Return the lamb to the pan and spread some of the onion mixture along the top and sides of the lamb, leaving the rest of the mixture on the bottom. Add the wine, plus 1 cup (235 ml) water, the bay leaves, cinnamon sticks, and sun-dried limes. Cover the pan tightly with aluminum foil and place in the oven to cook for 30 minutes. Then reduce the temperature to 350°F and continue cooking for 2 hours. →

1 bone-in leg of lamb
(about 10 to 12 pounds/4.5 to
5.4 kilograms)

1 cup whole garlic cloves

¼ cup kosher salt

2 tablespoons plus 2 teaspoons
freshly ground black pepper

3 tablespoons ground turmeric

2 tablespoons smoked paprika

⅓ cup (45 grams) all-purpose flour

⅓ cup (80 ml) neutral oil, such as
vegetable or canola oil, for frying

1 large yellow onion, halved and
sliced into half-moons

1 cup (112 grams) tomato paste

3 cups (¾ liter) red or white wine

12 dried bay leaves

2 cinnamon sticks
(about 3 inches long)

2 whole sun-dried limes,
crushed into pieces

7 Check to see if the lamb has enough cooking liquid, but do not flip it. Cover and continue cooking for 1 hour more. At this point, it's your call: use a cake tester or sample a piece from the side. If the lamb isn't falling off the bone, but it tastes really good, it's done. But I like mine falling off the bone, so, if you like, flip it, and continue cooking, covered, for another 30 minutes.

8 Transfer the lamb to a serving platter, fat side up, and allow it to sit for 10 to 15 minutes before serving. If you have remaining liquid, reduce it and pour it over the lamb for serving.

MEATBALLS with MINT and VINEGAR SAUCE

KOOFTEH SHIRAZI | *makes about 10 meatballs*

Koofteh translates as "meatballs," but their name has its root in the word *koobideh*, which means "ground" (as does *kabab koobideh; see* page 152). Home cooks make giant meatballs by kneading ground meat with short-grain rice, split peas, or bulgur wheat and stuffing their centers with any and every dried fruit and nut combination imaginable. Each city in Iran has its signature meatball variation. I prefer making a more delicate version of *koofteh*, using chickpea flour in my mix for a lighter, softer texture. This sweet and sour *koofteh* recipe comes from my grandmother's birth city of Shiraz, and includes carrots and golden raisins, giving it a sweetness that contrasts with the mint-vinegar sauce.

1 Take out a large baking sheet and set it close by.

2 Prepare the meatballs: Add the onions, carrots, lamb, turmeric, chickpea flour, salt, pepper, and egg to a large bowl and mix to combine. Roll 3½ to 4 ounces (100 to 112 grams) of the mix by hand to form 10 oval-shaped meatballs. Press your finger into the center of each, making a shallow hole, and fill each one with a few raisins (whatever raisins you have remaining will be added to the sauce). Seal the meatballs closed and transfer to the baking sheet. Cover with plastic wrap and place them in the refrigerator to chill.

3 Prepare the sauce: Add the onions and 4 tablespoons olive oil to a large, heavy-bottomed pot with a tight-fitting lid and sauté over medium heat, adding more oil if needed, so that the onions turn golden, their edges darken, and they soften, about 5 to 7 minutes. Add the turmeric, a bit more oil, and stir, allowing the turmeric to bloom and release its fragrance, about 1 minute more. Add the dried mint and a bit more oil (so that the mint doesn't burn), and stir to release its fragrance. Add 3 cups (¾ liter) water, the vinegar, lemon juice, and salt, and bring to a gentle boil.

4 Warm about ¼ cup (60 ml) of the neutral oil (or more if needed) in a large sauté pan. Remove the meatballs from the refrigerator. Add them to the pan and lightly fry on all sides, working in batches if necessary.

5 Once the meatballs are fried, add them to the sauce, along with the remaining raisins and the sugar, and cover with the lid. Lower the heat to a simmer and cook, covered, for about 30 to 40 minutes.

6 Remove the lid, and taste and adjust the seasoning. Serve with Saffron Basmati Rice (page 56) or pita bread.

For the meatballs

1 extra large yellow onion, grated

1 small carrot (about 4 ounces/ 112 grams), peeled and grated

1 pound (454 grams) ground lamb

1 tablespoon ground turmeric

3 tablespoons chickpea flour

1 tablespoon kosher salt

½ teaspoon freshly ground black pepper

1 large egg, lightly beaten

1 cup (160 grams) golden raisins

For the sauce

1 small yellow onion, finely diced

Light olive oil

1 tablespoon ground turmeric

3 tablespoons dried mint

½ cup (120 ml) red wine vinegar

⅓ cup (80 ml) bottled lemon juice

1 tablespoon kosher salt, plus more to taste

Neutral oil, such as vegetable or canola oil, for frying

1 tablespoon granulated sugar

Beef *(Ghusht-e Ghav)*

AMIR'S MAKARONI with POTATO TAHDIG

makes 4 to 6 servings

I was babysitting for my two younger brothers, Reza and Amir, when Giti Joon rang: "There are cousins on the way over; I need you to put lunch together!" I was fourteen, and it was the first time she had put me in charge of a meal. I quickly took inventory: Lamb patties? Yes! Onions, garlic, and tomato paste? Of course. I crumbled the lamb patties to make an aromatic meat sauce, and to increase the portion size, I improvised, adding peas, and topping it with crunchy fried potatoes. Of the dozen or so people gathered that day, I'll never forget my mother's cousin when he told me between bites, "You have some hands, young lady!" It was the first time that an adult acknowledged that I had a talent for cooking. Later, my mom suggested that I make the same meat sauce with *makaroni*—the general term for any shape of pasta in Iran—because my brothers and father loved this popular foreign dish that she disliked making. And so, *makaroni* making became my job. The first time I returned home from university, Amir, who is ten years younger than I and was still a little boy, ran to me, saying, "Feed me *makaroni*!"

Amir joined me in the United States in 1993, living with my brother Reza, who had also followed. While Reza eventually returned home to Iran, Amir instead set down new roots in New York, making his home in Brooklyn. While in college earning his engineering degree, he worked for a brief time at my copy shop and later worked with Akis. When we were in the process of opening Sofreh, it made sense for Amir to take an apartment above the restaurant because I was the nanny to his young son, my nephew Sapand. When we finally opened, Amir became a presence in our dining room. He has beautiful ease and warmth, a kind heart, and generosity that make him beloved by all, especially me.

And here is the *makaroni* I made for him.

1 Prepare the potatoes for the *tahdig:* Combine 3 cups (¾ liter) water and ¼ cup (72 grams) of the salt in a medium bowl. Peel and slice the potatoes into ½-inch-thick rounds. Don't slice them too thin or they may stick to the bottom of the pot. Place the sliced potatoes in the salted water for about 30 minutes. →

For the potato *tahdig*

¼ cup (72 grams) plus 1½ teaspoons kosher salt

2 medium russet potatoes

⅓ cup (80 ml) light olive oil, plus more as needed →

2 Meanwhile, prepare the sauce: Add the onions and 4 tablespoons olive oil to a large, heavy-bottomed pot with a tight-fitting lid and sauté over medium heat, adding more oil if needed, so that the onions turn golden, their edges darken, and they soften, about 5 to 7 minutes. Make a well in the center of the pot, add the garlic and a bit more oil (so that the garlic doesn't burn), and sauté until fragrant, about 3 minutes more. Add the turmeric, a bit more oil, and stir, allowing the turmeric to bloom and release its fragrance, about 1 minute more.

3 Add the ground beef to the onion mixture and stir. Season with the salt and cook, stirring, until the meat is lightly browned.

4 Add the pepper, cinnamon, cumin, and sugar, and mix thoroughly to combine. Add the tomato paste and stir to incorporate. Next, add the lemon juice, ½ cup (120 ml) water, and the peas. Stir to combine, cover with the lid, lower the heat to low, and cook for about 15 minutes.

5 Meanwhile, bring a large pot of generously salted water to a boil and cook the pasta until al dente, according to the directions on the package. Drain and set aside.

6 Taste and adjust the meat sauce for seasonings. Remove the lid, stir in the parsley, and set aside.

7 Prepare the *tahdig:* Drain the reserved potato slices from the water, pat them dry, and season generously on both sides with the remaining 1½ teaspoons salt. Add the ⅓ cup olive oil to a 5-quart (4.7-liter) nonstick pot and place it over medium heat. Place the potato rounds in a single layer on the bottom of the pot without overlapping or touching, and allow them to warm and sizzle for 1 minute. Remove the pot from the heat.

8 Layer the *makaroni:* Using a large spoon, layer about 2 cups of the pasta over the potato layer, adding enough to make a small mound in the center. Using the same spoon, add a generous spoonful of the meat sauce over the pasta. Continue the process of layering the pasta and meat sauce, building a pyramid-shaped mound in the pot as you layer.

9 Cover with the lid and set over medium-high heat until the pot begins to steam, about 10 minutes. Lower the heat to medium-low and remove the lid. Wrap the bottom side of the lid in a clean kitchen towel and place the lid back on the top of the pot. Cook for about 45 to 50 minutes.

10 Turn off the heat and allow the pasta to rest for 2 to 3 minutes with the lid ajar. (Don't let it sit longer or the potato *tahdig* will get soggy.) If using a good-quality nonstick pot, place a serving dish on top of the pot and flip to invert the *makaroni* for a beautiful presentation. Or, gently remove the pasta from the pot and transfer to a serving bowl, placing the *tahdig,* crispy side up, on top of the pasta or on the side. Serve with yogurt, if you like.

For the sauce and serving

1 medium yellow onion, finely diced

Light olive oil

6 to 8 garlic cloves, finely chopped

1 tablespoon ground turmeric

¾ pound (340 grams) ground beef

2 tablespoons kosher salt, plus more as needed

1 tablespoon freshly ground black pepper

1 tablespoon ground cinnamon

1 tablespoon ground cumin

2 tablespoons granulated sugar

1 cup (225 grams) tomato paste

½ cup (120 ml) bottled lemon juice

1 cup (160 grams) frozen green peas

1 pound (454 grams) pasta (I prefer a thick noodle, such as bucatini, but any shape will work)

4 ounces (112 grams) fresh flat-leaf parsley, leaves and tender stems, roughly chopped

Homemade Yogurt (page 32) or store-bought Greek yogurt for serving (optional)

BEEF MEATBALLS with CARROTS and POTATOES

KOOFTEH GHELGHELI | *makes 4 to 6 servings*

If there is one food that I want to be remembered for, it is the tiny beef and chickpea flour meatballs that I would roll for Soshy when she was little. As she grew, so did my meatballs! These soft and cozy *koofteh* are typically found in Isfahan. They simmer in a fragrant broth of onions, turmeric, and lemon juice that gets thick and rich as it cooks. The addition of carrots and potatoes makes this a wonderful one-pot meal that's great year-round. To fancy it up, during the last 15 minutes of cooking, add sour plums or cherries in the summer and quinces or apples in the fall. I spent years rolling tiny meatballs, but my daughter tells me that Giti Joon's meatballs are "nicer" than mine. It's okay, I can take it. She also tells me if she has children of her own one day, these are the meatballs she will make for them.

Note You can also make these with lamb, or a combination of 8 ounces (226 grams) lamb and 8 ounces (226 grams) beef. I like to serve them with Saffron Basmati Rice (page 56) or pita bread.

1 Take out a large baking sheet and set it close by.

2 Make the meatballs: Add the meat, onions, salt, pepper, and turmeric to a large bowl and mix to combine. Add the chickpea flour and mix completely. Using your hands, mix until you cannot see the meat's red color and you have a soft, uniform texture. Roll by hand to form about 30 walnut-size meatballs. Transfer the meatballs to the baking sheet, cover with plastic wrap, and place them in the refrigerator to chill. Meanwhile, prepare the sauce.

3 Make the sauce: Add the onions and 4 tablespoons olive oil to a large, heavy-bottomed pot with a tight-fitting lid and sauté over medium heat, adding more oil if needed, so that the onions turn golden, their edges darken, and they soften, about 5 to 7 minutes. Add the turmeric, a bit more oil, and stir, allowing the turmeric to bloom and release its fragrance, about 1 minute more. Add 2 cups (470 ml) cold water and raise the heat to medium-high. Add the lemon juice, salt, and pepper, and bring to a boil, then lower the heat to a simmer. →

For the meatballs

1 pound (454 grams) ground beef or lamb

2 medium yellow onions, grated

3 teaspoons kosher salt

1 teaspoon freshly ground black pepper

1 tablespoon ground turmeric

⅓ cup (30 grams) chickpea flour

For the sauce

1 yellow onion, finely diced

Light olive oil

2 tablespoons ground turmeric

⅓ cup (80 ml) bottled lemon juice

3 teaspoons kosher salt

1 teaspoon freshly ground black pepper →

4 Remove the meatballs from the refrigerator. Gently add them to the simmering broth and cook for about 5 minutes. Add the carrots, potatoes, and sour grapes. Bring to a boil for 5 minutes, lower the heat to low, and cover. Leave the pot undisturbed and simmer for 40 minutes.

5 At this point, you should have a thick sauce—if not, uncover, increase the heat, and bring to a boil for a few minutes to reduce.

6 Pour the saffron water, if using, over the meatballs just before serving with Saffron Basmati Rice (page 56) or pita bread.

4 medium carrots, peeled and cut into ¼-inch-thick rounds

2 medium Yukon Gold potatoes, peeled and cut into 1-inch cubes

1 cup (228 grams) pickled sour grapes in brine *(gooreh;* see Resources, page 317), drained

Saffron Water (page xxxiv) for serving (optional)

BEEF and POTATO PATTIES

KOTLET | *makes 8 to 10 patties*

The name of these aromatic, comforting minced beef and potato patties is Russian in origin (*kotleti*) due to the fact that the countries have shared the northern Caspian Sea border for centuries. It was during the nineteenth century that several Russian dishes, including *salad olivieh* (see page 162) and beef *piroshki,* made their way into the repertoires of home cooks in our northern provinces. I love serving these little oval-shaped patties with Salt-Brined Cucumbers (page 256) and fresh tomatoes for a light dinner.

1 Preheat the oven to 450°F.

2 Poke holes in the potatoes, wrap them in aluminum foil, and bake. Peel and allow the potatoes to cool before moving on to step 2.

3 Using a box grater, grate the onion into a large bowl. Using a clean kitchen towel or paper towels, squeeze the grated onion to remove excess moisture. Next, using the same box grater, grate the cooled potatoes into the bowl with the onions. Add the beef, salt, pepper, 2 tablespoons of the turmeric, and the dried mint to the bowl, and using your hands, mix thoroughly to combine.

4 Add the egg and mix well. Cover the bowl with plastic wrap and place it in the refrigerator for 30 minutes (this helps prevent breaking).

5 In a medium bowl, combine the bread crumbs with the remaining ½ teaspoon turmeric.

6 Add enough oil to coat the bottom of a large stainless-steel pan, and warm over medium heat until hot but not sizzling. Remove the beef mixture from the refrigerator and taste for salt, adding more if needed. To test if the oil is ready, drop a bit of the meat mixture into the pan, and if it sizzles, the oil is hot enough.

7 Working in batches, roll 8 to 10 small, egg-shaped pieces of meat in the bread crumbs to coat, and then gently flatten them in the palm of your hand before placing them in the hot pan. Depending on the size of your pan, add 3 to 4 *kotlets* at a time (be careful not to overcrowd) and cook on one side, undisturbed, until the undersides are golden brown, about 2 to 3 minutes. Turn and continue cooking on the other side, adding more oil if needed, about 2 to 3 minutes more. Transfer the first batch of cooked *kotlets* to a plate lined with paper towels to absorb excess oil, and continue cooking, adding more oil if needed.

8 Once all of the *kotlets* are cooked, serve immediately with the cucumbers and tomatoes.

1½ pounds (680 grams) medium Idaho potatoes

1 medium yellow onion

1 pound (454 grams) ground beef

2 tablespoons kosher salt

2 tablespoons freshly ground black pepper

2 tablespoons plus ½ teaspoon ground turmeric

1 tablespoon dried mint

1 large or 2 small eggs

1 cup (119 grams) good-quality, plain bread crumbs, store-bought or homemade

Neutral oil, such as vegetable or canola oil, for frying

Salt-brined cucumbers, store-bought or homemade (page 256), for serving

Fresh tomatoes for serving

ABGOUSHT-E BOZBASH

BEEF AND BEAN STEW WITH GARLIC CHIVES

makes 4 to 6 servings

Bozbash is a specialty of Isfahan, and my province's variation of *Abgousht* (page 138). I make it with a fatty cut of beef, which works great with the strong umami depth and complexity of flavor from the garlic chives. Serve *bozbash* with pickles, raw onions, and bread, as we do.

Note Soak the chickpeas, kidney beans, and white beans for a minimum of 4 hours and up to overnight before making this recipe. If you do not have a *ghusht kub*—a traditional wooden meat masher—use the bottom of an empty wine bottle.

1 Put the chickpeas, kidney beans, and white beans in a large bowl, cover with water by 2 inches, and soak for a minimum of 4 hours and up to overnight.

2 Add 3 cups (¾ liter) water to a medium bowl and soak the potatoes. Set aside until ready to use.

3 Add the onions and 4 tablespoons olive oil to a large, heavy-bottomed pot with a tight-fitting lid and sauté over medium heat, adding more oil if needed, so that the onions turn golden, their edges darken, and they soften, about 10 minutes. Add the turmeric, a bit more oil, and stir, allowing the turmeric to bloom and release its fragrance, about 1 minute more.

4 Pat the beef dry and add to the onion mixture. Season with the salt and pepper, cover with the lid, lower the heat to low, and cook, allowing the meat to release its juices, about 10 minutes. Remove the lid, raise the heat to medium-high, and continue cooking until the meat is glossy and any remaining liquid in the pot evaporates.

5 Add 6 cups (1.4 liters) water, return the lid, and bring to a boil. Lower the heat to a gentle boil and cook for about 30 minutes. Remove the lid and add the sun-dried limes. Drain the beans and add them to the pot, too, and continue cooking, covered, for 1 hour.

6 Remove the lid and add the garlic chives, cilantro, and parsley and continue cooking, covered, for 30 minutes. Next, add the potatoes and cook until the meat is fork-tender, and the beans and potatoes are softened, about 20 minutes more. Taste and adjust the seasoning.

7 To serve, separate the broth and offer it in a large bowl. I like to reserve some of the meat, potatoes, and beans as a garnish, before mashing the rest with a *ghusht kub* (see headnote) and dividing it among individual bowls.

½ cup (100 grams) dried chickpeas

½ cup (92 grams) dried red kidney beans

½ cup (92 grams) dried white beans

4 small Yukon Gold potatoes or 2 large russet potatoes, peeled and halved

1 large yellow onion, medium diced

Light olive oil

2 tablespoons ground turmeric

1½ pounds (680 grams) fatty beef, such as a rump, cut into large cubes

2 tablespoons kosher salt, plus more to taste

1 tablespoon freshly ground black pepper, plus more to taste

6 sun-dried limes, halved

About 1 pound (454 grams) garlic chives, cut into 1-inch pieces

4 ounces (112 grams) fresh cilantro, leaves and tender stems, finely chopped

4 ounces (112 grams) fresh flat-leaf parsley, leaves and tender stems, finely chopped

Kababs

When I was a kid, going out for *kababs* was reserved for a special Friday lunch with friends and family only when my brothers and I had completed our homework and chores. I advocate for any food that opens the door to an understanding of my culture, but for better or for worse, *chelo kabab*—rice served alongside variations of *kababs*—have become the food most representative of Iranian cooking in the United States. With Sofreh, I set out to change that perception. I showcase dishes that culturally are representative of women home cooks.

Honestly, I can't remember once when the women in my family set themselves near a charcoal grill with skewers of meat—it seems it is always men who gravitate toward a live fire. Take my *kabab*-obsessed cousins. One of them always arrives at my parents' house for a family get-together lugging his charcoal, skewers, and meat, even though Giti Joon assures him, "My butcher is great; tell me which cut you want!" My cousin always answers, "No, thanks." And even though for these family affairs we spread the *sofreh* with home-cooked dishes, I know his heart is with his fire; I watch him get the grill going one or two hours ahead of time, and in the meantime, he marinates and massages and readies the meat. And when it comes time for serving, his wife acts as his assistant to ready the warm lavash and rice plates. And truly, his *kababs* are magnificent!

Historically in Iran, *kababs*, which refer to any skewered meat cooked over an open flame, are either Cornish hen, such as *juje kabab* (see page 173), chicken, ground lamb, or lamb sirloin. However, these days, in restaurants across Iran and, of course, in the United States, you'll find a mix of ground beef and lamb, which in my opinion is a tastier blend. So, do feel free to use lamb for the *kabab* recipes in this section, if you wish.

MINCED MEAT KABAB

KABAB KOOBIDEH | *makes 4 to 6 servings*

Kabab koobideh, also called *chelo kabab,* because we eat it with plain basmati rice, is Iran's popular ground meat *kabab.* Its ingredient list is short: ground meat, onions, and a bit of excess water from the onion juice, giving it lots of onion flavor. There are a few secrets to a good *koobideh;* begin with excellent-quality fresh meat with just the right fat content and, if possible, freshly grind it at home so that you can grind your onions into it on the second pass (as directed below). Also, be sure to chill both the meat and onions, and allow the mixture to rest before shaping it onto the skewers. Each of these elements will affect the moisture content of the meat mixture, and if it is out of balance, your *kabab* won't adhere properly to the skewer. I've also included my easy Oven-Ready *Kabab Koobideh* (page 154) if you'd like to skip the grill.

Note Wide metal skewers, about 7 to 8 inches long or longer, are preferable. If you can, remove the grill grate from a standard American grill so that you can rest the skewers from one end of the grill to the other, about 1 to 2 inches away from the charcoal. If you do not have a meat grinder, have your meat freshly ground by your butcher or buy it already ground.

1 Trim the silver skin and sinew from the lamb and beef and discard. Cut the meat into chunks small enough to fit into your meat grinder. Set the meat in the refrigerator to chill until very cold, 30 minutes.

2 Meanwhile, set up your meat grinder with the large grinder plate. Grind the onions through the meat grinder and set the onions in the refrigerator for 30 minutes. After 30 minutes, place the ground onions into a fine-mesh sieve set over a bowl, and using a clean kitchen towel or paper towels, squeeze out most of the excess water, leaving just a bit of moisture.

3 Remove the meat mixture from the refrigerator, season with the salt and pepper, and grind through the large grinder plate. Next, combine the onions and ground meat in a mixing bowl until incorporated. Return the mixture to the refrigerator.

1 pound (454 grams) lamb belly or boneless lamb ribs (70% fat, 30% lean)

1½ pounds (680 grams) beef chuck or brisket (70% fat, 30% lean)

½ pound (226 grams) yellow onions, roughly chopped

1 tablespoon kosher salt, plus more as needed

1 teaspoon freshly ground black pepper

1 tablespoon Saffron Water (page xxxiv)

4 Switch to the small grinder plate on your grinder, remove the meat and onion mixture from the refrigerator, and grind again into a mixing bowl. Add the saffron water and knead for about 3 to 5 minutes. Return the mixture to the refrigerator and allow to rest for 1 to 2 hours.

5 Set out a bowl of cold water. Dip your hands in the water and, keeping your hands wet, shape the desired amount of meat around the skewers.

6 Preheat a charcoal grill until the embers are glowing and any excess soot has burned off. Place the skewers on the grill (see headnote), turning every 20 to 30 seconds until cooked through.

7 Have plates of lavash ready, and place the *kababs* on top. Season immediately with more salt and sumac to taste. Serve with plain basmati rice garnished with more sumac, if you like.

Store-bought lavash bread or homemade *Naan-e Taftoon* (page 6) for serving

Sumac, as needed

Plain basmati rice for serving

Sumac *(Somagh)*

Native to North America, and widely used throughout the Middle East, the sumac bush's cluster of red berries are dried and ground into a spice with a zesty citrus flavor and a beautiful color. I use it predominantly as a garnish to sprinkle over plain basmati rice or *chelo* (see page 56) that I serve with *kababs,* as well as over thinly sliced red onions. And it is the spice that gives za'atar spice blend its signature lemon zing.

OVEN-READY KABAB KOOBIDEH

makes 4 to 6 servings

I love skipping the grill when I can, turning out juicy Saffron-Marinated Cornish Hens (page 173) from my oven, as well as this variation of *kabab koobideh*. You can get *kababs* and rice ready in less than 30 minutes.

Note If possible, have your meat freshly ground by your butcher or buy it already ground.

1 Preheat the oven to 400°F. (Turn on the convection, if you have it.)

2 Using a box grater, grate the onions into a large bowl. Add the beef, salt, pepper, turmeric, and 1 tablespoon of the sumac, and using your hands, combine well until the mixture easily pulls away from the sides of the bowl.

3 Transfer the meat to a 9 x 13-inch broiler-safe baking dish, lightly pressing down to spread the meat in an even layer. Sprinkle the remaining 1 teaspoon sumac over the top, and cook for about 10 minutes, or until the meat releases its liquid.

4 Remove from the oven and turn on the broiler. Using a sharp knife, cut the layer of meat lengthwise into 1-inch-wide *kabab* strips. Carefully turn each one over and place the dish under the broiler to cook for 4 minutes more, or until the top gets crispy.

5 Remove from the broiler and allow to rest, about 10 minutes, or until the liquid is absorbed back into the beef. Serve with plain basmati rice.

1 pound (454 grams) yellow onions

2 pounds (907 grams) ground beef (90% fat, 10% lean)

1 tablespoon kosher salt

1 teaspoon freshly ground black pepper

1 tablespoon ground turmeric

1 tablespoon plus 1 teaspoon sumac

Plain basmati rice for serving

KABAB SOLTANI

makes 4 to 6 servings

When this *kabab* is served alone, it's called *kabab barg,* and when served alongside *kabab koobideh,* it's given the additional name *soltani,* derived from *soltan* (sultan) in Turkish, which means it's a meal "fit for a king." I like to serve *kabab barg* with grilled tomatoes and long chili peppers.

Note Chateaubriand is also called beef tenderloin or tenderloin roast.

1 Trim any excess pieces of fat and sinew from the meat and discard.

2 Divide the tenderloin into even segments, about 3 inches in width.

3 Working with one segment of meat at a time, butterfly each, opening it up two or three times, depending on the thickness of the beef. (Once butterflied, each meat segment should look like a rectangle.)

4 Working with one butterflied section at a time, cut each piece into sections about 2 inches wide and thread each section onto a long metal skewer. Use the blunt side of your knife's spine to gently tenderize the meat, working from the center outward, breaking up its fibers. Combine the onion juice with the saffron water. Brush the onion juice and saffron water on top of each section of meat. Allow to marinate at room temperature for 10 to 15 minutes.

5 Preheat a grill (charcoal is best) to high heat—you want very strong heat about 2 inches away from the skewers. Season with salt before laying the skewers across the grill. Grill to your desired doneness, and season again with a bit of salt before serving.

2 pounds (907 grams) chateaubriand (*shatoo biyran*)

Juices from ½ medium onion, grated (save the grated onion for another use)

¼ cup (60 ml) Saffron Water (page xxxiv)

Kosher salt as needed

KABAB CHENJE

makes 4 to 6 servings

These easy *kababs* are all about using a well-marbled cut of beef to ensure that they turn out juicy and tender. Take care to cut the meat in uniform 1½-inch cubes so all the pieces will be done at the same time. When I make *kabab chenje,* I cover a tray with *Naan-e Taftoon* (page 6) to catch the drippings and to keep the *kababs* warm while they rest. Since the tomatoes take more time on the grill, start them about 10 minutes earlier than the *kababs.*

1 Use a food processor to roughly chop the onion, then transfer the onions to a large mixing bowl.

2 Add the olive oil and meat cubes to the bowl with the onions, and marinate, covered, for a minimum of 4 hours and up to 12 hours in the refrigerator.

3 Remove the meat from the refrigerator, season with salt, then thread the meat onto 12-inch metal skewers and set aside at room temperature to rest for 30 minutes. Meanwhile, prepare the tomatoes.

4 Generously season the tomatoes with salt and thread onto separate skewers.

5 Preheat a grill (charcoal is best) to high heat—you want very strong heat about 2 inches away from the skewers. Spread the flatbread out on a large tray and set aside.

6 Place the tomato skewers on the grill and grill until slightly charred, about 10 minutes. Remove from the grill and set aside. Next, place the meat skewers on the grill and grill them for 3 to 4 minutes on each side, flipping them only once or twice.

7 Immediately transfer the cooked *kababs* to the prepared tray and brush them with the saffron water. Keep the *kababs* warm while the meat rests. Sprinkle with sumac, if you like, before serving with the tomatoes.

1 large yellow onion

⅓ cup (80 ml) extra-virgin olive oil

3 to 4 pounds (1.3 to 1.8 kilograms) well-marbled beef, such as London broil or New York strip, cut into 1½-inch cubes

1 tablespoon kosher salt, plus more as needed

¼ cup (60 ml) Saffron Water (page xxxiv)

Fresh tomatoes, your choice, halved or quartered depending on size

Store-bought flatbread, such as lavash, or *Naan-e Taftoon* (page 6)

Sumac for serving (optional)

KABAB HOSSAINI

makes 4 to 6 servings

Kabab hossaini is a style of layering beef skewers with tomatoes, bell peppers, and onions, giving you the tender, succulent comfort of a beef stew. I love to make *kabab hossaini* in a clay or cast-iron pot instead of using the grill. It's an excellent *kabab* to make a day ahead of time, so the next day, you can reheat it in the same pretty pot and bring it from the oven to the table for serving with Saffron Basmati Rice (page 56).

1 Alternate threading the beef cubes with the bell pepper cubes onto skewers about 6 to 8 inches long. You should get about 8 to 10 skewers, depending on how tightly you thread them. Sprinkle 1 teaspoon of the salt and the black pepper all over them.

2 Add the half-moon-sliced onions and 4 tablespoons olive oil to a large, heavy-bottomed pot with a tight-fitting lid and sauté over high heat, until just softened. Scoop the onions out with a slotted spoon and set aside.

3 To the now-empty pot, add the skewers and brown on all sides over high heat, then transfer to a cast-iron or clay pot, if using.

4 Preheat the oven to 400°F.

5 To the same now-empty pot, add the diced onions and more oil if needed, and sauté over medium heat, adding more oil if needed, so that the onions turn golden, their edges darken, and they soften, about 5 to 7 minutes. Add the garlic and a bit more oil (so that the garlic doesn't burn), and stir. Add the turmeric, a bit more oil, and stir, allowing the turmeric to bloom and release its fragrance, about 30 seconds. Next, add the tomato paste, a bit more oil, and sauté, stirring occasionally until the tomato paste takes on a shiny color, about 1 minute more (the mixture will pull away from the bottom of the pot). Deglaze with ½ cup (120 ml) water and lower the heat. Add 1 teaspoon of the salt, the dried lime powder, and taste and adjust the seasoning, adding more salt and pepper if needed. Pour the mixture over the skewers and arrange the reserved half-moon slices of onion on top.

6 Add the cinnamon and the remaining 1 teaspoon salt to the tomatoes and pour over the *kababs*. Cover with the lid, place in the oven, and cook for 30 minutes. After 30 minutes, reduce the heat to 375°F and cook until the meat is tender, about 2 hours. Serve with saffron basmati rice.

1½ pounds (680 grams) beef chuck, cut into 1- to 1½-inch cubes

1 green bell pepper, stemmed and seeded, cut into 1- to 1½-inch cubes

3 teaspoons kosher salt, plus more to taste

1 teaspoon freshly ground black pepper

Light olive oil

2 medium yellow onions (about 8 to 9 ounces each), 1 sliced into half-moons (not too thin), 1 small diced

3 to 4 garlic cloves, thinly sliced

1 tablespoon ground turmeric

2 tablespoons tomato paste

1 teaspoon dried lime powder

1 teaspoon ground cinnamon

One 28-ounce (794-gram) can whole San Marzano tomatoes with juice, or 6 skinned fresh tomatoes, medium diced

Saffron Basmati Rice (page 56) for serving

CHICKEN MORGH

I discovered my joy of cooking for a crowd while attending the University of Tehran. My first year as a law student coincided with the beginning of the Iranian revolution in 1979. Everything in the universities that represented the old regime was swept away by the student movement—including the people running the student cafeteria in my school, causing the cafeteria to shut down, a major inconvenience for many students who had no better way to get lunch. During a meeting among my law school classmates, I stood up, a skinny, shy freshman, and asked, "What about the cafeteria? Why don't we just open it?" There was a strange reaction in the room because the meetings typically dealt with more ideological issues, far from the mundane daily lunch. "Open it?" (I can't be sure it was a question, because I can't find anyone to corroborate the details; it may have simply been, "Open it.") Here is where the memory—like so many from that time of my life set to the soundtrack of the demonstrations and destruction of 1979—breaks into fragments.

The next thing I remember, the student-led organization appointed me and two others as kitchen staff and set us on a bus headed to Tehran's Grand Bazaar for provisions. We returned with bags the size of our bodies filled with onions, beans, and potatoes. We washed, cleaned, and prepped through the night to create a thick bean appetizer and a delicious, shredded, creamy chicken salad with pickles called *salad olivieh* (see page 162). Just before we opened our doors, I remember running to the campus soccer field to pick dandelion flowers to place in empty salt shakers to adorn the tables. I knew our mission was a success because we ran out of food!

My classmates and I operated our cafeteria until one day a lock appeared on the cafeteria door, with a sign that read THOSE WHO BREAK AND ENTER WILL BE SUBJECT TO PROSECUTION. And our cafeteria became too risky to continue. But the *feeling* of what we accomplished is unforgettable—to this day, I consider it my "first restaurant." Forty years later, I am doing the same work—only this time I have my family and dedicated team beside me to help with the planning and managing of the business, as I continue my love of cooking for a crowd at Sofreh.

Our *salad olivieh*, like so many chicken dishes, was a mealtime lifesaver. In this chapter, I give you the most fantastic chicken I've enjoyed, from Giti Joon's Stuffed Chicken (page 167)—brimming with herbs, prunes, and walnuts and that is wonderful for a special occasion—to my Sour Cherry and Apple Stew with Chicken (page 164)—a recipe template for a *khoresht* that gives you room to play with seasonal fruit. And then there is *mosama bademjoon* (see page 170)—a chicken and eggplant stew from my best friend, Minoo, which incorporates the sweet and slightly spicy flavor and aroma of cinnamon that cooks use throughout the south. And finally, there is my succulent, juicy version of *juje kabab* (see page 173)—one that I showcased in culinary school while waiting for the doors of Sofreh to finally open.

CHICKEN and POTATO SALAD

SALAD OLIVIEH | *makes 10 to 12 servings*

Iranians adopted this chicken salad from Russia in the early nineteenth century, and it has since become a staple of picnics, casual parties, and virtually every afternoon get-together. It varies from home to home, but growing up, I noticed everyone tended to puree the potato and shred the chicken to bits almost everywhere I ate it. Once, for a high school friend's birthday, I dedicated half a day to hand-shredding a whole chicken to death. My friend's father took one bite and said, *"Morgh kojast?"* ("Where's the chicken?") My teenage heart sank. I still haven't recovered.

On that day, I learned a lesson that I've carried forward in my cooking ever since; I follow my instincts and make my food as I wish, often challenging expectations about traditional dishes. My version here is chunky, forgoing a ton of mayonnaise for lots of lemons, good extra-virgin olive oil, and yogurt. When I want to treat myself, I toss in diced, pistachio-studded pieces of Italian mortadella, taking the dish to another level.

Note Further reducing the chicken stock adds a ton of flavor to this perfect picnic salad. You can also use Yukon Gold potatoes. I prefer to boil them instead of roasting them.

1 Preheat the oven to 350°F.

2 Place the potatoes on a baking sheet and bake until fully cooked, about 45 minutes. When the potatoes are cool enough to handle, peel and grate 2 of them using a box grater. Finely dice the remaining potatoes. Set all aside to fully cool.

3 While the potatoes are baking, add the onions and 3 tablespoons light olive oil to a large, deep skillet with a tight-fitting lid and sauté over medium heat until the onions turn golden, adding more oil as needed, so that their edges darken, and they soften, about 5 to 7 minutes. Add the turmeric, a bit more oil, and stir, allowing the turmeric to bloom and release its fragrance, about 1 minute more.

4 Place the chicken, breast side down, into the onion mixture and add ⅔ cup (157 ml) water. Reduce the heat to medium-low, cover, and cook for 1 hour. Remove the chicken, reserving the cooking liquid, and set aside. Return the reserved liquid to high heat and reduce to about ½ cup. Set aside.

3½ pounds (1.5 kilograms) russet potatoes, skin on but scrubbed

1 large yellow onion, medium diced

Light olive oil

1 teaspoon ground turmeric

1 whole chicken (about 2½ to 3 pounds/about 1.1 to 1.3 kilograms)

2 tablespoons plus ½ teaspoon kosher salt

1½ teaspoons freshly ground black pepper, or more to taste

1½ cups (240 grams) frozen green peas

5 Once the chicken is cool enough to handle, use a fork and knife—or your clean hands—to remove and discard the skin, and separate the chicken from the bones. Then, use two forks to shred the meat, place it in a large bowl, and discard the bones. Season with 1 tablespoon of the salt and 1 teaspoon of the pepper.

6 Prepare an ice water bath by filling a large bowl (preferably metal) with cold water and ice cubes. Set aside.

7 Add 2 cups (240 ml) water to a medium saucepan and bring to a boil. Add the peas and ½ teaspoon of the salt and boil until cooked but still firm. Transfer to the prepared ice bath, then drain and set aside.

8 Prepare the dressing: In a large mixing bowl, whisk the reserved chicken liquid, the mayonnaise, lemon juice, yogurt, and the remaining 1 tablespoon salt and ½ teaspoon pepper. Taste and adjust the seasoning and level of acidity, adding more lemon juice if needed.

9 To the bowl with the shredded chicken, add all the potatoes, the peas, and pickled cucumbers, and then pour the dressing over and mix well to combine. Taste, adding more salt and lemon juice if needed, then pour over the extra-virgin olive oil and parsley. Set aside in the refrigerator to chill before serving cold, with more parsley leaves for garnish.

1 cup (230 grams) good-quality store-bought mayonnaise

½ cup (120 ml) bottled lemon juice, or more as needed

½ cup (143 grams) Homemade Yogurt (page 32) or store-bought Greek yogurt

One 24-ounce (680-grams) jar pickled cucumbers in brine, drained and diced into ⅛- to ½-inch pieces (depending on the size of the cucumbers or personal preference)

⅔ cup (157 ml) extra-virgin olive oil

1 to 2 ounces (28 to 56 grams) fresh flat-leaf parsley, leaves and tender stems, finely chopped, plus more leaves for garnish

SOUR CHERRY and APPLE STEW with CHICKEN

KHORESHT-E ALBALOO BA SIB | *makes 4 to 6 servings*

Through genetic testing, scientists have traced the migration of domesticated apples in the West and other parts of the world back to Iran, due to its location along the Silk Road trade route. Caucasus crab apples, whose origins are thousands of years old, still flourish in lush forests near the Caspian Sea, near the border of Iran and Azerbaijan.

You can use any apple variety that you like for this stew, but I love sweet-tart Pink Lady apples. During the fall, I serve a variation of this dish, skipping the sour cherries and adding dried plums and Honeycrisp apples. Although, if you use plums, I recommend beef or lamb, instead of the more delicate chicken.

1 Generously season the chicken thighs with salt and pepper. In a large, heavy-bottomed pot with a tight-fitting lid, warm 2 tablespoons olive oil over high heat. Add the thighs in a single layer and fry, about 2 to 3 minutes per side or until lightly browned. Remove from the pan and set aside.

2 To the now-empty pot, add the onions, lower the heat to low (the onions will release their liquid), and deglaze the bottom of the pot with the onion juice. Next, add 2 more tablespoons olive oil, raise the heat to medium, and sauté the onions until soft and browned, about 5 to 7 minutes. Add the turmeric, a bit more oil, and stir, allowing the turmeric to bloom and release its fragrance, a few minutes more. Next, add the tomato paste, a bit more oil, and sauté, stirring occasionally, until the tomato paste takes on a shiny color, about 1 minute more (the mixture will pull away from the bottom of the pot).

3 Add the reserved sour cherry brine, ½ cup (120 ml) water, 1 tablespoon salt, the lemon juice, and sugar, and stir to combine. Return the chicken thighs to the pot, fatty side down, cover with the lid, lower the heat to low, and cook until the chicken is cooked through, about 30 minutes.

4 Lift the lid, add the sour cherries and vanilla, if using, and check the liquid. If it is too thick, add ½ cup (120 ml) water, stir, then taste and adjust the seasoning. Continue cooking, covered, for 10 minutes more. Remove the lid and cook for 10 minutes more.

5 Chop the apples into bite-size pieces and gently stir them into the stew, cooking for about 3 to 4 minutes. Allow the stew to rest with the lid ajar before serving.

8 skinless, bone-in chicken thighs (about 2½ to 3 pounds/ 1.1 to 1.3 kilograms)

Kosher salt

Freshly ground black pepper

Light olive oil

1 medium yellow onion, finely diced

1 tablespoon ground turmeric

2 tablespoons tomato paste

One 24-ounce (680-gram) jar sour cherries in brine, drained, brine reserved

⅓ cup (80 ml) bottled lemon juice

2½ tablespoons granulated sugar

1 tablespoon pure vanilla extract (optional)

2 Pink Lady apples or another firm variety

GITI JOON'S STUFFED CHICKEN

makes 6 servings

You'll find as many variations on a stuffed chicken in Iran as you do for *a'ash* (see pages 189–209). Some people add pomegranates, nuts, and herbs; others omit the nuts but add plums. And then, there is my mother, Giti Joon's, signature chicken—a stuffed bird that gently cooks in a fragrant sauce that she would make for special get-togethers and that I love so much. Over the years, her stuffing kept evolving to include plums, dried herbs, barberries, and walnuts. A few years back, my mother and I were standing side by side in my New York apartment as she was stuffing her chicken for a dinner we were hosting. *"Madar,"* she said, sweetly calling *me* the Farsi word for "mom." "You make the sauce for my chicken." Caught off guard, I stammered, "But your sauce is delicious." And she replied, "I know, but I prefer *yours.*" Well, isn't this something, I thought, so happy and proud. From then on, each time we've made this chicken dish together, Giti Joon prepares her perfect stuffing—I wouldn't change a thing—and I make the sauce.

1 Soak the barberries in cold water for 10 minutes, if fresh, or up to 25 minutes, if they are older. Drain and set aside.

2 Rinse the outside and the cavity of the chicken under cold running water. Pat dry with paper towels and generously season the cavity with salt.

3 Add the thinly sliced onions and 2 tablespoons olive oil to a medium skillet and sauté over medium heat, adding more oil if needed, so that the onions turn golden, their edges darken, and they soften, about 5 to 7 minutes.

4 Combine the cooked onions, drained barberries, the walnuts, basil, tarragon, and prunes in a large bowl, and using your hands, fill the cavity of the chicken with the mixture, being careful not to overstuff (so that the chicken doesn't burst). Either sew the chicken closed, as I like to do, or truss it with kitchen twine. Set aside.

5 In a small saucepan, bring 1½ cups (360 ml) water to a boil and set aside.

6 Add the diced onions and 4 tablespoons olive oil to a large, deep skillet with a tight-fitting lid, and sauté over medium heat, adding more oil if needed, so that the onions turn golden, their edges darken, and they soften, about 5 minutes. Add 1 tablespoon of the turmeric, a bit more oil, and stir, allowing the turmeric to bloom and release its fragrance, a few minutes more. Add the stuffed chicken, breast side first, and give it a quick sauté, rotating it so that it's lightly browned and coated in the turmeric, about 3 minutes on each side. Add the boiled water to the skillet. →

⅓ cup (37 grams) dried barberries

1 whole chicken (about 3 to 4 pounds/1.3 to 1.8 kilograms), skin on

Kosher salt

2 medium yellow onions, 1 thinly sliced into half-moons for stuffing, 1 medium diced

Light olive oil

⅔ cup (70 grams) chopped walnuts

¼ cup (24 grams) dried basil

⅓ cup (30 grams) dried tarragon

1 cup (174 grams) California prunes, pitted

2 tablespoons ground turmeric

1 cup (225 grams) tomato paste

½ cup (120 ml) lemon juice, bottled or fresh

¼ cup granulated sugar

1 teaspoon saffron powder

1 teaspoon ground cumin

1 tablespoon freshly ground black pepper

7 In a small bowl, mix the remaining 1 tablespoon turmeric, the tomato paste, lemon juice, sugar, saffron powder, cumin, 1 tablespoon salt, and the pepper. Taste it. It should be sweet, sour, and slightly salty. Making sure the chicken is breast side up, season with more salt (but be careful, as the sauce is salty) and pepper. Next, pour the sauce over the chicken. (The sauce is thick, but the steam from cooking will loosen it.)

8 Bring the pot with the chicken to a boil, then cover with the lid, lower the heat to low, and cook for 1½ hours—you'll notice steam coming out of the pot. Check for doneness by lifting the lid and pressing the side of one of the chicken's legs. It should not bounce back. Depending on the size of the chicken, it may need more cooking time, so increase if necessary. Remove the pot from the heat.

9 Allow to rest, partially covered, until slightly cool, before serving the chicken.

MINOO'S CHICKEN and EGGPLANT STEW

MOSAMA BADEMJOON | *makes 4 to 6 servings*

Minoo, my dazzling best friend of more than twenty years, was raised in the Abadan southwestern Khuzestan province of Iran that borders the Persian Gulf. There is a fun musicality, free spirit, and live-out-loud love for life in the heart of Iranians who live on the coast, and you can taste it in the mouthwatering spiciness of their food, which often uses tamarind and red chili flakes. I appreciate these flavor profiles and expressions of personality in my cooking—so much so that Minoo likes to joke that I'm an Abadani baby who was mistakenly dropped off in the more reserved and old-fashioned mountain and desert province of Isfahan.

When we first opened Sofreh, Minoo gave me the wise advice and emotional support I needed as a first-time restaurateur. This *mosama bademjoon* is her recipe, and it is a tribute to my love for her.

1 Working with one eggplant at a time, use a sharp knife to trim any spines along the stem, but leave the stems intact. Peel 4 narrow stripes lengthwise on each eggplant, then halve lengthwise. Sprinkle liberally with salt and stand the eggplants upright in a colander to drain for 1 to 3 hours.

2 Preheat the oven to 450°F.

3 Generously season the chicken thighs with salt and pepper. Warm 3 tablespoons olive oil in a large sauté pan set over high heat, add the chicken, and quickly brown on all sides, about 1 to 2 minutes. Remove the chicken from the pan and set aside.

4 To the now-empty pan, add the diced onions and sauté until golden and soft, about 5 to 7 minutes. Next, add the turmeric, a bit more oil, and stir to allow the turmeric to bloom and release its fragrance, about 1 minute. Add the tomato paste and a bit more olive oil, and sauté until the tomato paste opens up and the color gets shiny. Add 1 tablespoon salt, 1 tablespoon pepper, the cinnamon, and lemon juice, and deglaze the pan. Next, add ½ cup (120 ml) water and the sugar, and stir to combine. Taste and adjust the seasoning. Remove the sauce from the heat and set aside.

5 Meanwhile, fry the eggplants: Pat the eggplants dry with paper towels. Coat the bottom of a large skillet with the neutral oil and warm over medium heat. Place the cut side of the eggplant halves facedown in the skillet and fry until brown but still firm, about 2 to 3 minutes per side. Remove the eggplants from the pan and set aside. →

2 pounds (907 grams) small Italian or other farmers' market varietal eggplants

Kosher salt

1½ pounds (680 grams) skinless, bone-in chicken thighs

Freshly ground black pepper

Light olive oil

1 medium yellow onion, medium diced, plus 1 small yellow onion, sliced into half-moons

1 tablespoon ground turmeric

¼ cup tomato paste

1½ teaspoons ground cinnamon, plus more to taste

¼ cup (60 ml) bottled lemon juice

1 tablespoon granulated sugar

¼ cup (60 ml) neutral oil, such as vegetable or canola oil, for frying

2 large tomatoes, sliced diagonally into 1-inch slices, or a small bunch sweet cherry tomatoes on the vine

¼ cup (60 ml) Saffron Water (page xxxiv) for garnish

6 To the now-empty pan, add the reserved browned chicken, return the heat to medium, and quickly sauté the chicken on all sides. Transfer the chicken to a 9 x 13-inch Pyrex dish. Next, layer the eggplants on top of the chicken, followed by the sauce. Cover the dish loosely with aluminum foil and bake for 10 minutes. Lower the heat to 375°F and continue baking for 50 minutes more.

7 Meanwhile, prepare your choice of onion garnish: Add the sliced half-moon onions and 2 tablespoons olive oil to a medium skillet and sauté over medium heat until the onions turn golden, their edges darken, and they soften, about 5 to 7 minutes. Set aside. (Alternatively, continue frying longer until the edges are crispy and golden brown, or really go for it and glorify the dish with Crispy Fried Onions [page 194] as I do at Sofreh.)

8 Remove the dish from the oven, top with the tomatoes, sprinkle with 1 teaspoon salt, more sprinkles of cinnamon, if you like, and return the dish to the oven, partially covered, to allow the tomatoes to cook, about 10 minutes more. Garnish with the fried onions and saffron water before serving.

SAFFRON-MARINATED CORNISH HENS

JUJE KABAB | *makes 4 servings*

On my first day at culinary school, after introducing myself, my instructor said, "You're from Iran? Ha! Your food is so barbarian." I thought: Challenge accepted. So, for my end-of-the-year thesis project menu, I presented Sour Cherry Rice (page 67), Sofreh Roasted Eggplant with Tomato Sauce and Feta (page 109), and my saffron and lemon–infused version of *juje kabab*— a classic dish traditionally grilled over a bed of glowing charcoal. That dish had become a staple at my home parties, and it's especially great for picky eaters because it's saucy, tender, and comforting. It's also convenient to make in advance. You can serve it at room temperature or if you like, place it under the broiler for a quick char before serving. Because in school I was always one of those nerds who wanted to take home every award, my version of *juje kabab* won the final project! There are two methods for you here: a quick weeknight oven-baked method and, for when you have more time, a spatchcock method whereby you butterfly the hens by removing the backbones and laying them out flat. See the photograph on page 158.

Note While the hens are resting, if there is excess liquid, transfer it to a small pot and cook on high heat for a few minutes to reduce it to a thick sauce to cover the hens.

1 Make the marinade: Combine the onions, paprika, turmeric, pepper, saffron powder, salt, and olive oil in a large mixing bowl. Mix thoroughly, and taste and adjust the seasoning.

2 Add the hens to the bowl, and using your clean hands, rub them all over with the marinade. Cover and refrigerate for at least 2 hours or up to 4 hours.

3 Preheat the oven to 450°F. Lightly oil a 9 x 13-inch broiler-safe baking dish.

4 Place the marinated hens, breast side down, in the dish and pour the marinade over them, followed by the lemon juice. Partially cover the dish with aluminum foil and bake for 20 minutes. The hens will be slightly cooked.

5 Remove the foil, and using tongs, flip and continue cooking the hens on the other side for an additional 20 minutes, or until a thermometer inserted into a thigh reads 165°F and the onions brown.

6 Turn on the broiler. Carefully transfer the hot dish to the broiler and broil for 5 minutes to crisp the skin. Allow to rest before serving (see headnote).

2 small yellow onions, grated and drained of excess liquid

1 tablespoon smoked paprika

1 tablespoon ground turmeric

2 tablespoons freshly ground black pepper

½ teaspoon saffron powder

2 tablespoons kosher salt, plus more as needed

⅓ cup (80 ml) light olive oil, plus more as needed

4 Cornish hens (about 1 pound/ 454 grams each), cut into pieces, as you wish, or spatchcocked (see headnote)

⅓ cup (80 ml) bottled lemon juice

FISH AND SEAFOOD MAHI

Before the revolution in Iran, a distant relative was the head of the Caspian Sea fishery, which later became SHILAT, an acronym for the government division that oversees aquaculture. He ran the entire operation to import caviar and *mahi sefid,* an incredibly juicy, rich, and fatty whitefish that is eaten smoked or fried throughout Iran during Nowruz, Persian New Year. One year, when I was a teenager, my relative came to visit. To thank Giti Joon for her incredible meals and hospitality, he arranged to have a private government jet deliver to us some of the most valuable fish pulled from the waters of the Caspian Sea.

When the package arrived, my mother opened it to find delectable *karaburan* (wild sturgeon), cod, and massive *mahi sefid,* and said, "Oh lord, it stinks. Ring everyone to come and take this off my hands!" Our relatives were at our house within half an hour. Besides the fish, included in the package were also two long, black sacks holding large, steely-gray pearls. My mother took one look at and smell of them and promptly dumped them into the garbage.

A few days later, Giti Joon called to thank her guest for his gift. "How were the eggs?" he asked. I'll never forget my mother's face, with the phone to her ear, as a look of shock and surprise crept over her. She had unknowingly thrown away two large containers of pure Iranian beluga caviar, aka "black gold." I stared at her. What was she going to say? I wondered. I knew she couldn't own up to having thrown the caviar away, and yet she couldn't tell him how much she had enjoyed it. I watched her compose herself, and then quickly recovering, she said, "How would *you* enjoy eating them?" There was a long pause as my mother listened to his expertise on the other end of the line. And then she said, "Oh my God, I wish I knew. I made an omelet with mine!"

That, my dear, sums up the role of fish in my home as I grew up on the landlocked Isfahan plateau.

My appreciation for the seafood traditions of other parts of Iran blossomed only when I began traveling to Gilan and Mazandaran, near the Caspian Sea, and to the Persian Gulf coast province of Bushehr. In Bushehr, walking through fish markets at the crack of dawn, I watched fishmongers unload the most incredible array of fish, silver- and gold-streaked and every color of the rainbow, that they had pulled from the long, narrow, warm-water coastline. They'd empty tubs of smaller sardines and drums of crustaceans, as local women, eager to bring home their catch and get lunch started, gathered around with their heads covered, baskets in hand, waiting for the fishmongers to chop off the heads of the still-squirming catch of the day. At my brother Amir's wedding in 2008, I ate beautifully fried whole grouper that was more than three feet long and set down, intact, on our table for feasting. I was awestruck at the expertise of the *a'ashpaz*, and to this day, I wonder, How large was *that* pot?

Once, while on a *lenj*—a wooden fishing boat made by hand and that has been integral to the life of Iranian mariners for more than four hundred years—I watched as my hosts, waiting for the tide to recede, lit a small glowing fire onboard to do some cooking. The idea of fire on a wooden boat sounds crazy. But back then, I was too interested in the cooler that held the ingredients they needed to make *mahi shekam por* (see page 186), a southern-style whole stuffed fish.

You can do so much with fish and shrimp with the flavors you'll find in this chapter: gorgeous saffron, musky dried lime powder, sour tamarind, tangy barberries, crunchy walnuts, pomegranate molasses, and the aroma of fresh and dried herbs. (With these flavors on hand, you may even be able to make yourself one hell of an omelet!)

SOFREH GHALIEH MAHI

makes 6 servings

Soon after the Iran-Iraq war in the 1980s, a migration of war refugees from coastal, southern parts of Iran made its way north carrying its seafood-rich cuisine to Isfahan, and increasing the demand for fish in my province. When I returned to Iran with Akis for the first time, my aunt Mihan set out a celebratory feast for my arrival, but more so, I think, to impress my then-new husband! Among her dishes was a traditional bone-in fish stew that her neighbor from the south had taught her called *ghalieh mahi—ghalieh* being the Arabic word for "stew." I fell in love with the mouthwatering flavors that unfold from the base of musky fenugreek, fried herbs, and sour tamarind. My aunt told her neighbor how much we had enjoyed it, and a few days later her neighbor brought us more *ghalieh mahi* to savor. My aunt's version had been outstanding, but this lady's version was otherworldly.

I tried making *ghalieh mahi* at home in New York many times, coming close but not quite nailing it the way I remembered it. One day, my best friend, Minoo, raised near the Persian Gulf, made *ghalieh mahi* for a party, and there it was! Her version had captured all of the expressive flavors that had been so memorable. When I was creating my menu for Sofreh, I wanted to include several regional specialties to honor my country, and *ghalieh mahi* was top of my list. But I didn't want to misrepresent such a traditional dish that was not from my home province; it had to have approval from Minoo. Soon after we opened, *The New York Times*'s Melissa Clark asked me for my *ghalieh mahi* recipe, bringing a lot of attention to Sofreh. But more important, it brought so much joy and pride to Minoo and her southern Iranian mother, who said, "We were kicked out of our land, but today, we're in *The New York Times*!"

Note You can make the herb and tamarind sauce to serve with seared sea scallops, or make it vegetarian and serve with cauliflower or fried tofu. If using store-bought tamarind paste, taste and adjust the seasoning for sugar and salt to achieve a balance of sweet and sour.

1 Prepare the sauce: Add the onions and 4 tablespoons olive oil to a medium sauté pan with a tight-fitting lid over medium-low heat and sauté, stirring occasionally, until the onions are dark golden brown, about 10 minutes. Stir in the garlic and cook for 2 minutes more. Next, add the chili flakes and cook, stirring, for 30 seconds more. Add the turmeric and a bit more oil (so the turmeric doesn't burn), and stir, allowing the turmeric to bloom and release its fragrance. Remove the onion mixture from the pan and set aside. $\longrightarrow$

For the herb and tamarind sauce

1 medium yellow onion, finely diced

Light olive oil

5 large garlic cloves, chopped

2 teaspoons red chili flakes, or to taste $\longrightarrow$

2 To the now-empty pan, add the parsley, cilantro, chives or scallions, and fresh fenugreek, and stir continuously, until they release all of their liquid and start sticking to the bottom of the pan. Next, add the dried fenugreek and slowly add ¼ cup (60 ml) olive oil, in batches. Continue frying until the herbs are dark and you have used up all the oil.

3 Deglaze the pan with the lemon juice, scraping up the charred herbs. Add the reserved onion mixture to the herbs, along with the salt, pepper, tamarind paste, and 2 cups (470 ml) water, and stir until incorporated. Bring to a boil, then taste and adjust the seasoning (adding sugar, more tamarind paste, or both if necessary, to achieve a balance of sweet and tart). Lower the heat to low and cook, covered, stirring occasionally, until a thick stew forms, about 15 to 20 minutes. Set aside to rest, partially covered.

4 Prepare the fish: Generously season the fillets with salt and pepper. In a medium skillet over medium-high heat, warm the olive oil until almost smoking. If you are using fish with skin, place the fish, skin side down, in the skillet and cook until brown and crispy, 4 to 5 minutes. If necessary, work in batches so you don't crowd the pan, adding more oil as needed. Turn the fish and cook on the other side, until opaque and cooked through, about 1 to 2 minutes more.

5 Divide the herb and tamarind sauce among serving bowls, place a piece of fish on top of each, and garnish with drizzles of extra-virgin olive oil and fresh chives, if using. Serve with Saffron Basmati Rice (page 56).

2 tablespoons ground turmeric

8 ounces (226 grams) fresh flat-leaf parsley, leaves and tender stems, roughly chopped

8 ounces (226 grams) fresh cilantro, leaves and tender stems, roughly chopped

6 ounces (170 grams) fresh chives or scallions, both white and green parts, finely chopped

4 ounces (112 grams) fresh fenugreek, leaves and tender stems, roughly chopped

⅓ cup dried fenugreek

¼ cup (60 ml) bottled lemon juice

2½ teaspoons kosher salt, plus more as needed

1 teaspoon freshly ground black pepper

⅓ to ½ cup (80 ml to 120 ml) Tamarind Paste (opposite), homemade or store-bought (see headnote)

Granulated sugar to taste

For the fish

6 thick fillets (4 to 6 ounces/112 to 170 grams each) meaty whitefish, such as striped bass or cod (preferably skin on), patted dry

Kosher salt

Freshly ground black pepper

1 tablespoon light olive oil, plus more as needed

Extra-virgin olive oil for finishing

Fresh chives, finely chopped, for serving (optional)

TAMARIND PASTE

makes 1½ cups or more thick paste

A block of dried, pressed tamarind will contain the roots, seeds, and pulp of the tamarind fruit. Once the softened tamarind is strained and the pulp extracted, it is ready for immediate use as tamarind paste. To purchase a good-quality block of tamarind, make sure it is pliable instead of rock hard to the touch.

1 Place the tamarind in a glass bowl, pour 1 cup (235 ml) warm water over it, and cover with plastic wrap. Soak at room temperature for at least 4 hours or up to overnight.

2 Place your hands in the softened tamarind and water mixture and separate the skins, seeds, and fibers from the fruit pulp and discard. And then, working in small batches, press the mixture through a fine-mesh strainer to collect a thick paste.

3 Repeat the straining process, using another 1 cup (235 ml) or more warm water to help dilute the pulp that remains in the strainer and discarding any remaining seeds and skins. Use immediately or store in a glass jar in the refrigerator for up to 1 week.

6 ounces (170 grams) pressed tamarind block, cut into smaller pieces

Tamarind *(Tambre Hendi)*

Tamarind comes from the Arabic *tamar hind,* meaning "Indian date." The fruit of the tamarind tree is a hard-shelled fruit pod with a dark brown, fleshy, sour pulp inside. In some parts of Thailand, sweet tamarind trees yield sweet fruit, but sour tamarind is used in Persian cooking. It's an incredibly versatile ingredient—you can bake, cook, and marinate with it. Many dishes in the southern provinces near the Persian Gulf incorporate tamarind into their fish dishes, such as Spicy Shrimp Rice (page 65). It has an irresistible sweet and sour flavor that kids love. When I was growing up, one of my favorite treats was tamarind paste packaged for snacking, called *tambre hendi*. I'd slice open a little corner of the bag and suck it down. In grocery stores you will see premade tamarind paste labeled as tamarind concentrate or tamarind paste. Prepared pastes vary in acidity levels, contain preservatives that leave a bitter aftertaste, and lack the sour depth of flavor that making your own tamarind paste from compressed tamarind pulp offers.

PANFRIED SAFFRON SHRIMP

MAYGOU ZAFFERANI | *makes 2 to 4 servings*

In addition to the 150 varieties of fish in the waters of the Persian Gulf, you'll also find giant *maygou* (prawns). Home cooks around the gulf use them in *ghalieh mahi* (see page 179) as well as in the layered *polo* rice called *maygou polo* (see page 65*). Here, they are seasoned with lime powder and quickly panfried in a gorgeous, colorful saffron sauce for a delicious weeknight dinner. Once the shrimp turn opaque, they are done, so be careful not to overcook them. And if you want to throw a ton of them on the grill for a party, you can do that, too. Just make the dish less saucy by reducing the lemon juice to ¼ cup (60 ml).

1 Season the shrimp with the saffron powder, and using your hands, massage the powder into each one. Continue seasoning with pepper, followed by the dried lime powder.

2 Warm a medium sauté pan over medium heat, melt the butter, then add the shrimp, shells down. Next, season the shrimp generously with salt, add the lemon juice and olive oil, and raise the heat to high.

3 Toss the shrimp in the mixture, cooking until slightly firm and opaque, about 3 minutes. Lower the heat and continue to spoon the sauce over the shrimp, for about 1 minute more (being careful not to overcook the shrimp). Serve immediately.

2 pounds (906 grams) 22/25 shrimp, shells on, butterflied, and deveined

½ teaspoon saffron powder

Freshly ground black pepper

1 teaspoon dried lime powder

4 tablespoons (½ stick/56 grams) salted butter

Kosher salt

½ cup (120 ml) bottled lemon juice

⅔ cup (157 ml) extra-virgin olive oil

SHRIMP with DOUBLE ONIONS

MAYGOU DOPIAZE | *makes 4 servings*

This dish—popular at restaurants and roadside shacks near the Persian Gulf, and always served with crispy potatoes—is named for the two-to-one ratio of onions to shrimp. The pureed onions melt away in the umami-rich sauce of tomato paste and tangy dried lime that gets some heat from the red chili flakes. I took to making this at home, because, let's face it, not all roadside shacks are created equal.

1 Prepare the potatoes: Combine the potatoes with 3 cups (¾ liter) water and ¼ cup (72 grams) salt in a medium bowl and soak for about 30 minutes.

2 Drain the potatoes, pat them dry, and season generously with 1½ teaspoons salt. Warm the neutral oil in a medium sauté pan over medium heat, add the potatoes, and sauté until golden, stirring occasionally, about 10 minutes. Set aside.

3 Meanwhile, working in batches, add the onions to the work bowl of a food processor, and pulse until they are pureed.

4 Add the onions and the olive oil to a large sauté pan and heat over medium heat until the onions shrink in volume and turn golden, about 5 to 7 minutes. Make a well in the center of the pot, add the garlic and a bit more oil (so that the garlic doesn't burn), and sauté until fragrant, about 3 minutes more. Add the turmeric, a bit more olive oil, and stir, allowing the turmeric to bloom and release its fragrance, about 1 minute more. Next, add the chili flakes, stir, and then add the tomato paste, dried lime powder, and a bit more oil. Sauté the mixture, stirring, until the tomato paste takes on a shiny color, about 1 minute more (the mixture will pull away from the bottom of the pan).

5 Season the shrimp with 1 tablespoon salt and the pepper. Add them to the sauté pan with the onion mixture and sauté, stirring occasionally, until slightly firm and opaque, about 3 minutes. Lower the heat, add the butter, and continue to mix the shrimp in the sauce for about 1 minute more (being careful not to overcook the shrimp).

6 If needed, return the potatoes to heat and warm through for a minute before serving them topped with the shrimp.

1 pound (454 grams) Yukon Gold potatoes, peeled and cut into small cubes

Kosher salt

3 tablespoons neutral oil, such as vegetable or canola oil, for frying

2 pounds (907 grams) yellow onions, roughly chopped

¼ cup (60 ml) light olive oil, plus more as needed

2 tablespoons garlic finely chopped to an almost paste-like consistency (about 10 cloves)

1 tablespoon ground turmeric

1 teaspoon red chili flakes

¼ cup (56 grams) tomato paste

1 tablespoon dried lime powder

1 pound (454 grams) 41/50 shrimp, cleaned, peeled, and deveined

1 tablespoon freshly ground black pepper

3 tablespoons (42 grams) salted butter

FISH WRAPPED in GRAPEVINE LEAVES

DOLMEH MAHI | *makes 4 to 6 servings*

Wrapping a small fish, such as red mullet, or fish fillets in *dolmeh* (grape leaves) will not only make the fish supermoist, but the leaves, which char fast, will impart a terrific smoky flavor to the fish. Using jarred grape leaves is acceptable, but try to find fresh ones (see Resources, page 317) because they have such a wonderful, earthy flavor.

Note I always keep very thinly sliced, salted lemons in my refrigerator to use when cooking fish. The salt softens the lemons, so they cook faster, but they will still retain their zing. To make salted lemons, use a mandoline to slice and salt your lemons 2 days in advance and wipe off any excess salt before using. You can store salted lemons in a glass or plastic container for up to 2 weeks.

12 to 15 fresh grape leaves or jarred grape leaves in brine

Kosher salt

Four to six 4-ounce (112-gram) fresh fillets of a fatty fish, such as cod, halibut, or rainbow trout, or eight to twelve 2- to 3-ounce (56- to 85-gram) red mullet

Freshly ground black pepper

2 fresh lemons, 1 thinly sliced with a mandoline, 1 cut into wedges for garnish

Extra-virgin olive oil for drizzling

1 Line 2 large baking sheets or a large flat work surface with a clean kitchen towel or paper towels.

2 If using fresh grape leaves: Prepare an ice water bath. Next, bring a large pot of lightly salted water to a gentle rolling boil. Rinse the fresh leaves several times under cold water, then, working in batches, gently blanch the leaves for 30 seconds, or until they soften. Do not let them stick together or get mushy. Use tongs to gently remove them from the water and gently lay them in the ice water bath for a moment to stop the cooking process and cool. Lay the leaves flat on the lined baking sheet and pat dry. Use a sharp knife to trim the thick stem from the base of each leaf.

3 If using jarred grape leaves: Gently rinse the leaves under cold running water to remove the flavor of the brine. Lay the leaves flat on the lined baking sheet and pat dry. Reserve several leaves for layering the pan.

4 To assemble the *dolmeh:* Working with one fillet at a time, season with salt and pepper, and using at least 2 leaves per fillet, layer the leaves, making sure that you have enough surface area to cover the fish, and place them, vein side up, on a flat work surface. Place one lemon slice on the center of the leaves, followed by a fish fillet. Top the fish with an additional lemon slice, drizzle with the olive oil, then fold the leaves over to seal the fish. Repeat with the remaining fillets.

5 Preheat a grill to medium, drizzle the wrapped fillets with olive oil so they don't stick, and grill for 5 to 7 minutes on each side, depending on the thickness of your fillet, until the leaves are fully charred. Drizzle over more olive oil and serve with the fresh lemon wedges.

STUFFED WHOLE FISH, TWO WAYS

MAHI SHEKAM POR │ *makes 4 servings*

Iranians love to stuff all kinds of foods. We enjoy stuffed eggplants (*dolmeh bademjoon,* see page 119), meatballs, grape leaves (*dolmeh barg mo,* see page 133), and in both the northern and southern parts of the country, one of the most popular ways of eating freshly caught whole fish is to fill them with an herb stuffing. Because my mom reviled fish, cooking it became my aunt Mihan's game. The northern recipe that follows is a riff on what I remember from the *mahi shekam por* that she would make for us. It's a sublime mix of sour pomegranate molasses, walnuts, barberries, and lots of dried and fresh herbs. The joke was to never wear your fancy clothes to Aunt Mihan's because we'd always come home smelling of fish and fenugreek! See the photograph on page 174.

1 Prepare the fish: Working with one fish at a time, rinse under cold running water, pat dry, then use some of the vinegar to massage the cavity and exterior of the fish. Next, season the cavity and exterior generously with salt and 1 teaspoon of the ground turmeric. Repeat with the other fish, cover them with plastic wrap, and set aside in the refrigerator for 1 hour.

2 Meanwhile, prepare the stuffing: Add the diced onions and olive oil to a large, heavy-bottomed skillet and sauté over medium heat, adding more oil if needed, so that the onions turn golden, their edges darken, and they soften, about 5 to 7 minutes. Make a well in the center, add the garlic and a bit more oil (so that the garlic doesn't burn), and sauté until fragrant, about 3 more minutes. Add the dried fenugreek, dried mint, and hogweed powder, if using, and sauté for a few more minutes. Next, add the parsley and cilantro and sauté until they shrink and are fragrant, a few minutes more.

3 Add the walnuts and stir, then add the pomegranate molasses or bitter orange molasses. Taste and, if it is not sour enough, feel free to adjust the flavor by adding lemon juice to your liking. Simmer until the stuffing tightens, about 3 minutes. Stir in the barberries, if using, and continue cooking until most of the liquid cooks off, about 1 minute more. Taste and adjust the seasoning, adding more salt to taste, and remove the pan from the heat and allow it to cool before moving on to the next step.

4 Meanwhile, preheat the oven to 400°F.

4 whole fish (about 1 pound/ 454 grams each) with wide bellies for stuffing, such as red snapper, gutted, cleaned, and scaled

Distilled white vinegar

Kosher salt

4 teaspoons ground turmeric

3 large yellow onions, 1 small diced, 2 sliced on the diagonal

3 tablespoons light olive oil, plus more as needed

6 to 8 garlic cloves, thinly sliced

2 teaspoons dried fenugreek

2 tablespoons dried mint

1 teaspoon hogweed powder (see Resources, page 317; optional)

6 ounces (170 grams) fresh flat-leaf parsley, leaves and tender stems, washed and dried, chopped in a food processor

6 ounces (170 grams) fresh cilantro, leaves and tender stems, washed and dried, chopped in a food processor

5 Remove the fish from the refrigerator and fill each fish with the stuffing. I like to sew the cavity of the fish closed with needle and thread, but securing it shut with toothpicks works, too. Arrange the onion slices on a large baking sheet (so that the fish doesn't stick to the bottom) and place the stuffed fish on top. Use a knife to score 3 diagonal slices on the exterior of each fish, rub each one with olive oil, season generously with more salt, and roast, uncovered, until the skin is crisp and the flesh is cooked through, about 15 to 20 minutes, depending on the size of the fish.

Alternatively For a southern variation of *mahi shekam por,* substitute the pomegranate molasses with ⅓ cup (80 ml) Tamarind Paste (page 181), homemade or store-bought, and add dried lime powder and ½ teaspoon red chili flakes. Omit the nuts.

1⅓ cups (142 grams) finely chopped walnuts

⅓ cup (80 ml) pomegranate molasses or bitter orange molasses

⅓ cup (80 ml) fresh or bottled lemon juice if needed

⅓ cup (37 grams) dried barberries (optional)

A'ASH

When I describe *a'ash* to someone, I instantly make a circle with my arms stretched out in front of me and my hands linked together. I am conjuring a massive, imaginary pot from which you can feed a ton of people. It's a gesture to show the communal nature of *a'ash*. *A'ash*, as a category of food, I explain, lands somewhere between soup and stew. Its hearty and thick base, made from a combination of legumes, beans, cracked wheat or rice, and freshly chopped herbs, makes it something unique to our cuisine. I also add that some *a'ash* recipes include meat. Yet most don't, making the dish vegetarian or, in some cases, even vegan. My audience is gleeful. But they can tell that I need to expound on a more critical element of *a'ash*, its three traditional garnishes—Crispy Fried Onions (page 194), Crispy Garlic Chips (page 195), and Mint Oil (page 196). My massive pot shrinks in size and my arms drop to my lap to become a wide bowl. And I am transported, by memory, to another time, holding on to this pot-turned-bowl for dear life.

A'ASH IS ONE OF THE FIRST DOCUMENTED FOODS THAT WE KNOW OF, WITH PREPARATIONS DATING BACK TO THE SIXTEENTH CENTURY.

I am in my parents' car, young again in Isfahan. I am assuming the hunched-over position of a girl who has been tasked with the acrobatic responsibility of holding my mother, Giti Joon's, *a'ash* "just so" to protect the garnishes that she has carefully laid out in rows on top. We are en route to a Friday-afternoon lunch at my distant cousin's home. The garnishes' aromas fill our car—sweet fried onions, crunchy garlic chips, and heady mint oil. Each one lends an irresistible texture and variance in temperature to the thick, soft *a'ash* beneath them. In addition to the traditional trio, my mom's *a'ash* was also often topped with the umami taste of *kashk* (page 43) or sometimes thick, creamy yogurt, adding another level of glory. "Can't we just garnish the *a'ash* when we get there?" I would beg her before setting off. And sharply, Giti Joon would flash *(No!)*. And why not? Because you never impose on someone else's kitchen in Iran; you are expected to behave as a guest and allow your host to anticipate your every need.

In late December 2003, a devastating earthquake left more than twenty-five thousand people dead and many more injured and homeless in Bam, in the southeastern Kerman province. The city holds a special place in the hearts of Iranians; its dates are treasured throughout the country, and it is the home of the world's oldest mud brick citadel, the Bam Citadel (Arg-e Bam). The citadel and its surrounding sprawl of medieval buildings, all made of adobe brick, were nearly leveled. In the midst of the chaos, the United Nations coordinated aid and medical supplies, search and rescue teams, and dozens of nongovernmental agencies that stepped in to help.

YOU NEVER IMPOSE ON SOMEONE ELSE'S KITCHEN IN IRAN; YOU ARE EXPECTED TO BEHAVE AS A GUEST AND ALLOW YOUR HOST TO ANTICIPATE YOUR EVERY NEED.

When we heard the news, I and others in the Iranian community in New York mobilized to collect funds for relief. And when it was deemed safe, I flew to Kerman to join a social worker from our *ashianeh* ("home" or "nest" in Farsi). The Ashianeh is a foundation that Akis and I had set up more than twenty years ago in Iran, to support single mothers and their children living in Tehran. We asked one of the social workers working with Ashianeh to focus her efforts on assisting in Bam, and she arrived on the scene and was set up in a makeshift, corrugated metal office. She had brought with her several sewing machines and fabric, and she helped the women in the community organize so that they could sew clothing and headscarves for themselves and their neighbors.

Once I arrived to see what more I could do, I realized that the food situation was terrible. Weeks after the earthquake, bodies were still being recovered, and the women and their families—who were still being sheltered in tents set up among the rubble—were reduced to begging for a bag of rice here or a potato there. One day shortly after arriving, we borrowed a huge pot from a mosque and gathered legumes, lentils, mung beans, and split peas—whatever we could get our hands on. We set the pot over a fire next to the United Nations rescue setup and the women began making their version of *a'ash-e reshteh* (see page 208).

Hours later, when the *a'ash* was ready, the women, who were so proud, invited the UN workers to eat, before feeding their own families. It was a tender, beautiful gesture that turned awkward because no one stepped forward. I remember two women standing next to their pot, eagerly waiting. The initial hesitation from the workers was fear for a food and culture that they didn't understand. Eventually, though, they sat and ate with us. And in the weeks that followed, the women came together and used their weekly food allowance to make an *a'ash* for anyone who presented an empty bowl to fill.

A'ash is one of the first documented foods that we know of, with preparations dating back to the sixteenth-century Safavid dynasty. *A'ash* is such a prominent part of Persian cuisine that it's the root of the word for "cooking" (*a'ashpazi*). *A'ashpaz* means "the cook," and the kitchen is the *ashpazkhane* or "cook's place." Ironically, there is no word for the home cook. We reserve the word *a'ashpaz* for those who cook professionally, as we use the title *chef* in English. It is a given that good cooking at home in Iran is just part of being a human, so why does it need a separate name?

Every city in Iran has one or two of its specialty *a'ash*. Still, Isfahanis, like me, celebrate many more, including *a'ash-e reshteh* (see Sofreh Herb and Noodle *A'ash*, page 208) and *a'ash-e anar* (see Pomegranate *A'ash* with Meatballs, page 201) and *a'ash-e somagh*—this tangy *a'ash* uses the dried and powdered red sumac flower berries in its base. A little joke among Iranians about people from Isfahan is that we are tightfisted. Historically, so much commerce, money, and wealth have passed through my ancient city that Isfahanis understand their goods' value! Perhaps the Isfahani love of *a'ash* is an extension of our resourceful nature.

The Garnishes: Crispy Fried Onions (*Piyaz Dagh*), Crispy Garlic Chips (*Sir Dagh*), Mint Oil (*Na'na Dagh*)

Making *a'ash* without some combination of garnishes is virtually unheard of. The fragrances and textures of garnishes hit all the sensory notes that make *a'ash* such a great comfort food. The recipes for crispy fried onions, crispy garlic chips, and mint oil that follow (see pages 194–196) are not complicated to make, but they are imbued with such emotional attachment and cultural nostalgia that my love for them lies in the careful details of their preparation. These garnishes pop up in several other dishes throughout this book. You can also use them to elevate any number of your favorite soups, mashed potatoes, and vegetables, such as bringing a simple roasted cauliflower to new heights. Batch cook and make a whole bunch of garnishes on the same day, because each will hold for a week or more. If you do not prepare your garnishes in advance, don't worry. To help you with time management, I have indicated a good time to make them throughout each recipe.

A'ashpaz Tips for A'ash

In Iran, *a'ash*'s identity rests on its being a one-pot dish, and traditionally, the ingredients cook together. But you'll notice in the recipes in this chapter that I cook my beans separately and then add them to the pot because I like to control their texture. Furthermore, the little step to discard the bean water after soaking is essential. (You may want a red kidney bean flavor in your famous chili, but for my *a'ash,* I like the flavor of the herbs to shine through.)

The cook times provided here are a guideline. While the beans call for presoaking to reduce your cook time, always consider your altitude when cooking. Iran is located at a high altitude, so my lentils take much longer to cook there. But when I cook my beans at sea level in New York, 1½ to 2 hours is enough. Perhaps *you* are in the high-altitude state of Colorado, for instance? If you toss chickpeas into a pot of water and wait for it to come to a boil, good luck. You'd start cursing me. So, bring your water to a boil first before cooking lentils, legumes, or beans. Also, I salt my lentils and split peas just before they are finished cooking (for larger beans, I add salt 10 to 15 minutes before they are entirely done). To salt earlier will toughen their texture.

Also, feel free to reinterpret these recipes. Use brown rice or quinoa, as well as pearled wheat, barley, or cracked wheat where you like. The cooking time will vary a bit, of course. Personally, for pillars of tradition like *a'ash-e jo* (see Barley *A'ash* with Lamb, page 206) or *a'ash-e reshteh* (see Sofreh Herb and Noodle *A'ash,* page 208), I stick to what's called for in the recipe. But I advocate making small changes as a great way to experiment, as well as an easy way to include more whole grains in your diet. And, as is the case in Persian stews and layered rice dishes, meat is used as a flavor enhancer. Most people in Iran can't afford eight ounces of protein per person like we see in restaurants and homes in the United States. So, think of the meat as optional. Or reduce the portion size if you want.

I know you may wake up one morning and want to make *a'ash* in one pot without going through the process of presoaking and cooking your beans separately, as directed in my recipes. Feel free to do so. Just add your beans to the pot, beginning with the larger beans, giving them a head start on their cooking time, followed by the smaller beans. Then, when the beans are almost cooked, add the herbs called for in each recipe and continue from there. While my tips ensure better texture and flavor, I want *a'ash* to be approachable for you, especially if you are pressed for time. Because *a'ash* is traditionally cooked to feed a crowd, if the yield in an *a'ash* recipe is too large, feel free to cut it in half to make a smaller portion.

And finally, allowing the *a'ash* to cool for 2 to 3 hours before serving enables the flavors to meld. And *a'ash* always tastes even better the next day. Just warm it through before serving.

CRISPY FRIED ONIONS

PIYAZ DAGH | *makes 1 cup*

The texture of the onion garnish used in *a'ash* varies in each household.
Many people in my family say onion garnishes need to be thinly sliced for
elegance, others say they must be diamond shaped, and still others call
for them to be square. And in families other than mine, cooks are proud to
showcase onions caramelized until they are sticky and gooey. I will eat them
all. But my preferred method—and the one that I am providing—is to make
a mountain of very crispy onions to pile on top. It is a double-step method—
first boiling the slices, then frying them—that ensures their crispiness. As far
as the cooking time goes, it will ultimately be determined by the thickness of
your onion slices, as well as the color that you want to achieve. Use common
sense and adjust the time according to your preference. After frying, reserve
the fragrant oil to drizzle over your *a'ash*.

2 medium yellow onions,
thinly sliced on a mandoline

Light olive oil

1 Before beginning, set out a couple of paper towel–lined large plates: one
to absorb the moisture after you boil the onions, and one to absorb the oil
and aerate the onions after frying.

2 Bring a medium saucepan of water to a boil, and using a large spoon, place
the onion slices in the water, using the spoon to make sure you completely
submerge them. Boil for 3 minutes. Use a slotted spoon to transfer them
to one of the plates, spreading them out in a single layer to extract any
remaining water. You don't want them to splash you when they hit the oil.

3 Pour enough olive oil into a medium saucepan so that it is one-third full,
and heat it over medium-low heat until it reaches between 350° and 375°F.
Or, if you don't have a thermometer, drop a slice of onion into the oil—if it
crisps up right away, the oil is ready.

4 Working in small batches, fry the onions, turning them gently while they
shrivel, the oil bubbles, and the onions begin to turn golden, about
5 minutes. Transfer to the other paper towel–lined plate. Continue frying
the remaining onions in batches.

Note Use immediately or allow to aerate before storing in an airtight
container for up to 1 week.

CRISPY GARLIC CHIPS

SIR DAGH | *makes 1 cup*

I like to cook my garlic chips to a uniform dark brown, while some people like to remove their garlic when the color is tawny and the edges are browned. Since my preference allows them to get really dark, mix them continuously while frying so that they cook evenly and don't burn. After frying, reserve the fragrant oil to drizzle over your *a'ash*.

2 garlic heads, cloves peeled and thinly sliced on a mandoline

Light olive oil

1 Before beginning, set out a couple of paper towel–lined large plates: one to absorb the moisture after you boil the garlic, and one to absorb the oil and aerate the garlic after frying.

2 Bring a medium saucepan of water to a boil, and using a large spoon, place the garlic slices in the water, using the spoon to make sure you completely submerge them. Boil for 3 minutes. Use a slotted spoon to transfer them to one of the plates, spreading them out in a single layer to extract any remaining water. You don't want them to splash you when they hit the oil.

3 Pour enough olive oil into a medium saucepan so that it is one-third full, and heat it over medium-low heat until it reaches between 350° and 375°F. Or, if you don't have a thermometer, drop a slice of garlic into the oil—if it crisps up right away, the oil is ready.

4 Fry the garlic, continuously stirring, until dark and crispy, about 5 minutes, or less if you prefer. Transfer to the other paper towel–lined plate to drain.

Note Use immediately or allow to aerate before storing in an airtight container for up to 1 week.

MINT OIL

NA'NA DAGH | *makes ½ cup*

When I use mint oil as a garnish for *a'ash,* as well as *Borani Bademjoon* (page 39), I prefer it to be thick. However, for garnishing roasted vegetables or Watermelon Feta Salad (page 278), I add more oil to dilute the texture before drizzling. Feel free to do the same. While this is so easy to make, one thing to note is that your oil does not need to be very hot. If the mint sinks to the bottom when you add it to the pan, the oil is ready.

Add the olive oil to a medium sauté pan and warm over medium heat until just hot. Add the dried mint, stir once, and turn off the heat. Allow the oil to sit for 15 to 20 minutes to darken in color and deepen in flavor and aroma before using.

Note You can store mint oil in an airtight container for up to 2 weeks in the refrigerator.

½ cup (120 ml) extra-virgin olive oil

5 tablespoons dried mint

GITI JOON'S TOMATO, BEANS, and HERB A'ASH

A'ASH-E GOJE FARANGI | *makes 6 to 8 servings*

My mother often met us in Greece for summer vacation when our twins, Soshy and Noony, were small. One summer, the skin-burstingly ripe tomatoes captured her imagination and insisted she make an *a'ash-e goje* (by the way, this was a dish I had *never* seen her make before). It was fantastic!

From then on, each time my mom visited us in New York, this tomato *a'ash* was in her repertoire. Once, we carted home a ton of vibrant heirloom tomatoes from the farmers' market at Union Square. Akis looked at us in disbelief, saying, "These tomatoes are the price of steak!" My quick-witted mom joked *(You married an Isfahani!)*. Seek out the best-quality summer tomatoes, garnish with plenty of aromatic Mint Oil (page 196), and enjoy with lavash or homemade *Naan-e Taftoon* (page 6).

Note You will need to soak the beans for a minimum of 4 hours and up to overnight before making this recipe. If you don't have fresh tomatoes, you may substitute 5 pounds (2.3 kilograms) good-quality canned diced tomatoes.

1 Put the beans in a bowl and cover with cold water by 2 inches. Soak for a minimum of 4 hours and up to overnight.

2 Halve the tomatoes. Working in batches, place them in a food processer and puree. Set aside until ready to use.

3 Drain the soaked beans, place them in a medium pot, and add water to cover by a few inches. Bring to a boil, then lower the heat and cook, uncovered, until they begin to soften but are not cooked all the way through, about 40 minutes. Season with 1 teaspoon of the salt 10 to 15 minutes before they are done. Drain and set aside.

4 Meanwhile, add the onions and 4 tablespoons olive oil to a large, heavy-bottomed pot with a tight-fitting lid and sauté over medium heat, adding more oil as needed, so that the onions turn golden and they soften, about 5 minutes. Make a well in the center of the pot, add the garlic and a bit more oil (so that the garlic doesn't burn), and sauté until fragrant, about 3 minutes more. Add the turmeric, a bit more oil, and stir, allowing the turmeric to bloom and release its fragrance, about 1 minute more. $\rightarrow$

½ cup (92 grams) dried pinto or cranberry beans

5 pounds (2.3 kilograms) ripe tomatoes, cleaned and stemmed (see headnote)

1 teaspoon plus 2 tablespoons kosher salt

1 large yellow onion, finely chopped

Light olive oil

8 to 10 garlic cloves, finely chopped

2 teaspoons ground turmeric

½ cup (45 grams) cracked bulgur wheat

½ cup (83 grams) barley

5 cups (1¼ liters) chicken stock, homemade or store-bought $\rightarrow$

5 Add the cracked wheat and barley to the onion mixture and stir to incorporate, then add the chicken stock, tomato puree, the remaining 2 tablespoons salt, and the pepper. Cover with the lid, bring to a boil, then lower the heat to medium-low and simmer until the barley softens a bit, about 30 minutes.

6 Add the celery, return the lid, and continue simmering until the celery is tender but still has a bite, 20 minutes more. Meanwhile, make the mint oil.

7 Add the dried tarragon, basil, and mint, and continue cooking, covered, until the celery is soft, about 10 minutes more.

8 In a medium saucepan, heat 2 cups (470 ml) water, then add it to the pot along with the reserved beans. Taste and adjust the seasoning.

9 Cool the *a'ash* for 3 hours. Garnish with the mint oil before serving.

3 teaspoons freshly ground black pepper

5 celery stalks, cut into ½-inch pieces

Mint Oil (page 196) for garnish

6 tablespoons dried tarragon

3 tablespoons dried basil

3 tablespoons dried mint

POMEGRANATE A'ASH
with MEATBALLS

A'ASH-E ANAR | *makes 4 to 6 servings*

In preparation for Yalda Night, a celebration that marks the longest night of the year, pomegranates, along with summer watermelon, are wrapped in a cotton cloth and stored in a cool, dark basement to preserve them. Families gather in their elders' homes to snack, eat, and keep each other company well into the night. The preserved fruits are sliced open to symbolize the crimson color of sunrise and served along with plenty of dried fruits and nuts.

When I was growing up, my favorite place to be on Yalda Night was tucked under the *korsi* at my paternal grandmother, Khanoom's, home. A *korsi* is a long, low table with a heater underneath and thick blankets draped across and over the table to trap the heat. At my grandparents' home, their *korsi* was fueled by coal (we'd roast potatoes in the fire, then pull them out and hit them with butter and salt—heavenly). My brothers and cousins and I ate there and slept there, only to wake up to eat our breakfast there. During Yalda Night, all of our family gathered around the *korsi* and my grandmother passed around a tray of dried apricots, peaches, nectarines, raisins, and nuts, doting on us all, tucking us kids underneath, and offering tea. At some point, a large pot of *a'ash* would come to the table, and here the memory becomes a freeze-frame: hands, so many hands, little cousins, aunts and uncles, my parents, all reaching for their share. The combination of rich, tart *a'ash,* along with mint oil and the burst of fresh pomegranate seeds, served alongside tiny meatballs, is an indelible heartwarming memory for cold days.

When you blanket the entire surface of this *a'ash-e anar* with the crimson color of pomegranate seeds as I do, the presentation looks like a field of rubies gracing the surface of your dish. Allow *a'ash-e anar* to rest, serving it warm instead of hot.

Note Fresh pomegranates are easy to seed. Cut off the flower end. Next, using your knife, score along the ribs that run toward the bottom of the fruit, cutting into the white pith. Gently pull the pomegranate apart from the top and it will open up like a flower.

1 Bring 12 cups (3 liters) water to a boil in a medium pot. Turn off the heat and set aside.

2 Add the onions and 4 tablespoons olive oil to a large, heavy-bottomed pot with a tight-fitting lid and sauté over medium heat, adding more oil as needed, so that the onions turn golden, their edges darken, and they soften, about 5 to 7 minutes. Add 2 teaspoons of the turmeric, a bit more olive oil, $\rightarrow$

For the *a'ash*

1 large yellow onion, medium diced

Light olive oil

2½ teaspoons ground turmeric $\rightarrow$

and stir, allowing the turmeric to bloom and release its fragrance, about 1 minute more. Then add the parsley, cilantro, scallions or chives, and dried herb mix and quickly sauté until well incorporated.

3 Add the reserved hot water to the pot. Add 3 tablespoons of the salt and the pepper, stir, and cover with a lid. Raise the heat to high, bringing the mixture to a boil, then lower the heat to allow the mixture to gently boil for about 20 minutes.

4 Add 2 cups (470 ml) water to the now-empty pot you used to boil the water and bring to a boil. Add the split peas and the remaining ½ teaspoon turmeric, and bring to a boil, about 5 minutes. Lower the heat and simmer until the split peas are cooked but still firm, about 20 minutes more. Add the remaining ½ teaspoon salt in the last few minutes of cooking. Drain the split peas and set them aside.

5 Meanwhile, make the meatballs: Combine the ground beef, onions, turmeric, salt, and pepper in a medium bowl. Using your clean hands, mix to combine, being careful not to overwork the mixture. Shape the meat into small balls about the size of a kumquat and add them to the large pot.

6 Dilute the pomegranate molasses with 1 cup (235 ml) water and add it to the pot, along with the rice, lemon juice, and sugar. Return the lid and continue cooking until the rice is done, about 25 minutes more.

7 Add the drained split peas to the pot. Taste the *a'ash*—it should have sweet and sour notes. Adjust the flavor to your preference. Continue cooking for a few minutes more to allow the flavors to meld. Turn off the heat and allow to cool for 2 to 3 hours before serving. Meanwhile, make the mint oil.

8 Transfer the cooled *a'ash* to a large vessel, garnish with the mint oil, and cover the top with the pomegranate seeds before serving.

4 ounces (112 grams) fresh flat-leaf parsley, leaves and tender stems, finely chopped

10 ounces (283 grams) fresh cilantro, leaves and tender stems, finely chopped

6 ounces (160 grams) scallions, both white and green parts, or fresh chives, finely chopped

½ cup *sabzi a'ash* dried herb mix (see Resources, page 317)

3 tablespoons plus ½ teaspoon kosher salt, plus more to taste

1 tablespoon freshly ground black pepper

½ cup (112 grams) yellow split peas

1 cup (235 ml) pomegranate molasses

¾ cup (138 grams) jasmine rice, rinsed twice

½ cup (120 ml) bottled lemon juice

⅓ cup (66 grams) granulated sugar

Mint Oil (page 196) for garnish

2 large whole pomegranates, seeded, for garnish (about 2 cups/350 grams)

For the meatballs

1 pound (454 grams) ground beef

1 small yellow onion, grated

1 teaspoon ground turmeric

1 teaspoon kosher salt

1 teaspoon freshly ground black pepper

Pomegranate Molasses *(Rob-e Anar)*

Anar (pomegranate) is Iran's national fruit, and its glorious color and arils (seeds) are rich with the symbolism of life and rebirth. The thick molasses made from their juices is the base of several dishes, including *a'ash-e anar* and *khoresht-e fesenjan* (see page 285). Its flavor profile depends on the regional pomegranate varieties, ranging from very sour to sweet. Every cook should have a couple bottles of varying consistencies and colors to play with in the kitchen. I love to try all of them! It's incredibly versatile: make salad dressing with it, or drizzle it over smashed potatoes or crispy fried eggs. Even add it to cocktails.

MY CHICKEN SOUP

A'ASH MAAST | *makes 6 to 8 servings*

In Iran, *a'ash maast* traditionally includes meatballs, but I took the liberty of switching in chicken—a sort of homage to American chicken noodle soup.

Note If the texture of the *a'ash* is too thick, you can add a bit of hot water before serving to loosen it up.

1 Add the onions and 4 tablespoons olive oil to a large, heavy-bottomed pot with a tight-fitting lid and sauté over medium heat, adding more oil if needed, so that the onions turn golden, their edges darken, and they soften, about 5 to 7 minutes. Add 1 teaspoon of the turmeric, a bit more oil, and stir, allowing the turmeric to bloom and release its fragrance, about 1 minute more.

2 Pat the chicken dry and add it to the pot with the onion mixture. Season the chicken with 1 tablespoon of the salt, the pepper, and the remaining 1 tablespoon turmeric. Cover with the lid, lower the heat to low, and cook, allowing the meat to release its juices, about 10 minutes. Remove the lid, give the mixture a stir, and then raise the heat to medium-high and continue cooking, until the meat is glossy and any remaining liquid in the pot evaporates, about 6 minutes. Add 1 cup (235 ml) water and the chicken stock, return the lid, then lower the heat to low and cook until very tender, about 35 minutes.

3 Meanwhile, place the split peas in a small pot and cover with 2 cups (470 ml) water. Bring to a boil over medium-high heat, then lower the heat and simmer, uncovered, for 15 minutes. Add the remaining ½ teaspoon salt in the last few minutes of cooking. Drain and set aside.

4 Remove the chicken from the pot, reserving the liquid, and using your hands, pull the meat off the bone in large chunks. Return the pulled chicken to the pot and add the rice, parsley, cilantro, dill, scallions or chives, and 4 cups (1 liter) water. Stir, cover with the lid, and bring to a boil for 5 minutes. Taste and adjust the seasoning, adding more salt and pepper if necessary. Then lower the heat and cook, stirring occasionally, until the rice fully cooks and is very soft, about 20 minutes. Add the cooked split peas during the last 5 minutes of cooking.

5 Place the yogurt in a medium bowl, add a few tablespoons of the *a'ash,* and whip to thoroughly combine and temper the yogurt so it doesn't curdle. Slowly add the yogurt-*a'ash* mixture to the pot, stirring so that it is well incorporated. Set the *a'ash* aside to cool for 2 to 3 hours (I like to serve it lukewarm). Meanwhile, make the crispy fried onions and garlic chips.

6 Before serving, squeeze fresh lemon wedges over the *a'ash* and garnish with the crispy onions and garlic.

1 large yellow onion, medium diced

Light olive oil

1 teaspoon plus 1 tablespoon ground turmeric

1 pound (454 grams) skinless, bone-in chicken breasts

1 tablespoon plus ½ teaspoon kosher salt, plus more to taste

1 teaspoon freshly ground black pepper, plus more to taste

1 cup (235 ml) chicken stock, homemade or store-bought

½ cup (112 grams) yellow split peas

1 cup (185 grams) jasmine rice, rinsed twice

2 cups (about 4 ounces/112 grams) finely chopped fresh flat-leaf parsley, leaves and tender stems

2 cups (about 4 ounces/112 grams) finely chopped fresh cilantro, leaves and tender stems

1 cup (about 2 ounces/56 grams) finely chopped fresh dill, leaves and tender stems

1 cup (about 2 ounces/56 grams) finely chopped scallions, both white and green parts, or fresh chives

3 cups (855 grams) Homemade Yogurt (page 32) or store-bought Greek yogurt

Crispy Fried Onions (page 194)

Crispy Garlic Chips (page 195)

2 to 3 fresh lemons, cut into wedges (optional)

"EVERYTHING but the KITCHEN SINK" A'ASH

ISFAHANI SHOLE GHALAMKAR | *makes 6 to 8 servings*

If you ever hear an Iranian utter *"A'ash-e shole ghalamkar,"* that means that they have dug themselves into a messy situation yet can't help but pile on more mess. This *a'ash*'s ingredient list is so long and admittedly so cumbersome that its very name has become synonymous with getting yourself into trouble.

No one undertakes making *a'ash-e shole ghalamkar* lightly. If someone shows up at your home offering this dish, it's a gesture of love, considering how much time they took to make it for you. And so, I offer it to you, the intrepid home cook. This recipe is an Isfahani version. (I never looked beyond making my own city's version because every other city I turn to has ingredient lists even longer than this one!) During the holy month of Ramadan, when observant Muslims fast from sunrise until after dusk, there is a restaurant in Isfahan whose only two menu items are *haleem* (see page 23) to eat in the predawn hours and *a'ash-e shole ghalamkar* to eat after sunset.

Traditionally, a meat masher called a *ghusht kub* is used to shred the meat, but finely shredding it with two forks will also yield a good result. If you prefer a crispier texture to your onion garnish, spread the sautéed onions on a baking sheet and place in the oven at 350°F for a few minutes to crisp, or if you like, you can continue sautéing the remaining one-third of the onions for a few minutes more to allow them to get very crispy.

Note You will need to soak the beans for a minimum of 4 hours and up to overnight before making this recipe.

1 Put the chickpeas and kidney beans in a large bowl and cover with water by 2 inches. Soak for a minimum of 4 hours and up to overnight.

2 Add the diced onions and 4 tablespoons olive oil to a large, heavy-bottomed pot with a tight-fitting lid and sauté over medium heat, adding more oil as needed, so that the onions turn golden, their edges darken, and they soften, about 5 to 7 minutes. Add 1 teaspoon of the turmeric, a bit more oil, and stir, allowing the turmeric to bloom and release its fragrance, about 1 minute more.

3 Pat the lamb dry and add it to the onion mixture. Season with 2 tablespoons of the turmeric, the salt, and pepper. Cover with the lid, lower the heat to low, and cook, allowing the meat to release its juices, about 5 minutes. Remove the lid, give the mixture a stir, then raise the heat to medium-high and continue cooking, uncovered, until the meat is glossy and any remaining liquid in the pot evaporates, about 6 minutes more.

⅔ cup (126 grams) dried chickpeas

⅔ cup (126 grams) dried white kidney beans

1 yellow onion, medium diced, plus 2 large yellow onions, thinly sliced on a mandoline

Light olive oil

2 tablespoons plus 2 teaspoons ground turmeric

1 pound (454 grams) lamb or beef neck

3 tablespoons kosher salt, plus more to taste

3 tablespoons freshly ground black pepper, plus more to taste

4 Add 2 cups (470 ml) water to the meat pot and bring to a boil for a few minutes, then lower the heat to low and cook until the meat is very tender, about 2 hours. Once the meat is cooked, remove it from the pot, reserving the juices, and using two forks, shred the meat (discard any bones) and set aside in a large bowl.

5 Fill a large pot with 14 cups (3½ liters) water and bring to a boil. Add the chives, cilantro, and parsley to the pot. Drain the soaked chickpeas and kidney beans and add them to the pot as well. Taste and adjust the seasoning, and cook, uncovered, for about 1 hour. Add the mung beans and cook for 20 minutes more. Next, add the lentils and rice and cook for 20 minutes more.

6 Meanwhile, add the sliced onions and 5 tablespoons olive oil to a large sauté pan and sauté over high heat until the onions soften and their edges darken, about 10 minutes. Add the remaining 1 teaspoon turmeric, a bit more oil, and stir, allowing the turmeric to bloom and release its fragrance, about 1 minute more. Remove from the heat and set aside.

7 Examine the beans to make sure that they are all cooked, and if they require additional cooking, allow for that before proceeding to the next step.

8 Remove 2 cups of the herbs and beans and set aside. Add the shredded meat, along with the reserved juices, to the pot, and using a *ghusht kub* or the bottom of a clean, empty wine bottle, mash them together until the meat is fully incorporated. Return the reserved beans to the pot and continue mixing. Add three-quarters of the reserved sautéed onions to the pot, setting aside the rest for garnish (see headnote). If the *a'ash* is too thick, add a bit of hot water to loosen it. Taste and adjust the seasoning.

9 Allow the *a'ash* to rest for 2 to 3 hours before serving. While the *a'ash* is resting, make the saffron water, garlic chips, and mint oil and set aside until ready to use.

10. Before serving, top with plenty of garnishes. Serve with fresh lime segments.

5 cups (about 9 ounces/253 grams) finely chopped fresh Chinese chives or garlic chives

2 cups (about 4 ounces/112 grams) finely chopped fresh cilantro, leaves and tender stems

2 cups (about 4 ounces/112 grams) finely chopped fresh flat-leaf parsley, leaves and tender stems

½ cup (100 grams) mung beans

½ cup (100 grams) lentils, rinsed and drained

½ cup (92 grams) jasmine rice, rinsed twice

Saffron Water (page xxxiv)

Crispy Garlic Chips (page 195)

Mint Oil (page 196)

6 to 8 fresh limes, cut into segments, for serving

BARLEY A'ASH with LAMB

A'ASH-E JO | *makes 6 to 8 servings*

While most *a'ash* are reserved for food offerings or for large family gatherings, this comforting, creamy barley *a'ash* makes for a great weeknight dinner. Small cubes of beef or lamb are called for in this dish, but I also like to make *a'ash-e jo* with oxtail. I love the fermented, umami taste of *kashk*, so add as much as you like. Also, for this *a'ash*, you have the option to serve the tender meat on the side, making the *a'ash* vegetarian.

Note You will need to soak the beans and chickpeas a minimum of 4 hours and up to overnight before making this recipe.

1 Put the cranberry beans and chickpeas in a large bowl and cover with cold water by 2 inches. Soak for a minimum of 4 hours and up to overnight.

2 Add the diced onions and 4 tablespoons olive oil to a large, heavy-bottomed pot with a tight-fitting lid and sauté over medium heat, adding more oil if needed, so that the onions turn golden, their edges darken, and they soften, about 5 to 7 minutes. Add 1 tablespoon of the turmeric, a bit more oil, and stir, allowing the turmeric to bloom and release its fragrance, about 1 minute more.

3 Pat the meat cubes dry and add them to the pot with the onion mixture. Season the meat with 1 tablespoon of the salt and the pepper. Cover with the lid, lower the heat to low, and cook, allowing the meat to release its juices, about 10 minutes. Remove the lid, give the mixture a stir, then raise the heat to medium-high and continue cooking, uncovered, until the meat is glossy and any remaining liquid in the pot evaporates, about 6 minutes. Add 1½ cups (360 ml) water, return the lid, then lower the heat to low and cook until the meat is fork-tender, about 1½ hours.

4 Meanwhile, cook the cranberry beans and chickpeas: Add the cranberry beans, chickpeas, and 4 cups (1 liter) water to a large pot. Cover and bring to a boil for 5 minutes, then lower the heat to medium-low and continue cooking, until tender, about 45 minutes to 1 hour. Add the remaining 1 tablespoon salt in the last few minutes of cooking. Remove the beans and chickpeas from the heat and set aside.

5 Meanwhile, add the sliced onions and 5 tablespoons olive oil to a large sauté pan and sauté over high heat until the onions soften and their edges darken, about 10 minutes. Add the remaining 1 teaspoon turmeric, a bit more oil, and stir, allowing the turmeric to bloom and release its fragrance, about 1 minute more. Remove from the heat and set aside.

½ cup (92 grams) dried cranberry beans

½ cup (100 grams) dried chickpeas

1 medium yellow onion, medium diced, plus 1 medium yellow onion, thinly sliced on a mandoline

Light olive oil

1 tablespoon plus 1 teaspoon ground turmeric

1 pound (454 grams) boneless lamb shoulder or beef chuck, cut into 1-inch pieces

2 tablespoons kosher salt, plus more to taste

1 tablespoon freshly ground black pepper, plus more to taste

½ cup (100 grams) barley

10 ounces (283 grams) fresh spinach, leaves and tender stems, finely chopped

10 ounces (283 grams) fresh flat-leaf parsley, leaves and tender stems, finely chopped

10 ounces (283 grams) fresh cilantro, leaves and tender stems, finely chopped

10 ounces (283 grams) fresh chives or scallions, both white and green parts, finely chopped

½ cup *sabzi a'ash* dried herb mix (see Resources, page 317)

6 To a large, heavy-bottomed pot with a tight-fitting lid set over medium-high heat, transfer two-thirds of the sautéed sliced onions (reserve the remaining third for garnish), the barley, spinach, parsley, cilantro, chives, dried herb mix, and 10 cups (2.3 liters) water. Cover with the lid and bring to a boil for 10 minutes. Taste and adjust for salt, adding 1 more tablespoon if necessary.

7 Return the lid, lower the heat, and simmer until the barley softens, about 20 minutes. Add the lentils, return the lid, and continue cooking until the lentils are tender, about 20 minutes more.

8 Drain the reserved cooked cranberry beans and chickpeas and stir them into the pot. Whip the *kashk* in a medium bowl (otherwise it will split when added to the hot *a'ash*) before stirring it into the pot as well. The *a'ash* will be thick and creamy. Allow to cool for 2 to 3 hours before serving. In the meantime, prepare the mint oil and garlic chips.

9 To serve, offer the meat on the side, or divide it among each portion. Garnish with the mint oil, garlic chips, more *kashk,* if you like, and the reserved sautéed onions.

½ cup (100 grams) lentils, rinsed and drained

1½ cups (360 ml) *kashk*, store-bought, plus more for garnish

Mint Oil (page 196) for garnish

Crispy Garlic Chips (page 195) for garnish

SOFREH HERB and NOODLE A'ASH

A'ASH-E RESHTEH | *makes 6 to 8 servings*

Of all the *a'ash* in Iran, the one that provokes the most nostalgia is *a'ash-e reshteh*, and for that reason, it's the only one I offer at Sofreh. Iranians enjoy eating *a'ash-e reshteh* on Chaharshanbe Suri, also known as the Festival of Fire, which falls on the eve of the last Wednesday before the Persian New Year called Nowruz (see Nowruz: Persian New Year, page 236), and also on Sizdah Be-dar, which marks the end of the celebration. It's a perfect *a'ash* for chilly fall and winter days. Still, I offer it year-round. And I'm always kind of surprised to see people order it in sweltering July weather! See the photograph on page 188.

Note I like my *a'ash* tangy, so if my *kashk* isn't sour enough, I will add a touch of lemon juice. That is totally up to you. Also, it is always a great idea to cook this or any other *a'ash* a day ahead or several hours before serving. If reheating this *a'ash* the next day, add 1 cup (235 ml) water to loosen it. You will need to soak the beans for a minimum of 4 hours and up to overnight before making this recipe.

1 Put the chickpeas and kidney beans in a medium bowl and cover with water by 2 inches. Soak for a minimum of 4 hours and up to overnight.

2 Drain the chickpeas and kidney beans and place them in a medium pot with enough water to cover them by 2 inches, and bring to a boil. Reduce the heat to medium-low and cook until they are soft but retain a bite, about 45 minutes. Add 2 teaspoons salt in the last few minutes of cooking. Remove the chickpeas and beans from the heat and set aside in their cooking liquid.

3 Meanwhile, add the onions and ⅓ cup (80 ml) olive oil to a large, heavy-bottomed pot with a tight-fitting lid and sauté over medium heat, adding more oil if needed, so that the onions turn golden, their edges darken, and they soften, about 5 to 7 minutes. Add the flour and stir until fragrant, about 2 minutes, then add the turmeric, a bit more oil, and stir, allowing the turmeric to bloom and release its fragrance, about 1 minute more.

4 Next, add 12 cups (3 liters) water, cover with the lid, and bring to a boil. Add the spinach, parsley, cilantro, scallions or chives, and dried herbs to the pot. Return the lid, lower the heat to medium, and cook for 20 minutes. Add the lentils and continue cooking for 15 minutes more.

½ cup (100 grams) dried chickpeas

½ cup (92 grams) dried red kidney beans

Kosher salt

1 large yellow onion, medium diced

Light olive oil

¼ cup (62 grams) all-purpose flour

2 tablespoons ground turmeric

4 ounces (112 grams) fresh spinach, leaves and tender stems, finely chopped

4 ounces (112 grams) fresh flat-leaf parsley, leaves and tender stems, finely chopped

4 ounces (112 grams) fresh cilantro, leaves and tender stems, finely chopped

4 ounces (112 grams) scallions, both white and green parts, or fresh chives, finely chopped

5 Taste and adjust the seasoning, adding 2 tablespoons salt and the pepper, or more if necessary. Add the noodles, stirring so that they don't stick to each other. Whip the *kashk* in a medium bowl with a bit of *a'ash* to temper it (otherwise it will split when added to the hot *a'ash*) and add that to the pot as well, stirring to incorporate. Continue cooking, uncovered, until the noodles are softened, depending on the type of noodles used, about 15 to 20 minutes.

6 Drain the reserved cooked chickpeas and beans, add them to the pot, and bring to a boil, uncovered, for about 5 minutes more. Allow to rest for 2 to 3 hours before serving. Meanwhile, prepare the fried onions, garlic chips, and mint oil garnishes.

7 Before serving, squeeze fresh lemon wedges over the *a'ash* and garnish with the crispy onions, garlic, and mint oil.

1 cup (90 grams) *sabzi a'ash* dried herb mix (see Resources, page 317)

1 cup (200 grams) lentils, rinsed and drained

2 tablespoons freshly ground black pepper

4 ounces (112 grams) *a'ash* noodles (see Resources, page 317) or ramen noodles, cut into 2-inch pieces

1 cup (235 ml) *kashk,* store-bought, plus more for garnish

Crispy Fried Onions (page 194) for garnish

Crispy Garlic Chips (page 195) for garnish

Mint Oil (page 196) for garnish

2 to 3 fresh lemons, cut into wedges, for serving (optional)

KUKU

It is the fall, 2010. My twins, Noony and Soshy, are in high school, and my husband, Akis, is at work. I'm fifty-one years old, and our Persian restaurant, Sofreh, in Brooklyn exists solely in my dreams. This afternoon, nine stories up in our apartment, I am on a mission; I'm demonstrating my obsessively detailed method for making the Persian Herb Frittata (page 214) known as *kuku sabzi* to a food writer from *The New York Times*. When she first read my recipe, she couldn't believe that the total cooking time was eighty minutes. So, I invited her to see the process for herself.

"*Sabzi* [herbs] give this rich Iranian frittata a gorgeous, forest-green color," I say. We're watching the mixture of eggs, walnuts, tangy barberries, and a mix of parsley, cilantro, scallions, and romaine firm up in the eleven-inch skillet that I have placed over medium heat, just as I had written to her. "Every household in Iran has varying assemblages of vegetables, slight alterations, and special touches to give their *kuku* personality," I tell her. "Some people add flour—I don't, but my mother adds walnuts." And then: "But I think it needs a little sour note, so I add dried barberries *and* walnuts to mine." I can feel my Giti Joon rolling her eyes at me from 6,298.97 miles away in Isfahan.

The writer has been tracking the details of my rustic interpretation all day. She watched me chop the herbs and vegetables by hand for more texture, and as I cooked, we talked. "I always make *kuku sabzi* during Nowruz, the celebration of our Persian New Year, which arrives during the spring equinox," I explain. Both the aroma of my *kuku* and threads of my life story fill the air. "The herbs symbolize the green, fresh start that comes with spring." She's taking in every word. "And now," I tell her, as I uncover my skillet, "I reduce the heat to low and let it cook for thirty minutes." She looks at me with wide-eyed disbelief. "But, I don't just stand here. While it's cooking, I take my dog, Bibi, for a walk." She laughs. "And then I return home, take a sharp knife, and I gently cut my *kuku sabzi* into four wedges and separate them slightly so that any liquid that has released in the skillet can evaporate." I know that she thinks that, by now, it's finally done. But no. "And then, I let the underside cook about ten minutes more, allowing it to get nice and crispy."

Since those days, I have let go of my excessively attentive approach to making such a carefree dish. And if ever there was a time to laugh, it's over my *kuku sabzi*. It's also a time to reflect on how far I have come as a cook.

The essence of *kuku*, which translates loosely as "omelet," is simple: eggs, herbs, and vegetables that you whip together into a flavor-packed snack. Or a whole meal. When potatoes are incorporated into the egg mixture, it's reminiscent of a latke, or potato pancake. And *kuku* sets the scene for a glorious feast when placed alongside bountiful *Sabzi Khordan* (page 88), sharp pickles, creamy yogurt, and bread. The truth is you can pull a *kuku* together in fifteen or twenty minutes. You can make them ahead of time and offer them at room temperature. Or send them right back into the oven for a minutes-long reheating, if you like.

And while *kuku sabzi* may very well be a famous Nowruz egg dish, the basic idea behind Iranian *kuku* is widely recognizable among many cultures. From Middle Eastern *eggah* to North African Tunisian tajine, which incorporate potato and chicken; the Spanish *tortilla española* to the Italian frittata. But what sets *kuku* apart is the addition of nuts, barberries, or raisins. As well as the prodigious use of herbs. And in Isfahan, some people like to enjoy a saffron and rosewater syrup–soaked *kuku ghandi* as a dessert after a rich meal of the fatty, cinnamon-laced minced lamb specialty we call *beryuni* (see page xix).

I can trace the arc of my life in the *kuku* I have cooked. My youth in Iran, when gathering with family and friends for a party or get-together meant an all-day affair (if we didn't have *a'ash* to carry along as a gift for our host, someone from the group would whip up a light vegetable *kuku* for our *asraneh*, or "snack," before dinner). The hustle of motherhood in New York, when my kids would rush into my kitchen in the middle of a playdate, looking hungry and headed for junk food. That was my cue to reach into the refrigerator, pull out some eggs and whatever vegetables I had on hand, and make my nutrition-packed, tasty *kuku* for them and their friends.

Once you master the fundamental concept of making *kuku*, *kuku* hold lots of possibilities, making them one of my favorite foods in the world. Use my recipe for Persian Herb Frittata (page 214) and swap in collard greens or kale in your version for a beautiful use of seasonal greens. Once I discovered that it was nearly impossible to use my painstakingly particular method of making *kuku* for larger-scale catering events, I devised an alternative oven method using a muffin pan. And while Zucchini Pancakes (page 218), called *kuku kedoo,* tops my list of favorite ways to cook with zucchini in the summertime, reach into your well of tradition for a selection of herbs as a counterpart to this delicate summer vegetable that I adore.

Here's to your unique *kuku* cooking personality. However long it takes you to find it.

PERSIAN HERB FRITTATA

KUKU SABZI | *makes 4 servings*

The bright green color of this *sabzi* (herb)-laden Persian egg frittata symbolizes spring, which is why we include it in our Nowruz spreads alongside *sabzi polo* (see page 74) and smoked fish, which symbolize good fortune for the new year. It's a perfect picnic food for the thirteenth day of the Nowruz, called Sizdah Be-dar ("getting rid of thirteen"), which marks the end of the New Year celebration (see Nowruz: Persian New Year, page 236). This recipe is my original method that appeared in *The New York Times* and one I continue to make for home gatherings. It's a time-consuming version that is well worth the love and effort for the compact, crispy wedges it yields. The muffin-pan variation (opposite) not only saves you time, but it's perfect for making individual *kuku* for a picnic or snack. See the photograph on page 210.

1 Soak the barberries in cold water in a small bowl for 20 minutes.

2 Meanwhile, in a large bowl, combine the parsley, cilantro, scallions, and romaine, and set aside. In a separate medium bowl, combine the eggs, salt, and pepper, and whisk just until frothy. Drain the barberries, discarding any small stones.

3 Add ¼ cup (60 ml) plus 2 tablespoons of the olive oil to an 11-inch stainless-steel pan with a tight-fitting lid over medium heat and heat until shimmering. To the bowl with the herbs and chopped greens, add the egg mixture, barberries, and walnuts, and stir well. Pour the mixture into the skillet. Cover and cook until set, about 10 minutes.

4 Uncover, lower the heat to low, and cook for 30 minutes more. Cut into 4 wedges, separating them slightly so the liquid can evaporate. Cook until the underside is browned, about 10 minutes.

5 Use a spatula to gently turn the wedges over. Drizzle the remaining ¼ cup (60 ml) olive oil around the pan's edges and between the wedges. Cook, uncovered, until compact and crisp, about 40 minutes. Serve hot or at room temperature, with yogurt, if desired.

Alternatively Feel free to adjust the texture, if you like, to make it less eggy and more vegetable dense. You can increase the herbs by adding 2 ounces (56 grams) more, or I like to add 4 ounces (112 grams) finely chopped kale or collard greens to this mix. Also, you may substitute cranberries for barberries if necessary.

½ cup (56 grams) dried barberries

4 ounces (112 grams) fresh flat-leaf parsley, leaves and tender stems, finely chopped

4 ounces (112 grams) fresh cilantro, leaves and tender stems, finely chopped

4 ounces (112 grams) scallions, white part only, finely chopped

⅔ cup chopped romaine lettuce

4 large eggs

2 teaspoons kosher salt

2 teaspoons freshly ground black pepper

½ cup (120 ml) plus 2 tablespoons light olive oil

½ cup (150 grams) walnuts, coarsely chopped

Homemade Yogurt (page 32) or store-bought Greek yogurt for serving (optional)

ALTERNATIVE MUFFIN PAN METHOD

makes 12 individual kuku

1 Preheat the oven to 375°F.

2 Spray a 12-cup muffin pan with cooking spray and set aside.

3 Combine the parsley, cilantro, scallions, romaine, and olive oil in a large bowl and mix well. In a separate medium bowl, combine the eggs, salt, and pepper. Whisk just until frothy.

4 To the bowl with the herbs and romaine, add the egg mixture and walnuts and mix well.

5 Divide the mixture evenly among the 12 cups in the muffin pan, leaving ¼ inch of space from the top in each cup. Bake for 35 minutes, or until the tops look somewhat dark. Insert a cake tester and, if necessary, continue baking a bit more until the tester comes out clean.

6 Allow the *kuku* to rest for 10 minutes so that they easily release from the pan. Garnish with the candied barberries before serving at room temperature with yogurt, if you wish.

Nonstick cooking spray

4 ounces (112 grams) fresh flat-leaf parsley, leaves and tender stems, finely chopped

4 ounces (112 grams) fresh cilantro, leaves and tender stems, finely chopped

4 ounces (112 grams) scallions, white part only, finely chopped

⅔ cup chopped romaine lettuce

3 tablespoons light olive oil

4 large eggs

2 teaspoons kosher salt

2 teaspoons freshly ground black pepper

½ cup (150 grams) walnuts, coarsely chopped

½ cup (56 grams) Candied Barberries (page 52) for garnish

Homemade Yogurt (page 32) or store-bought Greek yogurt for serving (optional)

CABBAGE PANCAKE

KUKU KALAM | *makes 2 pancakes, 4 servings*

Kuku kalam showcases my love for cabbage, but this recipe also makes a great template for using with any hearty vegetable, such as shredded carrots, cauliflower, or a mixture of both. This recipe makes two round 11-inch pancakes done in two batches.

Note If you want to get fancy, you can make smaller, individual *kuku,* using a 3-inch ring mold to help shape them.

1 Line a wire rack with paper towels and set aside.

2 Combine the salt, pepper, turmeric, onion with all of its juices, and cabbage in a mixing bowl. Using your hands, massage the cabbage to soften it.

3 Next, add the eggs, scallions, and flour, and mix well to combine. Finally, add the extra-virgin olive oil and stir to incorporate.

4 Add enough neutral oil to coat the bottom of an 11-inch stainless-steel pan with a tight-fitting lid and warm over medium-high heat until very hot but not smoking. Add half of the cabbage mixture to the pan, and using a spatula, shape the edges, so that the *kuku* is uniformly round. Lower the heat to medium, cover with the lid, and cook for about 8 minutes.

5 Remove the lid, lower the heat to medium-low, and continue cooking, about 3 to 4 minutes more, until the edges are dark golden. Flip the pancake onto a larger plate, then slide it back into the pan to fry on the other side, uncovered, for about 10 to 12 minutes. Transfer to the rack to drain of excess oil.

6 Repeat the process with the remaining half of the cabbage mixture, to make the second pancake.

7 Serve hot or at room temperature, with yogurt, if desired

2 teaspoons kosher salt

1 teaspoon freshly ground black pepper

1 tablespoon ground turmeric

7 ounces (198 grams) grated yellow onion, juices reserved (from about 1 medium onion)

1 whole green cabbage (about 2 pounds/907 grams), core removed, shredded with a mandoline or finely sliced

4 large eggs, lightly beaten

7 to 8 ounces (198 to 226 grams) scallions, mostly green parts, chopped into ½-inch pieces

1 cup (125 grams) all-purpose flour

¼ cup (60 ml) extra-virgin olive oil

Neutral oil, such as vegetable or canola oil, for frying

Homemade Yogurt (page 32) or store-bought Greek yogurt for serving (optional)

ZUCCHINI PANCAKES

KUKU KEDOO | *makes multiple pancakes, about 4 servings*

Zucchini are always on my shopping list, especially in the summer when they arrive at the farmers' market. This *kuku* is full of herbs, chopped walnuts for texture, a hint of raisin sweetness, and a kick of heat from the red chili flakes. I enjoy it at room temperature, along with bread and yogurt, for a light summer dinner.

1 Line a wire rack with paper towels and set aside.

2 Shred the zucchini using a box grater. Toss with 1 teaspoon of the salt. Allow to sit for about 15 minutes. Use a clean kitchen towel or paper towels to squeeze the zucchini to remove excess water, and put the zucchini in a large mixing bowl.

3 Meanwhile, do the same with the potatoes: Shred the potatoes, toss with 1 teaspoon of the salt, and squeeze to remove excess water. Then add the potatoes to the mixing bowl with the zucchini.

4 Add the dill, cilantro, parsley, scallions, dried mint, and onion to the zucchini and potato mixture and stir to combine. In a separate medium bowl, combine the eggs, the remaining 1 teaspoon salt, and the pepper, turmeric, and chili flakes. Whisk just until frothy.

5 Add enough oil to coat the bottom of a large stainless-steel pan set over medium heat and heat until shimmering. To the bowl with the zucchini mixture, add the egg mixture, then the walnuts and raisins, and stir well.

6 Working in batches, spoon some of the mixture into the pan, making the *kuku* as large or as small as you like. Cook for 3 to 4 minutes, until the underside is brown. Flip and continue cooking for 3 to 4 minutes, until the other side browns, too.

7 Transfer to the rack to drain of excess oil and continue cooking until you have used up all of your mix. Serve hot or at room temperature, with yogurt, if desired.

2 pounds (907 grams) zucchini (about 6 medium), ends trimmed

3 teaspoons kosher salt

1 pound russet potatoes, peeled

3 ounces (85 grams) fresh dill, leaves and tender stems, finely chopped

3 ounces (85 grams) fresh cilantro, leaves and tender stems, finely chopped

3 ounces (85 grams) fresh flat-leaf parsley, leaves and tender stems, finely chopped

3 ounces (85 grams) scallions, both white and green parts, finely chopped

About 6 tablespoons dried mint

4 ounces (112 grams) grated yellow onion, squeezed of excess water (from about 1 small yellow onion)

6 large eggs

1 teaspoon freshly ground black pepper

1 tablespoon ground turmeric

1 tablespoon red chili flakes

Neutral oil, such as vegetable or canola oil, for frying

1 cup (107 grams) chopped walnuts

1 cup (160 grams) golden or red raisins

Homemade Yogurt (page 32) or store-bought Greek yogurt for serving (optional)

CHICKEN FRITTATA

KUKU MORGH | *makes 4 servings*

I have never had this *kuku* outside of my home in Isfahan, so I think that it must be my mother's creation (*baleh*). One summer, when I didn't have time to make *a'ash* (see pages 189–209), I cooked this chicken and turned it into *kuku morgh* sandwiches, similar to Vietnamese *bánh mì*, using a light and fluffy French-style baguette called *naan-e fantezi*. The lemon juice at the end enhances the flavor, and I love to squeeze more fresh lemon over it before serving. *Kuku morgh* keeps well at room temperature for a fantastic picnic dish.

1 Line a wire rack with paper towels and set aside.

2 Add the diced onions and 4 tablespoons olive oil to a large, heavy-bottomed pot with a tight-fitting lid and sauté over medium heat, adding more oil if needed, so the onions turn golden, their edges darken, and they soften, 5 to 7 minutes. Add the turmeric, a bit more oil, and stir, allowing the turmeric to bloom and release its fragrance, about 1 minute more.

3 Add the chicken, breast side down, along with 1 tablespoon of the salt, the pepper, and ½ cup (120 ml) water. Cover and cook on low until fully cooked, about 1 hour.

4 Meanwhile, shred the potato using the grating blade of a food processor or a box grater. Toss with the remaining ½ teaspoon salt. Allow it to sit for about 15 minutes. Then use a clean kitchen towel or paper towels and squeeze to remove excess water and set aside.

5 Remove the chicken from the pot, and once it is cool enough to handle, use a fork and knife, or your clean hands, to remove and discard the skin, and separate the chicken from the bones. Then, use two forks to shred the meat and place it in a large bowl. Add any remaining liquid (there should be very little left), along with the cooked onions, to the chicken.

6 To the chicken bowl, add the potato, saffron powder, eggs, and more salt and pepper to taste, and mix well. Set aside.

7 Add the neutral oil to a large skillet set over medium heat and heat until shimmering. Use your hands to shape the *kuku* into small patties, and working in batches if necessary, cook until the undersides start to brown, about 5 minutes. Flip and continue cooking until the undersides also brown, about 3 to 5 minutes more. Transfer the cooked *kuku* to the wire rack to drain of excess oil. Continue cooking until you have used up all of the *kuku* mixture.

8 Return the cooked *kuku* to the pan, raise the heat to medium-high, pour the lemon juice over them, and cook until they absorb the juice, about 2 to 3 minutes. Turn off the heat.

9 Serve as you wish, as a sandwich or as is, with lemon wedges and yogurt.

1 large yellow onion, halved, 1 half medium diced, the other half grated, squeezed of excess water

Light olive oil

1 tablespoon ground turmeric

1 small whole chicken (about 2½ to 3 pounds/ 1.1 to 1.3 kilograms)

1 tablespoon plus ½ teaspoon kosher salt, plus more to taste

1 tablespoon freshly ground black pepper, plus more to taste

1 large russet potato, peeled

⅓ teaspoon saffron powder

3 large eggs, lightly beaten

¼ cup (60 ml) neutral oil, such as vegetable or canola oil, for frying

½ cup (120 ml) bottled lemon juice

Fresh lemon wedges for serving

Homemade Yogurt (page 32) or store-bought Greek yogurt for serving

SWEETS SHIRINI

While dessert signals the end of a meal in Western cuisines, in Iran, *shirini* can signal its start! *Shirini,* meaning "sweets," is the general name for the wide range of cakes, tiny cookies, and custard- or cream-filled pastries (called *shirini tar*) that greet you as soon as you enter an Iranian home for a dinner party. The *shirini* are offered with an abundance of roasted and salted pistachios, walnuts, and almonds, as well as dried, sweet fruits—figs, dates, and golden plums among them—and fresh melons and seasonal fresh fruit. It's an over-the-top welcome, and at each party I attend, inevitably, I think to myself, Are we even going to have dinner? Of course, we are! But first, tasty, salty offerings, and *shirini,* to occupy our hands, rouse our appetites, and awaken our senses with their aromas of saffron, rosewater, and cardamom.

In addition to our sweets sometimes taking on the role of hors d'oeuvres, many are inextricably linked to centuries-old religious rituals and holidays, and other special events—such as the sweet pudding called *kachi* (see page 313), made for mothers after childbirth. Muslims prepare the saffron-yellow rice pudding called *shole zard* (see page 228) during their holy month of fasting called Ramadan, and the comforting simplicity of smooth Persian halvah (see page 232), a confection traditionally made to memorialize loved ones and for religious ceremonies. Regardless of *shirini*'s religious implications, the nostalgia and traditions of those that follow in this chapter make them deeply appreciated by secular Iranians, such as I, as well. Indeed, the Persian New Year called Nowruz (see Nowruz: Persian New Year, page 236), which celebrates the arrival of spring, is beloved by religious and secular Iranians and Persians throughout the world. Some of the most common *shirini* included in Nowruz celebrations are tiny marzipan cookies called *toot* (see page 241), sugar-coated almonds (*noghi*), walnut cookies (*naan-e gerdui*), almond cookies, chickpea flour cookies called *naan-e nokhodchi* (see page 240), delicate rice flour cookies called *naan-e berenji* (see page 239), and almond brittle (*sohan*). I've included three of these cookies and an Isfahani almond and honey brittle known as *sohan asali* (see page 234) in this chapter. The recipes for my Nowruz cookies remain true to their spirit. And the tinier you roll them, the more you'll have, so expect several dozen for sharing.

REGARDLESS OF *SHIRINI*'S RELIGIOUS IMPLICATIONS, THEIR NOSTALGIA AND TRADITIONS MAKE THEM DEEPLY APPRECIATED BY SECULAR IRANIANS.

In Iran today, cream-filled cakes and delicate, French-inspired pastries are sold in upscale bakeries in Tehran, but the sweets that follow are a lineup of the more traditional, nostalgic *shirini* from my youth. Here you have the simple but divine combination of sweet and moist dates stuffed with fresh walnuts and bound by a light batter in a cake called *ranginak* (see page 224) that is just as perfect for a midday snack with hot tea as it is after a meal. And all of the moist-liquidy sweetness and fragrant spices of a flaky, phyllo dough *baghlava* come together in a lighter version called Baghlava Cake (page 227). Desserts that I offer at Sofreh are here for you, too: Sofreh *paloodeh* (see page 238), a tangle of starchy noodles frozen in rosewater sorbet that dates from ancient times, and my favorite Saffron-Rosewater Ice Cream (page 231).

WALNUT and DATE CAKE

RANGINAK | *makes about 10 servings*

I cannot imagine a more straightforward, satisfying treat to enjoy with a good cup of tea than *ranginak*. Moist, caramel-sweet dates, each one stuffed with a crunchy, earthy walnut, are layered side by side, drizzled with a light batter, and then sprinkled with cinnamon and sugar. My recipe comes from my mother's family in Shiraz, where *ranginak* originates, and I will never alter my simple method for making it. Some home cooks chop their walnuts and layer them with the dates and batter and chill it as pie. Others top it with ground pistachios. My preferred method is to make a large tray, set it on the counter at room temperature—where it will last, covered, for weeks—and nibble at it each day. Years ago, it was the perfect treat for my then-grumpy teenagers on cold winter days. Look for plump, ripe, and soft, excellent-quality Medjool dates.

Note To make *ranginak* vegan, substitute light olive oil or neutral oil, such as vegetable or canola oil, for the butter.

1 Stuff each date with a walnut and arrange the dates facedown and tightly packed together on a serving plate, tucking any remaining walnuts in between. Sprinkle the cardamom on top and set aside.

2 Toast the flour in a large, dry pan over medium-low heat, stirring continuously, until the color changes to light brown and clumps form, about 5 to 7 minutes. Pass the flour through a fine-mesh sieve to remove the clumps, and return the flour to the pan.

3 Add the butter or oil and continuously stir the flour and butter mixture over medium-low heat, until the batter turns caramel-colored and is fragrant, about 10 minutes. You want a thick batter, but one that is still thin enough to spread over the dates. If the batter needs more butter or oil, feel free to add it.

4 Cover the dates with the batter and sprinkle the cinnamon, then the sugar, over the top. Loosely cover with plastic wrap and set aside at room temperature.

Note *Ranginak,* loosely covered with plastic wrap, will last up to 1 week on the countertop.

About 25 large Medjool dates, pitted

5 ounces (143 grams) walnuts

1 tablespoon ground cardamom

1 cup plus 1 ounce (255 grams) all-purpose flour

4 tablespoons (½ stick/56 grams) salted butter, or ½ cup (120 ml) light olive oil or neutral oil, such as vegetable or canola oil, plus more as needed

1½ tablespoons ground cinnamon

2 tablespoons granulated sugar

BAGHLAVA CAKE

makes about 8 servings

Baghlava cake is lightly nutty, redolent with cardamom, and drenched in rosewater syrup. This cake is closely associated with weddings and special occasions in Iran and makes a lovely sweet to bring to a casual dinner party and a beautiful birthday cake. You may make this cake one day in advance, since, as the syrup soaks the cake, it tastes even better the following day. I loosely cover the cake if it is to be served the next day.

1 Set the oven rack in the middle position and preheat the oven to 350°F. Lightly grease and flour a 12 x 16-inch straight-sided aluminum cake pan.

2 Use a hand mixer to beat the eggs until foamy in a large mixing bowl. Add the sugar and continue beating on high speed until the mixture turns the color of cream and is sticky, about 4 to 5 minutes. Add the butter and beat for 1 minute to combine.

3 In a separate bowl, combine the saffron water, milk, and ¼ cup (60 ml) water, and stir to combine.

4 In another bowl, combine the all-purpose flour, almond flour, salt, baking powder, and cardamom and sift together.

5 With the hand mixer on low, alternate adding the flour mixture and the milk mixture to the bowl with the egg mixture, doing so in three batches, until combined. Take care not to overmix.

6 Pour the batter into the cake pan and bake for 30 minutes. Rotate the pan once and then continue to bake for 10 minutes more. Use a cake tester to make sure the cake is evenly cooked through. Allow to cool on a wire rack for 3 to 4 hours.

7 When the cake is cold, make the syrup: Bring the sugar and 1 cup (235 ml) water to a boil in a medium saucepan and cook until the sugar dissolves, about 2 to 3 minutes. Add the rosewater, stir to combine, and cook for 1 minute more.

8 Slice the cake into squares and pour the hot rosewater syrup over them to soak the squares. Serve cold.

For the cake

6 large eggs

1½ cups (300 grams) granulated sugar

9 ounces (325 grams) salted butter, melted, cooled to room temperature

2 tablespoons Saffron Water (page xxxiv)

1½ cups (360 ml) whole milk

3¾ cups (450 grams) all-purpose flour

1 cup (120 grams) almond flour

2 teaspoons kosher salt

3 tablespoons baking powder

3 tablespoons ground cardamom

For the syrup

1 cup (200 grams) granulated sugar

¼ cup (60 ml) rosewater

SAFFRON RICE PUDDING

SHOLE ZARD | *makes about 8 servings*

While Soshy and Noony were still crawling, we visited Iran during the holy month of Ramadan. I was neither fasting nor going to mosque or attending religious ceremonies, and there was not much to do except spend a lot of time indoors with the kids. One day, I heard the *adhan,* a Muslim call to prayer, for the first time in ten years. It's a soulful, haunting voice that pierces the air with unwavering intention, and it was being broadcast throughout the city. My emotion took me by surprise. Snap out of it, I told myself. After the revolution, I had so much anger and emotional baggage that the religious implication of the sound was nonsense to me. But I couldn't help myself. Feelings of nostalgia flooded over me as I kept thinking about the parties, bonfires, and exchanges of food, as people gathered in their homes to break their fast or, as is tradition, to cook collectively. During Ramadan, groups of people get together to make a wish, called *nazr,* and then cook a ton of food, including *shole zard* that they then donate to the needy. The sound of the *adhan* reminded me of the tumble of voices that say, "I'll pay for the rice!" or "I'll take care of the saffron" or "Count on me for the rosewater." Although *shole zard* carries no religious implications, for me, the tradition of showing up for one another, using food as a conduit, is poetic. And magical. It brings me back to the good food-related memories of Ramadan in Iran.

This pudding is dairy-free. The short-grain jasmine rice will give up all of its starches during the long cook time and make it very creamy. And I am sure it will come as no surprise to you that I like my *shole zard* (yellow pudding) to be strong in saffron color and flavor. Also, it is lower in sugar compared with traditional versions, so you may want to taste it and add more sugar, if you like.

1 Add 12 cups (3 liters) water, the rice, and salt to a 7½-quart (7-liter) stainless-steel pot set over medium heat and cook for 30 minutes, stirring frequently for best results. Next, add the sugar and cook for 10 minutes more.

2 Add the saffron powder, lower the heat to low, and continue cooking, stirring constantly, for 30 minutes. (Halfway through, adjust the oven rack to fit the pot and preheat the oven to 200°F.) At this point, the rice should be soft and creamy. If it is too thick, add a bit of water to loosen it. Add the almonds, stir, and cook for 10 minutes more.

¾ cup (138 grams) jasmine rice

1 teaspoon kosher salt

1½ cups (300 grams) granulated sugar

⅓ teaspoon saffron powder

½ cup (54 grams) slivered almonds

¼ cup (60 ml) rosewater, or more if you fancy more rose character

3 Add the rosewater and turn off the heat. Taste, adding more rosewater, if you wish. Look at the *shole zard*. If the rice is a very broken and thick paste, it is ready to go into the oven.

4 Place the pot in the oven for about 30 minutes. This will help the *shole zard* come together, so when you serve it, the water doesn't separate.

5 Allow the *shole zard* to come to room temperature before transferring it to a container and chilling it in the refrigerator for 6 to 8 hours. Serve cold.

Cardamom *(Hel)*

Cardamom pods, which grow on a species of tree in the ginger family that is native to India, are filled with intensely fragrant seeds that have been used for medicinal purposes in Iran since the ninth century. As far back as the Middle Ages, their use in cooking has been documented in the layered rice dishes of the Safavid court (*polo*) and in halvah. I love the scent of cardamom—it reminds me of the birds, sun, and beauty of my Isfahan—and I use it generously throughout my baking. I especially love the simplicity of a pod cracked open and dropped into a glass of tea. Cardamom is available in several varietals, with green being the most widely used.

SAFFRON-ROSEWATER ICE CREAM

BASTANI AKBAR MASHDI | *makes 6 to 8 servings*

Akbar Mashdi invented this recipe for ice cream, which combines the glory of saffron, rosewater, and salted pistachios, in the 1920s in Tehran. It's also known as *bastani sonnati—sonnati* meaning the "traditional" or "classic" way of making something. On visits to Shiraz when I was a kid, my great-aunt Borzogeh would take me and my brother Reza and our cousins to the ice cream parlor. On one trip, my little cone of *bastani* fell to the ground. My great-aunt comforted me in her arms, then, in one swoop, grabbed my brother's cone out of his hand and gave it to me instead. My brother started bawling his eyes out, and to this day, I have always known I was Khale Borzogeh's favorite. Among the sea of ice cream flavors that I have tasted on my travels, this remains my number one.

The use of salep, a powder made from the ground tubers of wild orchids, does not impart flavor, but it does give traditional *bastani* its signature stretchy texture and chewy mouthfeel. If you use too much, you wind up with super-stretchy ice cream that's the consistency of marshmallows. But try using it for fun, if you like.

Note You will need an ice cream maker to make this recipe. Also, the mixture needs to chill overnight, so begin this recipe 1 day before you plan on serving it.

1 Mix the salep, if using, sugar, and salt in a small bowl and set aside.

2 Combine the milk and cream in a stainless-steel pot and warm over low heat. Add the sugar mixture, saffron powder, and rosewater, and use a hand mixer on low speed to mix, about 2 minutes.

3 Cover the mixture with plastic wrap, place in the refrigerator, and cool overnight.

4 The next day, process in your ice cream maker, following the manufacturer's directions, until the mixture gets to a soft-serve consistency. Stop the machine, transfer the mixture to a freezer-proof container, and mix in the pistachios. Freeze for 3 to 4 hours, mixing now and then, until ready to serve.

Alternatively When I am craving this ice cream, sometimes I make a shortcut version by freezing dollops of whipped cream, then add them to good-quality, softened store-bought vanilla ice cream, along with enough rosewater, pistachios, and saffron to taste. Mix and allow it to freeze for a bit before eating.

1 tablespoon salep (see Resources, page 317; optional)

1 to 1¼ cups (220 to 250 grams) granulated sugar

Pinch of kosher salt

4 cups (1 liter) whole milk

¾ cup (200 grams) heavy cream

⅛ teaspoon saffron powder, bloomed over 1 ice cube

⅓ cup (80 ml) rosewater

½ cup (75 grams) salted pistachios, chopped

CARROT HALVAH

makes 1 large tray for a gathering

Most people are familiar with the dry, flaky-dense sesame tahini halvah made throughout the Middle East. However, in Iran, we use a mixture of flour, butter, sugar, and rosewater for a smooth-textured halvah made for Ramadan, weddings, and memorial offerings. My aunt Mihan, who has mastered sweet halvah, would make it for us as a snack on a cold winter's night. You need only flour, sugar, and oil to make this, but you can get as fancy as you like. I like to incorporate vegetables, such as sweet potatoes, carrots, and butternut squashes, into the traditional base to make it brighter in color and lighter and fluffier in texture. The tradition of making and offering halvah in someone's memory is very dear to me. To take a bite brings pause, and in the pause, there is comfort.

1 Preheat the oven to 425°F.

2 Place the carrots on a baking sheet and roast until tender, about 20 minutes. Process in the food processor until smooth and clump-free.

3 Add the sugar and carrots to a pot and cook over low heat for about 10 minutes. Turn off the heat. Add the cardamom, rosewater, salt, and saffron water, if using, and set aside.

4 Toast the flour in a pan over medium heat, gently stirring continuously, until the color changes to a very light brown/tan and smells nice, about 10 minutes. Pass through a fine-mesh sieve to break up any lumps.

5 Place the flour back in the pan and add the butter, if using, and the olive oil and continue stirring for 5 minutes more.

6 Remove the pan from the heat and add the carrot mixture to the flour, otherwise everything will sizzle, bubble, splatter, and may burn you, which isn't pleasant. Keep stirring, off the heat, until the mixture is well incorporated and releases from the pan easily. Return the pan to low heat and continue stirring, until it is one homogenous mixture. The texture will tighten up and you'll be able to fold it over on itself as one homogenous unit.

7 Transfer the halvah to a baking sheet to cool down. Once it is cool, place the halvah on a serving plate and smooth it into an even layer. You can get as fancy and creative as you like to decorate the halvah. I like to decorate the top of mine to look like a flower. Working outward from the center, use the flat tip of a butter knife to make rows of "petals" (indentations) around the circumference of the dish. Next, sprinkle a small mound of crushed

About 1¼ pounds (550 grams) carrots, trimmed and peeled

1 cup (200 grams) granulated sugar

2 tablespoons ground cardamom

½ cup (120 ml) rosewater

Pinch of kosher salt

2 tablespoons Saffron Water (page xxxiv; optional)

1 cup (120 grams) all-purpose flour

3 tablespoons (1½ ounces/ 42 grams) salted butter (optional)

½ cup (120 ml) light olive oil

Crushed pistachios for decoration (optional)

Rosebuds for decoration (optional)

Toasted sesame seeds for decoration (optional)

pistachios in the center for the flower "pistil," and place a rosebud in the middle. Alternatively, to serve halvah to a larger crowd, you can roll the halvah into small balls, then roll the balls to coat in toasted sesame seeds or crushed pistachios. Or for a nut-free garnish, top the halvah balls with a pretty rosebud instead.

Alternatively To make gluten-free halvah: Use Japanese rice flour instead of all-purpose flour.

To make vegan halvah: Replace the butter with oil and the granulated sugar with raw sugar.

I sometimes add half wheat flour for nutritional reasons to my halvah, and you can try that, too, although the all-purpose flour makes it lighter on the palate. You may also substitute sweet potatoes or butternut squashes for the carrots, but I recommend increasing the amount of sugar slightly to balance their earthiness.

Pistachios *(Pesteh)*

The English name for pistachios is derived from the Farsi *pesteh,* and the roots of pistachio cultivation in Iran reach back to antiquity. Iranian pistachios are beloved the world over for their vibrant green color, tender crunch, and notes of unmistakable sweetness, with Iran being one of the world's major exporters of the nut. Apart from our love of snacking on roasted pistachios, we use them in the kitchen to garnish rice dishes and sweets, and to make jams.

HONEY BRITTLE

SOHAN ASALI

Sohan (brittle) is a confection that originated in eighteenth-century Qom, the capital city of the Qom province in north-central Iran. There are several varieties of *sohan* there, many of them made with wheat germ and flour, earthy saffron, butter, and various nuts. Nowruz cookie platters are not complete without this crunchy, sweet almond brittle, and as kids, my brothers and I would sneak it off the tray to eat all day. You can use your choice of nuts for the brittle, and further garnish it as you wish. *Sohan asali* comes together in minutes and can be made days ahead of time.

Note If you don't have a candy thermometer, use the cold plate test. Place a small china plate in the freezer before you begin. To test if your honey brittle has set, drop a teaspoon of brittle onto the plate, and if it keeps its shape, it's ready.

1 Grease a baking sheet and set aside.

2 Combine the honey, butter, sugar, and 1 tablespoon water in a small stainless-steel pot and set it over medium heat. Quickly mix once to combine, then cook undisturbed until the sugar begins to foam and turns a light caramel color, about 10 minutes.

3 Add the almonds or your choice of nuts to the mixture and stir to combine. The mixture will thicken because of the change of temperature, so continue cooking, mixing every so often to loosen it, until the almonds turn golden, about 8 minutes. Or, if using a candy thermometer, it should read between 280° and 300°F. (If you don't have a thermometer, use the cold plate test; see headnote.)

4 Add the saffron water (the mixture will foam) and stir continuously for 2 more minutes. Turn off the heat.

5 Use two spoons to shape and drop the honey brittle onto the prepared baking sheet in whatever amounts you'd like, keeping some space between the pieces of brittle so they can spread. Immediately garnish with the sea salt flakes, chopped pistachios, and/or rose petals, if using. Let the brittle cool before removing it from the baking sheet. Alternatively, you can pour the entire mixture onto the prepared baking sheet, garnish, and cool. Once the brittle has cooled, break it into smaller pieces before removing it from the sheet.

Note *Sohan asali* keeps well for a few weeks stored in an airtight container in a dark, dry place.

About 4 tablespoons (45 grams) honey

3 tablespoons (1½ ounces/ 42 grams) salted butter

⅔ cup (135 grams) granulated sugar

1 cup (130 grams) sliced or slivered almonds, or 1 cup (140 grams) cashews or hazelnuts

1 teaspoon Saffron Water (page xxxiv)

Sea salt flakes for garnish (optional)

Chopped pistachios for garnish (optional)

Rose petals for garnish (optional)

Nowruz: Persian New Year

Nowruz, meaning "new day," originated more than three thousand years ago in Persia and was one of the holiest days in the ancient religion of Zoroastrianism. At the exact moment of the vernal equinox in the Northern Hemisphere, Zoroastrians celebrated the light of spring triumphing over the darkness of winter. Later, in the eleventh century, Nowruz was officially recognized as the start of a new year in the Persian solar calendar.

In Isfahan and central Iran, weeks before the vernal equinox marks the start of spring, you'll see flowers start to bloom and smell the scent of jasmine and roses in the air. Even in colder northern provinces, where thin layers of snow still blanket the ground, bright purple flowers poke through. The air is charged with the green, fresh feeling of a new day and everywhere you turn, there's a sense of bubbling anticipation. If you walk down the street in my Isfahan neighborhood, you'll see households hard at work with spring cleaning. Women beat the dust out of carpets hanging from their windows, storekeepers sweep sidewalks and reorganize shelves. Most everyone feels a natural lift in their energy when Nowruz is around the corner.

When I was growing up, my mother didn't start her khaneh takani (spring cleaning, or literally "shaking out the house") until one week before Nowruz, but she always got a jump start on growing her sabzeh—special Nowruz sprouts that vary from home to home and signify new life. Giti Joon went with easy-to-grow lentil sprouts, while Ame Zivar, my aunt on my father's side, expertly grew the most incredible mung bean sprouts—a tricky undertaking because the sprouts can get funky fast. She carried fragrant batches of them in ceramic containers to our house as a gift each year. And my great-grandmother made samanu, a labor-intensive sprouted wheat germ pudding that symbolizes rebirth. It must also represent patience, because it takes five to seven days to germinate the wheat, followed by six hours of continuously stirring and cooking. I leave the memory of homemade samanu to her and stick with the store-bought stuff. Once cooked, the samanu goes on a special sofreh called sofreh haft-seen.

The components of a sofreh haft-seen are personal and can be as simple or elaborate as you wish. The most common items are seeb (apples), sir (garlic), senjet (dried silverberry), sekkeh (vinegar), sumac (somagh), samanu, and sabzeh. At Sofreh, it's become my tradition to place gorgeous hyacinth flowers (*sanbol*) on my bar as well as to create a *haft-seen* near the entrance to our dining room. In homes, families gather around the *sofreh haft-seen* at the exact moment spring arrives for a broad range of traditions. For years, I would awaken Soshy and Noony at sometimes ungodly morning hours, flipping through my books of Persian poetry by Rumi or Hafiz to land on a random morsel of wisdom that I would read out loud for them.

On the Tuesday before Nowruz arrives, Chaharshanbe Suri—literally, the "eve of Wednesday"—celebrants light bonfires, symbolizing purification. People gather in the streets and take turns leaping over the fire, to represent crossing the threshold of winter to spring. On our jump, we proclaim *"Sorkhi-e to az man!"* ("Give me your beautiful red color!") followed by *"Zardi-e man az to!"* ("And take back my sickly pallor"). During our first Nowruz celebration at Sofreh, Akis made a small bonfire out front, and we invited friends and neighbors on the block, along with their kids, to take a leap! Akis threw a little alcohol on the flames to make them *whoosh*! And all the kids in Brooklyn yelled *"Yeah!"* as they jumped hand in hand with their parents.

Nowruz officially ends on the thirteenth day of the year, on Sizdah Be-dar, which translates as "getting rid of thirteen." Staying indoors that day is considered bad luck, so we pack a picnic and head outdoors with family and friends to be close to nature.

My love for Nowruz is boundless. It's primal, ancient, and necessary, as it calls for us to be one with the cycle of nature. And it's so powerfully embedded in our culture, regardless of religion or faith, that for centuries, repeated attempts by Islamic governments to eliminate it—from the time of the Arab conquest of Persia in the seventh century through to the modern day—have failed. Today, Nowruz is one of Iranians' few remaining pre-Islamic traditions, and it's celebrated with love and pride in every country once part of the Persian empire, including Tajikistan, Uzbekistan, Afghanistan, Turkey, and among the Parsi people of India, a diaspora of Zoroastrianism-practicing Persians. My dream is to create a Nowruz Brooklyn block party with communities from all walks of life one year. It hasn't happened yet. But, my dear, I will get it done.

ROSEWATER-LIME SORBET

PALOODEH │ *makes 6 to 8 servings*

Paloodeh (spelled *faloodeh* after the seventh century) is considered the first frozen treat in history, originating in the ancient Persian empire. It's made by freezing rice or wheat starch noodles in rosewater syrup. The resulting frozen noodle sorbet is garnished with bursts of fresh lime or, sometimes, sour cherry juice. Everyone in Iran knows the best *paloodeh* comes from Shiraz. During trips I took as a girl to visit my mother's relatives there, my uncle would take us to a hole-in-the-wall shop in the old part of the city that sold only authentic handmade *paloodeh* noodles. For generations, the owners have dedicated their lives to rendering (*paloodan* means "to refine") a perfect expression of this ancient treat, with the texture of the noodles so delicate and crunchy. But because you may not find yourself in Shiraz anytime soon, what follows is my shortcut version, which uses store-bought vermicelli rice noodles to re-create the pleasure at home. The icy texture will be more like granita, as you'll scrape the mixture every hour. See the photograph on page 230.

1 Combine the sugar and 1½ cups (360 ml) water in a saucepan and cook over low heat for a few minutes, stirring until the sugar dissolves. Mix in the rosewater and salt, and then let the mixture cool before transferring it to a freezer-proof container to freeze until slushy, about 1 hour.

2 Meanwhile, bring 2 cups (470 ml) water to a boil in a pot with a tight-fitting lid, add the noodles, and cover. Remove the pan from the heat and let it sit for 10 minutes. Drain the noodles, then lay them on a large plate layered with paper towels to absorb excess water. Transfer them to the refrigerator to cool for 2 hours.

3 Use a fork to break up the slushy syrup mixture, then add the cold noodles, mix well, and return to the freezer. Every hour, for the next 4 hours, scrape the mixture, until the noodles are frozen and crunchy.

4 Before serving, remove the sorbet from the freezer, divide it among bowls, pour the fresh lime juice over the top, and garnish with the lime zest.

1½ cups (300 grams) granulated sugar

¼ cup (60 ml) rosewater

Pinch of kosher salt

6 ounces (170 grams) vermicelli rice noodles, broken into small pieces

3 to 6 whole limes, juiced, 2 of them zested

Nowruz *Shirini*

NOWRUZ RICE FLOUR COOKIES

NAAN-E BERENJI | *makes a lot of cookies*

During Nowruz, my mother's labor of love was to make these tiny, fragrant, and oh so delicious rice flour cookies called *naan-e berenji*. She also made chickpea flour cookies called *naan-e nokhodchi* (see page 240) and mulberry-shaped marzipan confections called *toot* (see page 241). As I became the elder in New York, and everyone in my family came to *my* home for our Nowruz celebrations, I continued the tradition of making these cookies, and now I make them each year for my guests at Sofreh. They melt in your mouth, and the perfume of rosewater and cardamom will fill your kitchen while they bake. See the photograph on page 220.

Note The dough needs to rest for 1 day.

1 Use a hand mixer to combine the butter and confectioners' sugar in a large mixing bowl.

2 Add the egg and egg yolks and continue mixing until incorporated. Stir in the rosewater until combined.

3 Sift the rice flour, stir in the cardamom, and add to the bowl with the wet mixture. Use a hand mixer to combine.

4 Place the dough in a ziplock bag to rest in the refrigerator for 1 day.

5 The next day, preheat the oven to 350°F.

6 Drop cherry-size cookies, placed ¼ inch apart, onto a greased baking sheet and bake for 12 to 15 minutes.

7 Remove the baking sheet from the oven, place it on a wire rack, and allow the cookies to cool without disturbing them for a minimum of 3 to 4 hours.

8 Once the cookies have cooled, gently transfer them to an airtight container and store at room temperature for up to 1 week.

Note You can freeze these cookies in an airtight container for up to 3 months.

1½ cups (250 grams) clarified butter

1½ cups (200 grams) confectioners' sugar

1 large egg plus 2 large egg yolks

1 cup (235 ml) rosewater

3 cups plus 2 tablespoons (500 grams) rice flour

2 tablespoons ground cardamom

NOWRUZ CHICKPEA FLOUR COOKIES

NAAN-E NOKHODCHI | *makes a lot of cookies*

Naan-e nokhodchi are delightfully easy, cardamom-scented Nowruz cookies that are vegan and gluten-free. It requires patience to bring the soft dough together, but keep kneading and squeezing and it will stick. These cookies are traditionally shaped using mini clover-shaped cookie cutters, but you can use any shape you wish. Or, instead of cutting out the dough into shapes, pinch off little dough balls to bake.

Note The dough needs to rest overnight.

1 The day before baking, use a hand mixer to combine the butter and confectioners' sugar in a mixing bowl until very soft.

2 Sift the chickpea flour with the cardamom, then add it to the butter mixture, using your hands to mix until it forms a uniform ball.

3 Place the dough in a ziplock bag to rest at room temperature overnight.

4 The next day, line a baking sheet with parchment paper and preheat the oven to 300°F.

5 Place the dough between two pieces of parchment paper and roll it out to any thickness you like. Use small cookie cutters to stamp out the cookies, rerolling the dough scraps until you've used all the dough, and place them on the parchment-lined baking sheet.

6 Sprinkle the pistachios, if using, on top and bake for 12 to 15 minutes. Make sure the cookies are well baked or they will fall apart after they cool down.

7 Remove the baking sheet from the oven, place it on a wire rack, and allow the cookies to cool without disturbing them for a minimum of 3 to 4 hours.

8 Once the cookies have cooled, gently transfer them to an airtight container and store at room temperature for up to 1 week.

Note You can freeze these cookies in an airtight container for up to 3 months.

½ cup (100 grams) clarified butter

¾ cup (100 grams) confectioners' sugar

2 cups (200 grams) roasted, fine chickpea flour

1 tablespoon ground cardamom

¼ cup (25 grams) ground pistachios for decorating (optional)

NOWRUZ MARZIPAN COOKIES

TOOT | *makes a lot of cookies*

These fragrant, adorable marzipan cookies are our most iconic Nowruz treat. They are hand rolled to resemble *toot,* the Farsi name for mulberries. I like the natural color of marzipan, for tradition's sake, but you can make them any color you like. And because they don't require baking, they are very easy to make.

1 Place the granulated sugar in a shallow container and set aside. Set out a large serving dish or small storage container.

2 Mix the almond meal, confectioners' sugar, and cardamom in a small bowl.

3 Pass the mixture through a fine-mesh sieve into a medium bowl. Next, add the rosewater and food coloring, if using, and using your hands, gently work the mixture until it begins to come together into a smooth, pliable dough.

4 Shape the *toot* one at a time by pinching off a piece of dough about the size of a large hazelnut, and roll it into a ball. Next, while it's still in your hand, shape the ball into the conical shape of a mulberry (which looks like a long raspberry) by pinching it at one end and flattening the bottom. Drop the shaped *toot* into the container with the granulated sugar and toss until well coated. Remove from the sugar and stick a pistachio sliver in the flat end to resemble a stem; set it aside on the serving dish.

5 Repeat until you have used up all the dough. Cover the dish with plastic wrap and chill before serving.

Note These cookies will keep in an airtight container in the refrigerator for up to 1 week.

½ cup (100 grams) granulated sugar

¾ cup (175 grams) almond meal

½ cup (115 grams) confectioners' sugar

1 tablespoon ground cardamom

2 tablespoons rosewater

Food coloring, your choice of color (optional)

About ½ cup (55 grams) slivered pistachios for the stems

Almonds *(Badam)*

Almonds have grown in Iran for thousands of years and are used in both savory and sweet dishes. We celebrate the bounty of Iranian almonds—with varieties ranging in flavor from bitter to sweet—by eating them in all forms. They are salted for snacking and ground into a paste to make the endearing *toot*—a confection resembling the *shah toot* (mulberry fruit). And we eat fresh green, unripened almonds in the spring called *chaghaleh badam,* treasuring their pleasingly sour, soft centers. For my Jeweled Rice (page 81), I soak slivered almonds in rosewater for enhanced fragrance, and they offer lovely texture to desserts.

PICKLES AND JAMS AND MARMALADES
TORSHI and MORABA

The summer I turned eleven, there were tomatoes everywhere. Giti Joon would wash my and my younger brother Reza's feet and we'd climb into a giant copper container full of tomatoes to stomp on them and remove their skins. Then my father would come and move the container, following the trajectory of the hot Isfahan sun so that the tomatoes could thicken and dry before my mother would strain them for her tomato paste. Each day, along with one of her hired helpers, she'd work tirelessly, juicing her own lemons, chopping herbs, and pickling and preserving seasonal vegetables and fruit for her *torshi* and *moraba*.

Earlier that year, my father had left the security of his military job and settled us permanently in Isfahan to start his own business. Without his steady paycheck, my parents had fallen on tough times. Also that year, my mother lost her beloved grandmother, who had helped raise her. I remember my mother selling off pieces of her jewelry to help make ends meet, as well as my parents' sadness and their late-night arguments punctuated with the whistling pitch of my mother's asthma. For as much as I loved helping my mother with her projects, it was the first time I felt like she really needed me; she seemed so tired and overworked.

One morning at sunrise, I awakened in the tent outdoors on our balcony where my family and I had been sleeping to stay cool and surprised her by cleaning all of her sour grapes to make *abgooreh* (sour grape juice). I'd seen her do it before, noting how to get the sharp stem out, before washing the grapes and manually juicing them in a grinder; a lot of work by hand. A few hours later, Giti Joon woke up, saw me among the grapes, and pulled me close. Instead of words, she brought my dirty little hands to her lips and kissed them.

I realized years later that some of my mother's summer labor was for the practicality of stocking her pantry, but much more of what she was doing was trying to inject some life into our home. "Bad times pass," Giti Joon would say, "and good times return, but what you have on your plate, and what you have to offer people today, is everlasting."

For years, whatever life threw at me, I'd turn to pickling and preserving for comfort. I'd surround myself with pounds of vegetables, as my mother had done, and lose myself in the repetition of peeling, and chopping herbs, and the transformative process of vinegar and spices to yield exciting varieties of *torshi* for my home, and to give away as gifts. I'd love the thrill of going to the farmers' market in New York to seize any number of fruits whose seasons were fleeting and give them new life as a *moraba* for my breakfast table.

What follows in this chapter, my dear, is a tiny sliver of the hundreds of centuries-old Persian recipes for pickling and preserving fruits and vegetables. Let's begin with *torshi*.

Torshi (*torsh*, meaning "sour") are pickled vegetables and fruits preserved in vinegar brine or a salt-bath solution (*shoor*, meaning "salty"). They are an essential part of Persian cuisine. The multitude of *torshi* flavors—salty, sour, spicy—and textures—creamy, crunchy, a bit of both—unfold to complement our stews and rice dishes and are the perfect condiments for grilled and roasted meats. They cut through richness, they add punch, and when you have a great one, you never forget it. It is common for four or five variations of *torshi* to be on the *sofreh* at once, shown off in beautiful crystal bowls. Gone are the days when home cooks, like my mother, would break their backs making them. Today, you can go to any grocery store or bazaar in Iran and pick from dozens of open containers, have a taste, and bring home your favorites.

IT IS COMMON FOR FOUR OR FIVE VARIATIONS OF *TORSHI* TO BE ON THE *SOFREH* AT ONCE.

Although *torshi* exist throughout most Middle Eastern, Arab, and Balkan cuisines, as well as in Mediterranean cuisines, many historians believe that they originated in Iran, with the practice of drying, salting, and preserving going back thousands of years. The *torshi* you will find in stores, and in homes, are as diverse as the herbs, fruits, and vegetables that flourish from region to region, but more important, homemade *torshi* are as diverse, experimental, and personal as each home cook wishes them to be.

These recipes are portioned for you to make a lot of *torshi*. And while they are commonplace in Iran, you may need to build an audience for your pickles here in the States. As I grew up, I recall my father never really liking pickles, so there was no way in hell my mother was making all of her *torshi* for us. It dawned on me only when I returned to Iran for the first time after my long separation that she had, all along, been making them to give away.

Although no one makes *torshi* for me in New York—probably because I have such strong opinions about the ones I love—if you were to show up at Sofreh with some of *yours* for me, you'd have my heart.

MORABA APPEAR BY THE SPOONFUL AS A SWEET TREAT OR AS A SNACK WITH A CUP OF TEA.

Moraba is the word used for both fruit jams and citrus marmalades in Iran, and like *torshi,* there are hundreds of variations for preserving fruits, fruit blossoms, and flowers. Centuries ago, honey and molasses would have been used for preservation, with sugar coming onto the scene much later, in the Middle Ages. Indeed, you may use honey in the recipes that follow, if you wish. Use it at a one-to-one ratio in place of the sugar called for. While the *sofreh* is never complete without copious bowls of pickles at lunch or dinner, jars of jewel-colored *moraba* fulfill that role at breakfast. They also appear by the spoonful as a sweet treat to finish a meal, or are enjoyed as an afternoon snack with a cup of tea. The selection of jams for this chapter was easy. Quince Jam (*moraba beh;* page 257), Carrot Jam with Salted Pistachios (*moraba havij;* page 259), and Crunchy Butternut Squash Jam with Almonds (*moraba kadoo halvaii;* page 261) are the mainstays in my mother's repertoire. She would experiment with other varieties each year, choosing from every fruit imaginable. However, we would beg her to return to our favorites. Over breakfast at my parents' home in Iran, I watched as Ali tasted, for the first time, my mother's deep, wine-colored, perfectly textured quince jam. "Your mother's is better than yours," he said. Giti Joon smiled broadly *(I understand only compliments in English)*. I've journeyed for decades on a quest, through fruit, sugar, and spices, to bring these preserves as close as possible to Giti Joon's—for the flavor and textures, and the memories of a handful of summers and countless breakfasts at my parents' table.

Pickles *(Torshi)*

SPICY MANGO PICKLES

TORSHI ANBE | *makes 1 quart jar*

I first tasted a spoonful of this mango pickle while traveling in the south of Iran, and I fell in love with the sweet mangoes mingled with flavors of sour tamarind and chili pepper heat. But honestly, I thought the runny, mushy texture needed work. In this recipe, I recommend unripe Kent mangoes for their fleshy body, but you can use any type of mango available to you. The mangoes will soften in the brine but still retain their bite and shape, which I like better. I also adjusted the seasonings to my taste, combining the warmth of light anise, citrus notes from celery seeds, and a touch of bitter nigella seeds. It's such an easy pickle to make, but it gives you so many layers of mouth-puckering tang and piquancy. And it's especially great with minced and grilled *kababs* (see pages 151–157).

Note This recipe calls for a presterilized mason jar.

1 Place the mango slices in a large bowl, salt them generously, and refrigerate, uncovered, for 1 day.

2 Lightly toast the fennel seeds and celery seeds in a small pan over low heat, then grind them well in a spice grinder.

3 Place the mangoes in the presterilized 1-quart jar, followed by the ground spices, nigella seeds, garlic, chili pepper or chili flakes, tamarind paste, and enough vinegar to cover.

4 Seal the jar and leave at room temperature for 1 week, then refrigerate, and keep for up to 1 month.

3 to 4 unripe Kent mangoes, peeled, pitted, and sliced

Kosher salt

1 teaspoon fennel seeds

1 teaspoon celery seeds

1 teaspoon nigella seeds

4 to 5 garlic cloves, thinly sliced

1 whole spicy red chili pepper, such as Tianjin, or 1 teaspoon red chili flakes

⅓ cup (80 ml) Tamarind Paste (page 181), homemade or store-bought

White wine vinegar

SMOKED EGGPLANT PICKLES

NAZ KHATOON | *makes 1 quart jar*

My aunt Mihan's husband is always thrilled when Akis and I return to Iran. "Finally!" he says, "we'll eat smoked eggplant all week." Aunt Mihan, who has a labor-intensive system for smoking her eggplants outdoors, saves her hard work for our visits. And in addition to making her northern specialty of *mirza ghasemi* (see page 114), she often makes this richly textured, herb-laden, and creamy smoked eggplant pickle with soft verjus to serve alongside fish dishes from her husband's province of Mazandaran. Or sometimes, she eliminates the verjus and turns it into a dip, combining the cold eggplant and herb mixture with yogurt and crushed walnuts. You can do the same (see *Borani Bademjoon,* page 39). Whisk this up in a day, and then punch up any number of your favorite roasted vegetables, such as potatoes or cauliflower, all week. Or serve it as a condiment the next time you make boneless, slow-roasted Italian pork (*porchetta*)—it's impressive.

Note This is a refrigerator pickle and the jar does not need to be sealed.

1 Cover a stove-top range with a layer of aluminum foil for easy cleanup, making sure to keep the burner exposed. Pierce the eggplants with a fork and place them directly on the grate, over a medium flame, and roast, giving a quarter turn now and then, for 1 to 2 minutes on all sides, until the skin is uniformly charred and the flesh is soft. Remove from the heat and set aside on a baking sheet to cool.

2 When the eggplants are cool enough to handle, peel the skin, pulling out the most charred pieces and finely chopping them to the consistency of a paste. Next, chop the eggplants to a fine dice.

3 In a large mixing bowl, combine the garlic, basil, tarragon, rosemary, verjus or pomegranate-lemon mixture, chopped eggplants, turmeric, chili pepper, salt, and black pepper to taste. Add the charred eggplant skins, a little at a time. I like my *naz khatoon* really smoky, but not everyone appreciates both salt and smoked skin, so make yours to taste.

4 Transfer the mixture to a 1-quart jar and store in the refrigerator, where it keeps for up to 1 week.

2 pounds (907 grams) eggplants

1 whole garlic head, cloves peeled and roughly chopped

3 ounces (85 grams) fresh basil, leaves and tender stems, washed and thoroughly dried, finely chopped

3 ounces (85 grams) fresh tarragon, leaves and tender stems, washed and thoroughly dried, finely chopped

2 ounces (56 grams) fresh rosemary, leaves picked, washed and thoroughly dried, and finely chopped

1 cup (235 ml) verjus or ¼ cup (60 ml) pomegranate juice combined with ¼ cup (60 ml) bottled lemon juice

1 tablespoon ground turmeric

1 whole chili pepper, such as jalapeño

Kosher salt

Freshly ground black pepper

FRUIT PICKLES

TORSHI MIVEH | *makes about 3 pint jars*

In Iran, if sweet and sour, luscious, juicy fruits aren't eaten or cooked at their peak of freshness, we preserve them through pickling. My dried fruit version of *torshi miveh* was inspired by the simplicity and practicality of a household pickle that I was given each year in Isfahan. The mother of my father's nephew's wife(!) would, over the course of a summer, toss an array of sour cherries, peaches, and plums that had gone unconsumed into a massive vinegar-filled clay jar, about the size of her small-framed body. By summer's end, she had built up a divinely tangy-sweet fruit pickle that she would then portion out in jars and pass around our neighborhood. We all knew to be careful of the pits, which was part of the thrill of eating it! I serve my *torshi miveh* at Sofreh alongside potato *kuku*. Every night, guests ask for more of this fruit pickle to eat by itself. It's also great with roasted and grilled meats, especially roasted turkey, and you can make it year-round, adding fresh sour cherries if glorious spring, in your part of the country, is kind enough to bring you some great ones.

Note This recipe calls for a presterilized mason jar. And this is a refrigerator pickle and the jar does not need to be sealed.

1 cup (160 grams) golden raisins

1 cup (160 grams) currants

1 cup (160 grams) Craisins

2 cups (174 grams) dried plums, quartered

2 cups (320 grams) dried apricots, cut into very thin slices

1 cup (140 grams) pitted sour cherries, if available

⅓ cup (44 grams) crushed garlic (from about 15 cloves)

½ cup nigella seeds

⅓ cup lightly crushed hogweed seeds (see Resources, page 317)

⅓ cup (30 grams) coriander seeds, lightly toasted

¼ cup (28 grams) red chili flakes, or to taste (optional)

3 tablespoons kosher salt, plus more as needed

2 tablespoons granulated sugar, or to taste

¼ cup (60 ml) balsamic vinegar

White wine vinegar or another mild vinegar, such as sherry vinegar

1 Add the raisins, currants, Craisins, plums, apricots, sour cherries, garlic, nigella seeds, hogweed seeds, coriander seeds, and chili flakes, if using, to a large mixing bowl and toss well. Next, add the salt, sugar, and balsamic vinegar, and mix very well.

2 Add as much wine vinegar as needed to cover the fruit by 1 inch, then transfer to a nonreactive (preferably glass) container with a lid and allow to sit, covered, at room temperature for 1 day.

3 Taste and adjust the seasoning, adding more wine vinegar if necessary, before dividing the mixture among presterilized pint mason jars, leaving about 1 inch of space at the top. (You may need to add a bit more vinegar if it seems dry on top.) It will keep for several weeks in the refrigerator.

Date
Pickle

Once, I had a magnificent date pickle that a friend of a friend had made,
its flavor was a crack of lightning: Flash! Wow.
What's in this? I asked.
"Oh, just some dates and carrots and some stuff . . ."
What *else*?
"Tamarind?" she said. *What* ELSE? I pressed. "Vinegar?"
Let's call your friend and ask her, please?
(ring, ring) "*Alo*" (hello).
What's in your marvelous date pickle?
"*Khorma, havij . . . tambre hendi . . . serke.*"
I went home right away and tried to make it. (Long, dejected pause)
"Can you ask your friend for a bit more information?"
Two more tries, then I gave up.
Years later, bored with my pickling repertoire . . . (ring, ring)
It was then I found out that the lady was gone.
And so was her most exciting, memorable date pickle.

SOFREH HOUSE PICKLES

TORSHI LITEH | *makes about 3 pint jars*

Torshi liteh is our national mixed-vegetable pickle side dish, found on every table throughout Iran, and served with rice and stews. It's a permanent fixture on my menu at Sofreh, where my guests love it. But when they ask me what's in it, I notice their eyes drifting off into la-la land after the first ten seconds of me rattling off the lengthy ingredient list. I wake them up by mentioning a touchstone recipe, like Mexican salsa: "Just think of it as a salsa with five more vegetables," I tell them. Or Indian fruit chutney: "Just remove the sweetness of the fruit and replace it with a few more vegetables." Soon they are begging me to teach them to make it. At the end of the day, it's just a bunch of vegetables chopped up into small pieces and thrown together, but what makes it so irresistible is the smoky, creamy eggplant that binds them. I also adore it because it leaves so much room to express yourself. Feel free to add your favorite farmers' market vegetable to the list, as you wish.

Some home cooks boil their cauliflower in vinegar for just a little bit. I prefer not to cook mine at all, instead cutting the raw florets into smaller pieces to leave a bit of crunch. But you decide. *Torshi liteh* gets better tasting when you aerate it, so mix away. If you want to eat your *torshi liteh* sooner than my recipe recommends, go ahead. It may be a little chunkier in texture, but there are no rules on how you may enjoy it.

Note This recipe calls for presterilized mason jars.

1 Char the eggplants: Cover a stove-top range with a layer of aluminum foil for easy cleanup, making sure to keep the burner exposed. Pierce the eggplants with a fork and place them directly on the grate, over a medium flame, and roast, giving a quarter turn now and then, for 1 to 2 minutes on all sides, until the skin is uniformly charred and the flesh is soft. Remove from the heat and set aside on a baking sheet to cool, reserving any liquid that weeps from the eggplants. Alternatively, if using an oven, preheat the oven to 450°F. Poke the eggplants with a fork and place them on a baking sheet to roast until the skin blackens and deflates, about 20 to 30 minutes.

2 When the eggplants are cool enough to handle, peel the skin, pulling out the most charred pieces and finely chopping them to the consistency of a paste. Next, chop the eggplants into bite-size pieces.

3 In a large, nonreactive container with a lid (preferably glass), combine the smoked eggplant and as much of the smoky skin as you wish, to taste. Add the carrots, celery, cabbage, cauliflower, red bell peppers, green bell peppers, jalapeños, garlic, cilantro, parsley, fresh tarragon, rosemary, $\rightarrow$

12 Italian eggplants or 6 large eggplants (about 2 pounds/907 grams)

2 to 3 large carrots, trimmed, peeled, and shredded

½ celery head, inside green leaves and stalks, finely chopped

1 savoy cabbage head, cored, very thinly sliced

1 cauliflower head, cut into bite-size florets

1 red bell pepper, seeded, small diced

1 green bell pepper, seeded, small diced

4 jalapeño peppers, seeded, thinly sliced

1½ garlic heads, roughly chopped $\rightarrow$

fresh mint, nigella seeds, and hogweed seeds, as well as the dried tarragon, dried mint, turmeric, salt, and black pepper, and stir well to combine.

4 Add the white wine and red wine vinegars, plus more as needed to cover the vegetables by 1 inch, and place in a cool, dry place. Check on the mixture every day for 10 days, mixing and tasting, and adding more of each of the vinegars (or just one of them, depending on your taste), topping off the mixture so the vegetables are covered by 1 inch, as well as more salt, because the flavor will get milder.

5 After 10 days, divide the mixture among 3 presterilized pint mason jars and seal. Store in a cool, dark place for 6 to 8 weeks before eating.

1 large bunch fresh cilantro, leaves and tender stems, finely chopped

1 large bunch fresh flat-leaf parsley, leaves and tender stems, finely chopped

1 bunch fresh tarragon, leaves and tender stems, finely chopped

3 to 4 sprigs fresh rosemary, leaves picked and finely chopped

1 bunch fresh mint, leaves and tender stems, finely chopped

2 tablespoons nigella seeds

1 tablespoon hogweed seeds (see Resources, page 317)

½ cup dried tarragon

½ cup dried mint

1 tablespoon ground turmeric

3 tablespoons kosher salt, plus more as needed

2 tablespoons freshly ground black pepper

2 cups (470 ml) white wine vinegar, plus more as needed

2 cups (470 ml) red wine vinegar, plus more as needed

Hogweed Seeds *(Golpar)*

Persian hogweed is a flowering plant in the carrot family that is native to the northern Caspian regions of Iran. The seeds are encased in small, thin pods and are sold dried. They can be used whole or lightly crushed or ground into a powder. Their strong aroma and slightly bitter, earthy taste are wonderful for pickling. *Golpar* is also sprinkled on fresh fava beans, with a dash of salt, and eaten as a snack in the spring.

SALT-BRINED CUCUMBERS

KHIAR SHOOR | *makes about 3 pint jars*

Shoor, meaning "salty," is the defining trait that separates Persian cucumber pickles from the sweet cucumber pickles of other cultures, such as bread and butter pickles. Our method involves a ratio of mostly salt brine to a small amount of vinegar. There is a saying among some families that loosely translates as "We don't touch pickles"—indicating that to make homemade pickles brings bad luck. "Oh, the first time I pickled, someone died!" they'll say (*eye roll*). Wonderfully crunchy, spicy, and versatile, *khiar shoor* makes a great gift.

Note This recipe calls for presterilized mason jars.

1 Bring 8 cups (2 liters) water to a boil in a large pot, add the sea salt, and mix well. Next, add the vinegar, turn off the heat, and let the mixture cool down completely.

2 Place some of the tarragon and dill in the bottom of each of 3 presterilized pint jars, followed by the garlic cloves, chickpeas, and chilies. Next, divide the cucumbers among the jars, packing them in and filling in any gaps with the rest of the tarragon and dill.

3 Pour the vinegar brine into the jars, leaving ½ inch to spare at the top, and seal. Refrigerate for 1 week before eating. They will keep for up to 2 weeks in the refrigerator.

4 to 5 tablespoons coarse sea salt

½ cup (60 ml) white wine vinegar

3 ounces (84 grams) fresh tarragon leaves

2 ounces (56 grams) fresh dill sprigs

9 whole garlic cloves

A few raw chickpeas

A few dried red chili peppers, such as Indian Guntur chilies

2 pounds (907 grams) small, fresh, farmers' market cucumbers, washed and dried

Jams and Marmalades *(Moraba)*

QUINCE JAM

MORABA BEH | *makes about 5 pint jars*

Beh (quince) is native to Iran. One thing that sets apart a very special quince jam from the rest is a deep wine-red color that you can get by preparing it in an untreated copper pot. If you don't have one, that should not discourage you from making this, however. A stainless-steel pot will produce a great-tasting marmalade, although with a lighter red color.

Note Quince seeds contain a lot of pectin that helps thicken jam, so add them to the pot, if you like, but they are not absolutely necessary because the long cook time gives this jam a naturally firm texture. If not using, separate and dry the seeds, and store them in a jar for later. This recipe calls for presterilized mason jars.

1 Place the sugar and 7 cups (1.6 liters) water in a medium, nonreactive pot with a tight-fitting lid and mix until the sugar is well incorporated. Add the cinnamon sticks, cardamom seeds, salt, and quinces.

2 Cover with the lid and bring to a boil, then lower the heat to low and simmer for 2½ to 3 hours, mixing gently every 30 minutes.

3 Remove the lid, add the lemon juice, and check the consistency and depth of color—the texture should be thick and the color light red. Continue cooking, uncovered, until the color deepens to your liking. Remove from the heat and add the walnuts, if using.

4 Cool down the jam to warm and divide among 5 sterilized pint jars. Allow to cool completely before sealing and refrigerating. The jam will keep for up to 2 weeks in the refrigerator.

2½ pounds (1.1 kilograms) granulated sugar

2 large cinnamon sticks (about 3 inches long)

1 tablespoon cardamom seeds

Pinch of kosher salt

6 small to medium quinces (about 3 pounds/1.4 kilograms), washed and dried, cut into ½-inch-thick slices, seeds reserved

3 tablespoons fresh lemon juice

1 cup (125 grams) walnuts (optional)

CARROT JAM with SALTED PISTACHIOS

MORABA HAVIJ | *makes about 4 pint jars*

Giti Joon makes this for me when she visits New York and quinces are not in season. The salted pistachios add even more beauty to this bright, saffron-colored jam. Enjoy it with breakfast, but it's also wonderful with a simple piece of feta cheese or add spoonfuls to yogurt for a nice, sweet snack.

Note To bloom the gelatin sheets, cut them into sections and soak them in ⅓ cup (80 ml) cold water for 5 minutes. Drain the water and squeeze out any excess water from the sheets before adding them to the pot. Alternatively, if you have them on hand, use 1 tablespoon quince seeds, wrapped in cheesecloth, and add them to the pot because they contain a lot of pectin. This recipe calls for presterilized mason jars.

1 Place the carrots in a large, nonreactive pot with a tight-fitting lid (preferably glass) and add the sugar and 2 cups (470 ml) water. Cover with the lid and bring to a boil for 20 minutes.

2 Meanwhile, in a separate pot, add the orange peels and cover with water. Bring them to a boil and continue boiling for 2 to 3 minutes. Pull one out and taste it. If it is still bitter, continue boiling the peels for 2 minutes more before draining and adding to the pot with the carrots. Next, add the gelatin sheets, lower the heat to medium-low, and cook, partially covered, for 30 minutes more. Add the lemon juice and saffron powder. Keep an eye on the mixture and occasionally mix it gently with a wooden spoon, removing any foam that appears on the top—this can cloud the marmalade and may crystallize.

3 Add the pistachios to the pot and cook, uncovered, for 10 minutes more. Remove the pot from the heat.

4 Cool down the jam to warm and divide among 4 sterilized pint jars. Allow to cool completely before sealing and refrigerating. The jam will keep for up to 2 weeks in the refrigerator.

1½ pounds (680 grams) carrots, trimmed, peeled, washed and dried, and shredded

1½ pounds (680 grams) granulated sugar

1 orange, peeled, pith removed, and peels cut into very thin strips

2 bloomed gelatin sheets or 1 tablespoon quince seeds (see headnote)

1 tablespoon fresh lemon juice

¼ teaspoon saffron powder

⅓ cup (33 grams) thinly sliced salted pistachios

SEVILLE ORANGE MARMALADE

MORABA NARANJ | *makes about 2 pint jars*

Seville oranges—known in Iran as *naranj*—grow in abundance in the northern region of Mazandaran and in the south in Shiraz. Their intensely aromatic and beautiful blossoms, as well as their peels, are used to make incredible jams. And they are also used to make *rob-e naranj,* a bitter orange molasses used in cooking, and a bitter orange *sharbat* (syrup). Seville oranges have a very short season in the United States, but getting your hands on them at specialty markets is worth it for this vibrant, sour marmalade that I love.

Note If you don't have a candy thermometer, use the cold plate test. Place a small china plate in the freezer before you begin. To test if your jam has set, drop a teaspoon of the jam onto the plate, wait a few minutes, then run your finger through it. If it wrinkles, it is ready. This recipe calls for presterilized mason jars. You will need to prepare the orange peels 1 day in advance.

1 The day before making this recipe: Cut the oranges in half and juice them. Remove any pulp and seeds from the juice, as well as pulp from the oranges, and store in a covered container for later use in step 3. Store the orange juice as well in a separate, covered container for later use in step 3. Pour boiling hot water over the now-hollow oranges, cover with a lid, and let the oranges sit for 10 hours.

2 The next day, drain the oranges and slice them into thin strips. Carefully scrape off any pith underneath the strips with a paring knife.

3 To make the marmalade: Bring 9 cups (2¼ liters) water to a boil in a large pot with a tight-fitting lid. Place the reserved orange pulp and seeds in a piece of cheesecloth. Gather the corners and tie them together tightly to create a cheesecloth bag. Add it to the pot along with the reserved orange juice, the lemon juice, and salt. Cover and bring to a boil for 30 minutes.

4 Add the orange peels to the pot and simmer gently, uncovered, for 1½ hours.

5 Turn off the heat, let the mixture cool so that you can remove the cheesecloth bag, and squeeze out as much of the pectin as you can. Next, add the sugar to the pot and give it a good stir. Cook, uncovered, until the temperature reads 220°F on a candy thermometer (see headnote). Turn off the heat, remove any white foam from the top, and let sit for 10 minutes.

6 Cool the marmalade down to warm and divide between 2 sterilized pint jars. Allow to cool completely before sealing and refrigerating. The marmalade will keep for up to 2 weeks in the refrigerator.

2½ pounds (1.1 kilograms) Seville oranges, washed and dried

Juice of 2 fresh lemons

Pinch of kosher salt

2½ pounds (1.1 kilograms) granulated sugar

CRUNCHY BUTTERNUT SQUASH JAM with ALMONDS

MORABA KADOO HALVAII | *makes about 2 pint jars*

Food-grade pickling lime wasn't always available in Iran, so Giti Joon would send my father to a construction site to pick up a tiny piece of lime to get her butternut squash crunchy. The construction site stuff is poisonous, but I guess she knew what she was doing—rinsing and washing it fifty times to remove any residue—because we all survived, and her jam was perfect. A spoonful of any *moraba* is lovely swirled into yogurt, when you want something sweet, but the crunchy butternut squash chunks, and the aroma and warmth of cardamom in this jam, make it an especially satisfying after-dinner sweet.

Note If you don't have a candy thermometer, use the cold plate test. Place a small china plate in the freezer before you begin. To test if your jam has set, drop a teaspoon of the jam onto the plate, wait a few minutes, then run your finger through it. If it wrinkles, it is ready. This recipe calls for presterilized mason jars.

1 The day before making the recipe: Combine the pickling lime with 8 cups (2 liters) cold water in a nonreactive bowl (preferably glass) and mix well. Let sit until the lime settles at the bottom.

2 Add the squash to a large, nonreactive container, pour the lime water over it, and let it sit for 10 to 12 hours.

3 The next day: Drain the squash in a colander, rinse very well, and place in a clean container. Pour fresh cold water over it, and let sit for 20 minutes. Repeat this process three times, draining, rinsing, and soaking the squash in a fresh change of cold water, making sure on the last pass that the water runs clear.

4 Combine the sugar with 6 cups (1½ liters) water in a nonreactive pot with a tight-fitting lid (preferably glass) and boil until it thickens slightly and the temperature reads around 150°F on a candy thermometer.

5 Add the squash and cardamom to the boiling syrup, and if using gelatin sheets, add them now. Lower the heat to low, cover with the lid, and cook, partially covered, for 2 hours.

6 Add the lemon juice and almonds, if using, and cook, uncovered, for 10 to 15 minutes, stirring continuously. It's ready when the temperature reads 220°F, or use the cold plate test (see headnote). Remove the pot from the heat and let the jam sit. Remove any foam from the top.

7 Cool down the jam to warm and divide beween 2 sterilized pint jars. Allow to cool completely before sealing and refrigerating. The jam will keep for up to 2 weeks in the refrigerator.

2 tablespoons food-grade pickling lime (see Resources, page 317)

1½ pounds (680 grams) butternut squash, washed, peeled, seeded, and cut to desired shape (about the same size)

1½ pounds (680 grams) granulated sugar

10 to 12 whole cardamom pods, seeds removed, or ½ teaspoon cardamom seeds

2 gelatin sheets (optional)

2 tablespoons fresh lemon juice

½ cup (54 grams) slivered almonds (optional)

SOFREH

Brooklyn, May 2018. After six years of permit delays, the gas and electricity were finally in place at Sofreh. I had spent years meticulously researching and finalizing my menu. And our bright and airy dining room was ready and waiting to receive guests. But we still couldn't open our doors because we were woefully understaffed. Besides myself and a young Iranian sous chef working with me, Soroosh Golbabae, no one—besides a dishwasher who had stayed for two days and then quit—had responded to our ad for help. So, one day, desperate for new hires, I googled "best culinary agency" and landed on a restaurant staffing service. "This is expensive just to hire a cook, Nasim," said Soroosh. "Well, the hell with it, they must be top-notch," I told him.

Indeed, they were expensive! I came to find out later why: they were a nationwide placement agency for executive chefs and general managers. I didn't need an executive chef; I was the chef of Sofreh. What I needed was a cook. Still, staffed or not, I was determined to launch a soft opening for friends and family. With the game plan settled, Akis and I set the date. Unexpectedly, however, Akis had to leave for Greece. "Go to Greece," I remember telling him. "And while you are there, send the invitations out. I'll be swamped!"

The Friday before the event, Soroosh and I worked from early morning until midnight; finally, I retired to the upstairs apartment, where my best friend, Minoo, lived. I had every intention of waking at eight in the morning to receive my delivery of meat and herbs. But instead, that evening, I was overcome with a feeling of terror. Panicked, I began to shake and pace the floor as it dawned on me that I had set everything in motion for Sofreh's opening, but I was entirely unprepared for the amount of work required to pull it off. I took a seat in a cozy chair and, as was my practice, began repeating a mantra to calm myself.

And then, I passed out, waking up at 4:00 p.m. the following day.

Oh my God, what is happening? I thought, as I got in my car and drove to Enchantments, an occult store in the East Village and a place I'd often go in times of despair. I returned home and lit the white candle etched with silver and gold glitter I'd purchased. Then, from stress and exhaustion, I passed out again and woke up at 4:00 a.m. to see the candle flickering— and then, a moment later, go dead. Well, now, this is a sign, I thought. I immediately texted Soroosh and emailed Akis in Greece: DON'T ASK ME QUESTIONS. RETRACT THE INVITATIONS IF YOU HAVE SENT THEM. SOFREH'S SOFT OPENING IS POSTPONED. And it was then that I noticed a new, random message in my email.

> *Hello,*
>
> *My name is Ali Saboor. I saw your ad. And I looked at your website.*
> *Opening a new restaurant can be a scary process . . .*

Well, that struck a chord in me! Ali, a corporate chef, was running two ski resorts in Southern California. He had been surprised to see our job posting for a new Iranian restaurant opening that wasn't a *kabab* house. I continued reading: *I've never been to Brooklyn and can come for a few days, at my own expense. I can help you set up, wash dishes, organize your walk-in refrigerator, whatever you need.*

I immediately wrote him asking: *When can you come?*

Ali came to Sofreh within days of our email exchange to help with the now-rescheduled soft opening. I'll never forget meeting him in person for the first time. Because of the way the morning sunlight showers in through the front windows of the restaurant, all I saw was a backpack approaching me. But as I drew closer and offered my hand, I took one look at his face, and felt a sense of familiarity. "We don't have anybody," I said, giving him a tour of my walk-in refrigerator. "I don't know if it's New York or it's me, but opening a restaurant has been very difficult," I confided. "No," he said, with an understanding that immediately put me at ease, "it's kind of common." And before I knew it, he opened his backpack, took out his knives, and he, Soroosh, and I got to work chopping, butchering, and prepping over two days to feed our guests.

On the evening of the friends and family dinner, my circle of friends started trickling in. Ali surprised me. "Say hello to your guests," he said. "They are here for you." While Ali and Soroosh managed the kitchen, I set off to welcome everyone. It was a surreal whirlwind of celebrating that lasted until around 2:00 a.m., when our little crew finished cleaning up from a dishwasher that had stopped working and flooded the downstairs prep kitchen. We opened up a bottle of tequila and toasted.

The next day, Ali and I met near Brooklyn Bridge Park and ended up spending the day together. I found out that his mother had brought him and his brother to the United States from Iran when he was twelve, shortly after the Iran-Iraq war. He had grown up mainly in Southern California, and his first kitchen job, in high school, was at his aunt's restaurant. Over two decades, he rose through the ranks to manage multimillion-dollar corporate restaurants, where he had spent the previous ten years.

I REALIZED I WAS NOT JUST CREATING A SPACE TO SHOWCASE PERSIAN FOOD AND CULTURE; I WAS OFFERING, THROUGH FOOD, A RETURN HOME.

Ali canceled his plans to return home to California, agreeing to stay in New York for a few more days to help me and Akis hire staff and see us through to our official opening.

Sofreh opened to the public in June 2018, and from the start, we enjoyed tremendous success, most especially from our Brooklyn community. To my delight, I noticed that when Iranian guests entered the restaurant, they would take one look at the bright, airy space and immediately relax, as if they could tell that I wasn't out to prove that my *ghormeh sabzi* was better than their grandmothers'.

As much as I love food and live for food, for me, food doesn't make sense if it doesn't have a community to share it with. I live to see my guests' empty plates. I love carrying more warm bread, more yogurt, more rice. A shot of liquor on the house here, a taste of a new marmalade I am working on there. I am always looking for ways to show that, in Iran, food and the warmth with which it's offered are inextricably linked. Some nights, I stop in my tracks to take in the look of pleasure on someone's face as they experience, for the first time, the mouthwatering flavor of sun-dried lime laid bare. Early on, I realized I was not just creating a space to showcase Persian food and culture; I was offering, through food, a return home, if only through memory, for Iranians. And although I had done the cooking, I soon realized that I was being nourished tenfold in return.

One weekend, shortly after Pete Wells's review of Sofreh in *The New York Times* came out, I was about to head home after a sixteen-hour workday when a woman about my age stood up from her chair and approached me. "Congratulations," she said to me in Farsi. "I drove three hours from Long Island to be here tonight, and I wanted you to have this." And she presented me with a framed copy of the article decorated with a little ribbon. It was a moment of arrival for me.

In those early days, Ali revamped my mother's *khoresht-e aloo*, a one-pot stew of chicken with sour plums and barberries, into a gorgeous sheet of crispy Chicken with Prune Sauce (page 289) that our guests immediately loved. I'd look around the room and take in the smiles of satisfaction on their faces and knew that it could not have been a better choice to express my mother's stew. Admittedly, I had balked at first. I was so culturally and emotionally attached to my home-cooked version. Still, I couldn't deny that the flavors of my mother's *khoresht*, a sauce that carried the warmth of cinnamon, the sweetness of dried plums, and the tartness of barberries, were shining through. But I also felt other suggestions betrayed time-honored traditions of Persian cooking, and I could not put them on my menu because they didn't have the cultural context that I stood for. From the moment I had met Ali, I had known that he had come into my life, however randomly, for a reason. But at times, we found ourselves butting heads, as I was as protective and stubborn as a new mother with her firstborn.

One day, I sought the counsel of a wise friend. I knew, in my heart, that Ali and I had the potential for an incredible culinary partnership. I was a keeper of centuries of tradition. And he had a wealth of professional experience managing restaurants. But our communication in the kitchen had come to an impasse. She told me, "Nasim, show him your roots." Before we had opened Sofreh, my father had brought me a tiny grapevine tendril from his garden in Iran, the origins of which were from my grandmother Khanoom's village in Dehagh. Inches tall, the tendril had two leaves when he had planted it in June. "Ali," I said, pointing to the grapevine that had by now grown several feet up the sides of the garden wall. "I planted my roots in the soil of Brooklyn," I continued. "My culture and tradition are here, at Sofreh, and they can belong to you, too, if you claim them."

Ali and I continued working together at Sofreh, and I grew as a person, chef, and restaurateur in the process. We developed a process for creating new Persian dishes for our menu, and this chapter honors and celebrates those collaborations. Our approach looks to our shared roots, combining my knowledge of authenticity, history, and tradition and Ali's extensive experience in professional restaurant kitchens to bring a new world of Persian food to New York City, and now, to you.

The Journey of Sofreh Bread

NASIM: When I thought about the fresh bread I wanted to bake at Sofreh, there was no question that I wanted it to be *sangak.* First, it's a bread with a good amount of whole wheat flour. For years, I had been chasing the memory of the unprocessed whole grain, chewy flavor of my grandmother Khanoom's villager bread. But, more important, I wanted a naturally leavened bread with a long fermentation process, which breaks down the gluten proteins, making it easier to digest in this age of gluten sensitivities.

Over four or five years, I went back and forth to Iran to research and develop my recipe, often visiting the *sangak* bakery blocks from my parents' home in Isfahan. Because of *sangak's* high hydration, the bakers scoop up the very wet, heavy dough, then flatten it on the peel. Then they scoop more water on top to smash the dough into a superthin layer before heaving it into the oven. *Sangak's* signature pebble-dimpled crispy bottom is formed when the water hits the *sang*—little pebbles on the bottom of the oven. When I tried making it once at the bakery, it felt like I was trying to balance water on a stick! I kept dropping it, and everyone laughed. It was either that or the novelty of seeing a woman at the bakery oven. On those trips, I was seriously trying to figure out how to bring a *sangak* oven to Brooklyn. I was so determined that I even considered hiring a master baker from Iran to make me one. But the cost and logistics weren't working out, and when I came back, I started searching for an oven that could deliver similar results. I saw a family-owned Palestinian company online called Spinning Grillers that specializes in Middle Eastern kitchen equipment. The guy told me, "Your *sangak* bread sounds like a Palestinian bread my parents grew up with called *taboon*," so I made an appointment to test my recipe in their commercial pita oven. I jumped into my car, with my dough and my son, Noony, who came along for the two-hour ride to upstate New York. It was so hot that summer day that my bread dough began rising, and I kept yelling at Noony, "Beat it! Punch it down!" In a panic, I called the company from the road and told them to get the oven ready because my bread was rising right out of the container. When we arrived, the entire family was gathered around the oven, no doubt curious about the crazy lady coming from the city. I baked my dough on the premises, and while its look needed more work, the flavor was spot-on. I had my bread oven in place for many months before we opened Sofreh. But when we ended up opening for the friends and family event, it was all rush, rush, rush and my bread dough was too runny for my bread oven. So, I bought *barbari* bread from a bakery I knew in Brooklyn because I just didn't have time to get mine where I wanted it. But Ali said, "Give me two days."

ALI: She was being pragmatic, trying to balance all the moving parts of opening a restaurant, and I guess I was the one who was being unreasonable! But I had made bread at pretty much every restaurant I have ever worked. At Tony Mantuano's restaurant Lorenzo in Miami, I worked with Tony's great pizza dough recipe and that gave me a lot of experience with hydration, mixing, and aging. We had Nasim's recipe and we had the oven, so I really wanted to make bread in-house.

NASIM: Ali developed a love-hate relationship with my oven. It rotates, with heating elements on the top and bottom, so you can't shape the bread on a stone or a peel, as you would normally do for making a flatbread.

ALI: Well, necessity is the mother of invention, and I guess I grew to love that oven because it led me to the technique for shaping Sofreh bread. For the dough, we make the sponge in the morning on day one, raise it for two days, then we make the dough and age that overnight. The next day, we portion out doughballs and age them overnight again, so that the following day, when we are going to use it, we do a final proof before using water to hand shape each piece of dough on the rotating oven top, so that its bottom gets nice and crispy, like *sangak*. The crumb itself is proofed and fluffier, so although it has the flavor of *sangak*, it resembles *barbari*. And, we added nigella seeds from *sangak* and sesame seeds from *barbari*, too.

NASIM: It's been a journey that evolved organically, and with trial and error, Ali tweaking the amount of water, salt, and the aging of the dough each day. If you look at the picture of the first generation of Sofreh bread on our website, it looks like a baby version of what our bread is today. But I keep that image because it's a metaphor for how far we've come. We've matured, we're grounded, we're *ja-oftadeh,* as they say in Farsi. We've found our place with our bread.

ALI: Bread making is a humbling experience. You can fix a sauce, or change the way you braise a dish, but bread is the one thing that you can't forget about, lie about, or garnish your way out of it. If you don't take care of it, or if you try to rush it, your dough will let you know. And I think even after all these years, it still makes my day when I see beautiful bread at Sofreh. It just makes me a little happier.

NASIM: When Iranians come to Sofreh, they taste our bread and say, "Wow, what a strange-looking *sangak*!" But because they remember the flavor, the look doesn't matter. It's a bread that belongs to Sofreh. Every time I know somebody is going to Iran, I send them a pack of frozen Sofreh bread to take to my family. I can't even believe that I am sending bread to Iran—it's surreal. And when people from back home— my father, my uncle, the people who go every day to get bread at the local bakery—tell me they prefer our bread, I beam with pride.

SOFREH BREAD

makes 18 to 20 pieces

This bread is the first thing Ali and I worked on together. It's a crispy-bottomed flatbread with an airy crumb that's topped with sesame and nigella seeds, which release their aromas when they bake. We drew inspiration from two iconic Iranian breads—super-crispy *sangak,* which is made using a wet dough method, and a lighter, airier, twice-proofed and shaped *barbari.* If you take time and care, giving yourself space to practice, pulling these warm loaves out of the oven will come to feel very rewarding. The loaves freeze very well, so making a big batch ensures you have plenty on hand to enjoy with every meal.

Note This recipe requires several days to make.

1 Make the bread sponge: Combine the whole wheat flour, sugar, yeast, and about 1¼ cups (300 ml) room-temperature water in a mixing bowl, and using a large spoon, stir until well combined. Cover with plastic wrap and place in the refrigerator overnight.

2 After 12 to 18 hours, place the bread sponge and 2 cups (470 ml) cold water in the bowl of a standing mixer fitted with the dough hook. Combine the all-purpose flour and salt and add to the mixing bowl. Mix on low speed until the mixture forms a ball. Scrape down the sides and bottom of the mixing bowl with a rubber spatula, ensuring all ingredients are incorporated. Continue mixing/kneading the dough in the mixer on medium-low speed for 15 minutes, until the dough becomes soft and elastic. Allow the dough to proof in the refrigerator overnight.

3 The next day, portion the dough into 4-ounce (112-gram) balls. Lightly sprinkle the bottom of a container with all-purpose flour, place the balls inside, and cover with plastic wrap. Allow to proof overnight in the refrigerator.

4 On baking day, pull the doughballs from the refrigerator 2 hours before baking. Allow them to come to room temperature and finish proofing.

5 Next, shape the dough by flattening it with your hands or a rolling pin into a long, oval shape (if the dough is sticky, you may dust with flour), then use your fingers to press 3 lengthwise parallel lines into the dough. (Be sure to press firmly until you feel the work surface.) Next, place parchment paper on the back side of an inverted baking sheet and lightly sprinkle the paper with flour. Transfer your shaped bread dough by grabbing both ends with your hands and stretching it to about 9 inches long and 3 inches wide, then →

For the bread sponge
1½ cups (200 grams) whole wheat flour

1 tablespoon granulated sugar

1 tablespoon active dry yeast

For the main dough
8½ cups (1,070 grams) all-purpose flour

2 tablespoons kosher salt

For the topping
2 tablespoons sesame seeds

2 tablespoons nigella seeds

place it onto the floured parchment paper. Cover the dough with plastic wrap and allow it to rest for 45 minutes at room temperature.

6 In the meantime, place a baking stone or a large, inverted baking sheet inside the oven and preheat the oven and the stone to 450°F.

7 Gently uncover the bread. Sprinkle with the desired amount of sesame and nigella seeds. Open the preheated oven door and slide the parchment paper with the dough on it onto the baking stone in the oven. Bake for 12 to 15 minutes until golden brown. Transfer the bread to a cooling rack and allow to cool.

8 Work in batches to bake the rest of the bread, allowing the baking stone to reheat between batches. You may place the dough back in the refrigerator if the dough starts to overproof.

Note If you are consuming this bread within 24 hours, store it under a cake dome. Otherwise, wrap the loaves in plastic wrap and store them in the freezer for up to 2 months. Reheat them in a toaster oven before serving.

BEEF TONGUE SANDWICH

makes 8 large sandwiches or many small appetizers

Tongue sandwiches are an institution in Iran and are traditionally made with small lamb's tongues that are slow-cooked until soft and melt-in-your-mouth divine. After school, my friends and I would grab lamb's tongue on a baguette with pickles and onions from street-food places in much the same way kids in America go for a slice of pizza. Later in New York, when I couldn't easily find lamb's tongue, I swapped it out for beef tongue, and made canapés for my home parties. I enhanced my childhood sandwich by tucking slices of tongue into mini pitas, along with pickled jalapeños, lightly marinated red onions dusted with tangy sumac, slivers of sour lime, and a bit of parsley drizzled with excellent olive oil. Or sometimes, I would make tongue into a roll on lavash bread. When I offered this nostalgic sandwich at Sofreh, I fancied it up even further by adding jalapeño aioli. It was so wildly popular that I had to discontinue it because each sandwich required *à la minute* assembly, and our sauté guy couldn't keep up with the barrage of orders each night, slowing down service for the rest of the dishes!

Note Because beef tongue can weigh between 12 and 15 pounds (5.4 and 6.8 kilograms), you can make it in advance and freeze it in its juices until ready to slice and reheat.

1 Add the onions and 4 tablespoons olive oil to a large, heavy-bottomed pot with a tight-fitting lid and sauté over medium heat, adding more oil if needed, so that the onions turn golden, their edges darken, and they soften, about 5 to 7 minutes. Add the turmeric, a bit more oil, and stir, allowing the turmeric to bloom and release its fragrance, about 1 minute more.

2 Add the tongue to the center of the pot, along with the sun-dried limes, bay leaves, cinnamon sticks, peppercorns, salt, and 3 cups (¾ liter) water. Cover with the lid and bring to a boil, then reduce the heat to a gentle boil and cook, covered, for 3½ hours, checking often to make sure there is enough liquid to cover, adding more if necessary. Halfway through the cooking time, flip the tongue.

3 To test that the tongue is fully cooked, insert a cake tester into the thickest part, and if there is no resistance, it is done.

4 Remove the tongue from the pot, and when it is just cool enough to handle, remove the skin. (It should come off easily while the tongue is still warm.) Next, strain the cooking liquid and reserve for reheating. (Refrigerate the cooking liquid in a covered container until ready to use. If you are →

For the beef tongue

1 pound (454 grams) yellow onions, medium diced

Light olive oil

1½ tablespoons ground turmeric

5 to 6 pounds (2.2 to 2.7 kilograms) beef tongue, skin on, rinsed and trimmed of excess fat

2 large sun-dried limes

6 dried bay leaves

2 large cinnamon sticks (about 3 inches long)

1½ tablespoons whole black peppercorns

2 tablespoons kosher salt

Jalapeño aioli for serving (see page 274)

Store-bought pita or other sandwich bread →

freezing the tongue, slice it on the diagonal to your desired thickness first, and then freeze it in its cooking liquid.)

5 When ready to serve, slice the tongue on the diagonal, portioning for the number of sandwiches you'd like, and reheat by gently simmering it in the reserved liquid.

6 Prepare the jalapeño aioli: Grill or broil the jalapeño until soft. Remove the skin and seeds and add the jalapeño flesh, mayonnaise, garlic, lime juice, and salt to a food processor and pulse until well combined. Taste and adjust the seasoning.

7 Serve the warmed tongue on pita bread, with the jalapeño aioli and some sliced red onions tossed with sumac.

Red onion, thinly sliced on a mandoline, for serving

Sumac for serving

For the jalapeño aioli

1 whole jalapeño pepper

¾ cup (180 ml) good-quality store-bought mayonnaise

1 tablespoon minced garlic

¼ cup (60 ml) lime juice, fresh or bottled

¼ teaspoon kosher salt

SPICY TAHINI DATE SALAD

makes 4 salads, plus more chili paste and dressing for another use

Early in our collaboration, Ali suggested that we include a leafy green salad on the menu. Because I love making salad dressings with yogurt, it was a no-brainer for me to turn to yogurt to build my dressing's base. And then a lightbulb went off in my head! It was date season. I remembered visiting a friend in the south of Iran who had set out a platter of glorious, caramel-sweet dates, along with a bowl of tahini and another little bowl of spicy chili powder for us to dip the dates first in the tahini, then in a touch of spice. The combination of the sweetness, nuttiness, and heat was exquisite. I knew right away that I wanted these three flavors for my dressing. But what is a salad without a crunch? So, we toasted sesame seeds, of course.

Note You may also use romaine, or another crispy lettuce, if you like.

1 Prepare the chili paste: Toast the guajillo chilies and chile de árbol in a cast-iron skillet over medium-high heat, about 2 minutes per side, until fragrant.

2 Slice the chilies open, remove the seeds, add the chilies to a small pot with enough water to cover, and simmer until soft, about 10 minutes. Drain, reserving a bit of the liquid.

3 Using a blender or food processor, puree the chilies with a small amount of the simmering liquid to achieve the consistency of a paste and set aside.

4 Prepare the dressing: Combine the tahini, yogurt, sugar, salt, lemon juice, and chili paste in a mixing bowl, and use a hand mixer to mix until well blended. Next, slowly add 2 to 3 tablespoons ice water to the mixture, and continue mixing, adding more ice water if needed, until the mixture reaches the consistency of a creamy salad dressing. Taste and adjust the seasoning and set aside.

5 Toast the sesame seeds in a dry sauté pan over medium-low heat until dark golden brown, about 4 to 6 minutes. Remove from the pan and set aside. Next, using the same pan, add oil and lightly sauté the dates until warmed through and soft. Keep warm.

6 To assemble the salad: Julienne some of the lettuce to use as a filling, using the remaining leaves for lettuce cups. Fill the cups with the warmed dates, diced radishes, julienned lettuce, and tahini dressing. Top with the toasted sesame seeds.

Note You will have leftover chili paste and tahini dressing for later use. Store in separate airtight containers in the refrigerator for up to 1 week.

For the chili paste
4 whole dried guajillo chilies

1 whole dried chile de árbol

For the dressing and salad
¼ cup (60 ml) tahini (preferably Al Wadi or similar quality), mixed well before removing from the container

2 cups (570 grams) Homemade Yogurt (page 32) or store-bought Greek yogurt

2 tablespoons granulated sugar

1 tablespoon kosher salt

¼ cup (60 ml) bottled lemon juice

3 tablespoons chili paste (see above)

White sesame seeds

Neutral oil, such as vegetable or canola oil

8 to 10 Medjool dates, from California or similar quality, seeded and halved

4 Little Gem red lettuce heads, halved, washed and dried

2 watermelon radishes, diced or thinly shaved on a mandoline

WATERMELON FETA SALAD

makes 4 to 6 serving

As a kid, most of my summertime dinners were composed of our pick of luscious pears, muskmelons or watermelons, bread, and feta cheese. Isfahani watermelons are renowned for being juicy sweet, with bright red flesh and tiny seeds. Ali and I certainly didn't invent this sweet and salty combination that you'll find throughout the Middle East and the Mediterranean, but we have our own special spin. We dress frisée with lemon juice and excellent olive oil for a lovely acidic component. And instead of hunks of feta, we whip the cheese with cream until it's soft and delicate, then shape it into little feta balls. Ali added mint oil, traditionally used to garnish *a'ash* (see pages 189–209), as a complementary herbaceous pairing with the watermelon. And a surprising sprinkle of nigella seeds gives lovely texture and perfume.

1 Combine the feta and heavy cream in a food processor fitted with a steel blade and blend until creamy. Use a small cookie scoop to portion the mixture into round balls and set aside.

2 Place the frisée in a large bowl, season with salt and pepper, and add the olive oil.

3 To assemble the salad: Layer the frisée on a serving platter, place the feta balls in the center, and arrange the watermelon cubes around it. Garnish with the nigella seeds, followed by the lemon zest and drizzles of mint oil.

12 ounces (340 grams) feta cheese, drained and crumbled

¼ cup (60 ml) heavy cream

2 frisée heads, light green tender parts, washed and dried, torn into bite-size pieces

Kosher salt to taste

Freshly ground black pepper to taste

4 to 6 tablespoons extra-virgin olive oil

3 cups (about 356 grams) or more cubed, seeded, and chilled watermelon

1 tablespoon nigella seeds

Zest of 1 fresh lemon

¼ cup (60 ml) Mint Oil (page 196)

ROASTED CAULIFLOWER
with SHALLOT YOGURT
and PISTACHIOS

GOL KALAM JAGHOOR BAGHOOR | *makes 4 to 6 servings*

The idea for this dish comes from *jaghoor baghoor,* a popular street food in the northwestern city of Zanjan, where it is made with a sauté of lamb's liver glazed with a glorious sauce that is at once earthy, tart, and umami-rich. I've also seen it served as a *mazza* (little plate) to accompany rounds of vodka, because there's nothing like fatty, unctuous livers to stand up to harsh alcohol. Ali had an idea to pickle and roast hearty cauliflower, which mimics the mineral characteristics of offal. Apart from being so delicious, this dish is significant to us because it's the first time we cracked open the textures and flavors of a traditional Persian dish and created something entirely new. When older Iranians come to Sofreh and see *jaghoor baghoor* in Farsi, next to the English name on our menu, and say, "Where's the liver," I have a lot of explaining to do. See the photograph on page 262.

1 Prepare the cauliflower: Combine 4 cups (1 liter) water, the vinegar, lemon juice, salt, sugar, and turmeric in a large saucepan and bring to a boil. Lower the heat and simmer, stirring occasionally, for 5 minutes.

2 Place the cauliflower florets in a large bowl, pour the pickling mixture over them, lay a suitably sized plate over the top—with a weight on it if necessary—to keep them submerged for 30 minutes. Meanwhile, prepare the tomato chili glaze.

3 Add the onions and 4 tablespoons olive oil to a large sauté pan and sauté over medium heat, adding more oil if needed, so that the onions turn golden, their edges darken, and they soften, about 5 to 7 minutes. Add the salt, garlic, and ginger, then stir and cook for 2 minutes. Lower the heat to medium and add the turmeric, dried lime powder, and cinnamon. Stir and cook for 1 minute more. Add the chili paste, stir to incorporate, and cook for 2 minutes.

4 Next, add the guajillo chili puree and chile de árbol puree and cook for 1 minute more. Add the lemon juice and ½ cup (120 ml) water, and stir well to incorporate. Lower the heat to a simmer and cook, stirring occasionally, until the liquid is reduced by half.

5 Add the sugar, stir to incorporate, then remove from the heat. Use an immersion blender to puree; adjust the seasoning. Set aside to cool.

For the pickled cauliflower

½ cup (120 ml) white wine vinegar

¼ cup (60 ml) bottled lemon juice

1 tablespoon kosher salt

2 tablespoons granulated sugar

1 teaspoon ground turmeric

1 whole large cauliflower head, broken into florets, about 1- to 2-inch pieces

Shallot Yogurt (page 36) for serving

Salted pistachios for garnish

Pickled vegetables of your choice for serving (optional)

For the tomato chili glaze

1 large yellow onion, medium diced

Light olive oil

1 teaspoon kosher salt

2 garlic cloves, minced

1 tablespoon minced fresh ginger

½ teaspoon ground turmeric

6 Preheat the oven to 425°F.

7 Drain and transfer the pickled cauliflower florets to a mixing bowl and gently combine with the tomato chili glaze. Transfer the cauliflower to a shallow ovenproof pan and cook until well roasted and slightly charred, 5 to 10 minutes.

8 To serve, plate as you like with shallot yogurt, and garnish with salted pistachios and more pickled vegetables of your choice.

½ teaspoon dried lime powder

½ teaspoon ground cinnamon

2 tablespoons chili paste (see page 277), homemade or store-bought

2 tablespoons guajillo chili puree, homemade (chilies pureed as on page 277) or store-bought

1 tablespoon chile de árbol puree, homemade (chilies pureed as on page 277) or store-bought

2 tablespoons fresh lemon juice

1 teaspoon granulated sugar

POTATO PANCAKES with SOUR CHERRY MARMALADE

KUKU GHANDI | *makes 4 to 6 pancakes*

I love to include a seasonal *kuku* (see pages 211–219) on my menu, and this take came about when I told Ali that every summer Giti Joon serves her Sour Cherry Rice (page 67) with a sweet version of a savory potato pancake that's unique to Isfahan called *kuku ghandi*. He suggested that we offer the sour cherry as a compote to serve alongside the traditional pancakes at Sofreh. I tweaked my mom's pancake recipe, because it's too eggy for my taste, but I still glaze it in saffron and rosewater syrup to sweeten it, as she does. Once we garnished the *kuku* with the sunshine yellow of lemon zest, the beauty of dried rose petals, and the freshness of mint, we had a dish that distills the Isfahani summers of my childhood into one bite.

1 Prepare the saffron syrup: Combine the sugar and 1 cup (235 ml) water in a small saucepan, and heat over medium-low heat until the sugar melts, and the mixture reaches 200°F and has a syrup-like texture. Add the saffron powder and salt and continue cooking for 1 to 2 minutes, until the liquid reaches about 210°F on a candy thermometer. Remove from the heat, add the rosewater, and set aside at room temperature until ready to use.

2 Prepare the sour cherry compote: In a small saucepan, reduce the sour cherry liquid by half until the liquid thickens to a syrupy consistency and reaches 200°F. Next, add the sugar, lemon juice, and drained sour cherries. Continue to cook on high heat for about 5 minutes, until the mixture reaches 210°F. Set aside at room temperature until ready to use.

3 Preheat the oven to 450°F.

4 Prepare the pancakes: Pierce the potatoes with a fork, season with salt, and bake on a baking sheet for 45 minutes until tender. Peel and set aside.

5 When the potatoes are cool enough to handle, use a box grater to grate them. Combine the potatoes and onion in a large mixing bowl and add the chickpea flour, salt, and turmeric. Taste and adjust for salt, adding more if needed. Next, add the egg and mix to combine.

6 Shape the mixture into small round or oval-shaped patties and place them on a baking sheet in the refrigerator to firm up for a minimum of 30 minutes.

7 Coat the bottom of an 11-inch sauté pan with the neutral oil and warm over medium heat. Remove the pancakes from the refrigerator and panfry, working in batches, until golden brown, adding more oil if needed, about →

For the saffron syrup

2 cups (400 grams) granulated sugar

⅛ teaspoon saffron powder (about 10 to 15 threads ground)

Pinch of kosher salt

¼ cup (60 ml) rosewater

For the sour cherry compote

One 32-ounce (907-gram) jar sour cherries in light syrup, drained, both liquid and cherries reserved (12 ounces/350 ml liquid, 6 ounces/170 grams sour cherries)

⅓ cup (66 grams) granulated sugar

1 teaspoon fresh lemon juice

For the potato pancakes

3 medium russet potatoes

Kosher salt

1 small yellow onion, finely grated, squeezed of excess water

2½ tablespoons chickpea flour

1 tablespoon kosher salt, or more to taste

2 teaspoons ground turmeric →

1 minute per side. Next, lower the heat and pour the saffron syrup mixture over the pancakes, coating them generously with the syrup. Simmer for 1 minute, then remove them from the pan and place on a cooling rack to drain the excess syrup.

8 To serve, sprinkle the sea salt flakes on top of each pancake and garnish each with spoonfuls of sour cherry compote, lemon zest, dried rose petals, and micro mint.

1 large egg, lightly beaten

Neutral oil, such as vegetable or canola oil, for frying

Sea salt flakes for finishing

Lemon zest for garnish

Dried rose petals for garnish

Fresh micro mint leaves for garnish

DUCK FESENJAN

makes 4 servings

Khoresht-e fesenjan (*fesenjan* stew) has been cooked in Iran since the days of the First Persian Empire more than two thousand years ago. It's an enticing, darkly crimson-colored stew of finely ground walnuts and tart pomegranate molasses and is synonymous with wedding celebrations, wealth, and royalty. Its heavenly aroma, sublimely rich texture, and layers of sweet and sour are transporting—one bite has you hooked. So, of course, I wanted to offer it at Sofreh. You'll find *khoresht-e fesenjan* throughout Iran, most commonly made with chicken slow-cooked in the sauce, as well as served with meatballs, and I cook it both ways in my home. But, Ali and I wanted to make a more exultant version for our guests. We took inspiration from the northern Gilan province's tradition of making *fesenjan* with wild ducks, but I didn't want to add even more layers of fat to an already decadent dish. So, we decided to prepare the duck two ways. We slowly roast the duck legs, set them in the *fesenjan* until they are fall-apart tender, and then serve a lightly cured, pan-seared duck breast alongside.

You won't find duck *fesenjan* on the menu year-round. (My father used to say, "What's the point of calling something special when you can have it every day?") But, if you've fallen in love with my *fesenjan,* I'll tell you what I tell my daughter, Soshy, who complains that I don't make it for her often enough at home: "Now is an excellent time to learn how to cook it so you can eat it anytime you want."

Note The flavor profile of *fesenjan* in Gilan can be very sharp, because cooks there use a highly prized, low-production molasses made from a very sour, wild pomegranate. But for me, a great *fesenjan* strikes a perfect balance of sweet and sour on the palate, known as *malas* in Farsi.

1 Prepare the *fesenjan* sauce: Grate the butternut squash in a food processor fitted with the S blade and set aside.

2 Add the onions and 4 tablespoons olive oil to a large, heavy-bottomed pot with a tight-fitting lid and sauté over medium heat, adding more oil if needed, so that the onions turn golden, their edges darken, and they soften, about 5 to 7 minutes. Add the squash, a bit more oil if needed, and continue sautéing until well browned and tender, about 10 to 15 minutes. Add the turmeric, a bit more oil, and sauté for a few minutes, and then add the walnuts, stirring to coat well.

3 Add 3 cups (¾ liter) water, mix well, and cover with the lid. Raise the heat to high and bring to a boil, then reduce the heat to low and cook, →

For the *fesenjan* sauce

¾ pound (340 grams) butternut squash, peeled, seeded, and cut into pieces small enough to fit in a food processor

1 large yellow onion, medium diced

Light olive oil

1 tablespoon ground turmeric

1 pound (454 grams) walnuts, finely chopped in a food processor

1 to 2 tablespoons granulated sugar →

covered, for about 1 hour. Remove the lid, add the sugar, salt, pomegranate molasses, and lemon juice. Mix well and taste for seasoning. Return the lid and continue cooking for 30 minutes more.

4 At this point, uncover and cook on low for 1 hour more, until the color starts changing, stirring gently and often, so it doesn't stick. The longer you cook uncovered, the darker the sauce will get. When the oil separates on top, it is a sign the sauce is perfect. Remove from the heat and set aside.

5 Meanwhile, lightly cure the duck breast: Toast the coriander seeds, black peppercorns, and cinnamon in a dry pan over medium heat, until the spices are fragrant. Transfer to a mortar and pestle and pound until the seeds are cracked and the cinnamon is in large pieces. In a separate mixing bowl, combine the salt, sugar, bay leaf, and spice mixture from the mortar and pestle and set aside.

6 Gently score the duck breast and place in a small, nonreactive container. Cover the entire breast with the dry rub cure and place in the refrigerator for 45 minutes to 1 hour. Remove the duck breast from the cure rub, rinse it, and pat it dry with paper towels. Refrigerate until ready to cook.

7 Meanwhile, cook the duck legs. Preheat a medium sauté pan over medium-low heat for 1 minute. Season the duck legs with a pinch of salt and sear over low heat until golden brown on all sides, about 3 to 5 minutes. (No oil is needed as the duck legs will render out their own fat.) Next, transfer the duck legs to a medium stockpot with a tight-fitting lid and add enough reserved *fesenjan* sauce to cover them halfway (saving any remaining sauce for plating). Next, add enough water or chicken stock, if using, to cover the duck legs completely. Cover with the lid and cook over low heat for 1 to 1½ hours, until tender and falling off the bone. Allow to cool in the sauce.

8 Meanwhile, when you are ready to cook the breast, remove it from the refrigerator and allow it to come to room temperature for 10 to 15 minutes.

9 Place a medium sauté pan over low heat for 1 minute, then place the duck breast, skin side down, in the pan. Slowly allow the duck breast to render out its fat and crisp up, removing the excess fat from the pan as needed. Continue to cook for 7 to 8 minutes on the skin side until golden brown and the duck breast begins to firm. Next, flip the breast and continue to cook on low heat, basting it with its own fat, for 2 to 3 minutes. Remove the duck breast from the heat. For medium temperature, the breast should feel slightly firmer to the touch and the internal temperature should read 135° to 140°F on a meat thermometer. Allow to rest for 5 to 7 minutes prior to slicing.

10 To serve, cover the plate with some of the sauce and place the duck legs on top, followed by the sliced breast. Top with more sauce or serve extra sauce on the side.

Kosher salt to taste

1 cup (235 ml) pomegranate molasses (preferably Al Wadi)

¼ cup (60 ml) bottled lemon juice

For the duck

1 teaspoon coriander seeds

1 teaspoon black peppercorns

1 cinnamon stick (about 2 inches long)

Kosher salt

½ cup (100 grams) granulated sugar

1 dried bay leaf

One whole Long Island duck (4 to 5 pounds/about 1.1 to 2.2 kilograms), legs and whole breast separated

1 cup (235 ml) or more chicken stock, homemade or store-bought (optional)

CHICKEN with PRUNE SAUCE

makes 4 servings

For the soft opening of Sofreh, I served *khoresh-e aloo*—a comforting chicken stew from Isfahan that I grew up eating—and made it with plump, sweet and sour, golden *aloo baraghani* prunes that I had brought back with me from Iran. I spent the night going table to table, warning my guests to be careful, fearing that someone would choke or break a tooth, because the prunes still had pits in them! Shortly after, Ali suggested that we marinate and grill a beautiful, air-chilled Bell & Evans half chicken, rendering the skin crispy and then strewing my prune sauce over the bird.

Note Marinate the chicken overnight before making this recipe.

1 One day before cooking, marinate the chicken: Grate the onion on a box grater's largest holes into a large mixing bowl, keeping all the juices in the bowl. Next, in a small saucepan, combine the lemon juice, 1 tablespoon salt, the turmeric, paprika, peppercorns, and bay leaves, and bring to a simmer over medium heat until everything is incorporated, about 30 seconds. Remove the pan from the heat and add the ice to cool down the mixture, then add the cooled mixture to the bowl with the grated onion.

2 Place the chicken in a container large enough to accommodate the 4 halves, pour the marinade over them, massage, and place in the refrigerator to marinate overnight.

3 The next day, make the sauce: Add the prunes and ½ cup (120 ml) water to a medium saucepan and bring to a boil. Transfer the mixture to a food processor and puree to the consistency of a thick paste. Meanwhile, heat the chicken stock and keep it hot until ready to use in the next step.

4 Add the onions and 4 tablespoons olive oil to a large, heavy-bottomed pot with a tight-fitting lid and sauté over medium heat, adding more oil if needed, so that the onions turn golden, their edges darken, and they soften, about 5 to 7 minutes. Add the turmeric, a bit more oil, and stir, allowing the turmeric to bloom and release its fragrance, about 30 seconds. Add the tomato paste and a bit more oil, and continue mixing until the tomato paste gets shiny, about 1 minute more (the mixture will pull away from the bottom of the pot). Deglaze the pan with the lemon juice, add the reserved hot chicken stock (adding hot liquid preserves the tomato color), the salt, pepper, cinnamon, sugar, and pureed prunes. Adjust the seasoning and add a little water if the sauce is too thick. →

For the chickens

1 small yellow onion

½ cup (120 ml) bottled lemon juice

Kosher salt

1 teaspoon ground turmeric

½ teaspoon smoked paprika

½ teaspoon whole black peppercorns

2 dried or fresh bay leaves

½ cup ice

2 whole chickens (3 pounds/ 1.3 kilograms each), butchered into 4 halves

Neutral oil, such as vegetable or canola oil, for frying

For the sauce

About 12 prunes, pitted

4 cups (1 liter) chicken stock, homemade or store-bought

2 large yellow onions, lightly processed in a food processor

Light olive oil

1 tablespoon ground turmeric

½ cup (112 grams) tomato paste

½ cup (120 ml) bottled lemon juice →

5 Cover with the lid and bring to a boil, then lower the heat and cook for about 1 hour. Once the oil separates, it is ready. (If not ready, remove the lid and continue cooking a little longer.) Remove from the heat and let sit at room temperature until an oil film forms on top.

6 Preheat the oven to 350°F.

7 To cook the chicken: Remove the chicken from the marinade and pat the skin sides dry with paper towels. Season the skin sides of the chicken with a pinch of salt and set at room temperature for 10 minutes before cooking.

8 Place a large baking sheet close by. Next, heat a large ovenproof sauté pan over medium heat, add 1 tablespoon neutral oil, and heat until shimmering. Working in batches if necessary, and adding more oil as needed, place the chicken, skin sides down, in the pan, holding the chicken away from you so that the oil does not splash you. Do not overcrowd the pan. Reduce the heat to medium-low and allow the chicken skins to crisp up in the pan slowly, letting the fat render out. Continue to cook for 3 to 5 minutes, until the skins are golden brown and crispy.

9 As you cook each chicken piece, remove the piece from the pan and transfer it to the baking sheet, skin side up. Once all the chicken pieces are golden brown, transfer the baking sheet to the preheated oven and cook for 15 to 25 minutes, until the internal temperature reaches 165°F. Remove the chicken from the oven and allow it to rest for 10 minutes prior to serving with the sauce.

1 tablespoon kosher salt

1 tablespoon freshly ground black pepper

1 tablespoon ground cinnamon

1 tablespoon granulated sugar

SOFREH RIB-EYE "KABAB"

makes 4 to 6 servings

I have always loved the combination of sour pomegranate molasses, crushed walnuts, and herby, aromatic flavors in the marinade for *kabab torsh,* a *kabab* from the northern Caspian Sea regions of Gilan and Mazandaran. And when I opened Sofreh, I had intended to remain true to its look by serving the meat on skewers. But after months of back-and-forth sampling cuts of meat with my butcher, to no avail, Ali landed on gorgeously marbled rib-eye to take on the robust flavors of the marinade. He then grilled it, glazed the top with more marinade and walnuts, and set it under the broiler to char. Our "*kabab*" hits your table sliced and ready to eat with grilled Campari tomatoes. I think our version enhances all the wonderful flavors of *kabab torsh* without the skewers. And it's so easy to make at home in a cast-iron skillet.

1 Use a food processor to finely chop the cilantro, parsley, fenugreek or mint, and garlic. Add the salt, pepper, 2 tablespoons water, and the pomegranate molasses to the bowl of a food processor and mix to combine everything.

2 Rub the steaks with most of the herb-pomegranate mixture (reserve some to make the glaze) and marinate in the refrigerator for a minimum of 4 hours and up to 8 hours before cooking.

3 Remove the steaks from the refrigerator 15 minutes before cooking. Season generously with salt and pepper. Preheat the broiler.

4 Combine the reserved herb-pomegranate mixture with the walnuts and olive oil to make a walnut glaze.

5 Add the neutral oil to a cast-iron skillet and heat until smoking. Working in batches, add one steak at a time, adding more oil as needed, and cook for 3 to 4 minutes on one side, then flip and baste with some of the walnut glaze on the cooked side. Cook for 3 to 4 minutes more before transferring the skillet to the broiler to crisp the top for a minute.

6 Allow to rest for 5 minutes, then slice and serve.

Alternatively Grill the steaks over medium heat or under the broiler until charred on both sides and the internal temperature reaches 125° to 130°F.

2 ounces (56 grams) fresh cilantro, leaves and tender stems

2 ounces (56 grams) fresh flat-leaf parsley, leaves and tender stems

2 ounces (56 grams) fresh fenugreek, or 2 ounces (56 grams) fresh mint, or 1 ounce (28 grams) dried fenugreek

6 to 8 garlic cloves

1 tablespoon kosher salt, plus more to taste

1 teaspoon freshly ground black pepper, plus more to taste

1 cup (235 ml) pomegranate molasses (preferably Al Wadi)

Four to six 8- to 12-ounce (226- to 340-gram) rib-eye steaks

½ cup (54 grams) finely chopped walnuts

⅓ cup (80 ml) light olive oil

2 tablespoons neutral oil, such as vegetable or canola oil, plus more as needed

ROSEWATER and CARDAMOM CUSTARD with a COOKIE CRUST

makes 12 individual tarts

In our first year, I served a chilled rosewater custard called *yakh dar behesht,* or "ice in paradise," that I garnished with pistachios and rose petals. When I was a kid, one of the highlights of strolling through Isfahan's Naqshe Jahan Square was stopping at a stand next to the bazaar to gulp down a warm version of this custard that the vendor handed to me in a plastic cup (some families even brought their own cups). It's still, to this day, my first stop after I see my family. This humble little custard dates back to ancient Persia and was later brought to India, where it's known as *phirni*. One day, as I watched Ali from the corner of the kitchen, he added gelatin to give my custard the texture of *panna cotta*. And then, I watched as he added sour cherry brûlée.

Oh, how fancy, I thought. At that point, I felt Ali was going too far in parting with tradition, but guests at Sofreh loved this version! I eventually removed the gelatin from the custard, and increased the cooking time to thicken the custard. It was important to me to strike a balance between my tradition and Ali's vision. Our current version is set in a graham cracker mold and topped with sour cherry brûlée. And every time it goes to a table, I see my guests' eyes light up. "Oh, it's so pretty!" they say. And it is.

1 Make the crust: Place the almond flour, graham cracker crumbs, and sugar in a food processor and slowly add the melted butter until you achieve a texture like wet sand. Leave at room temperature until ready to use.

2 Make the custard: Use a whisk to combine the wheat starch, sugar, and milk in a mixing bowl. Let the mixture sit for about 1 hour for the starch to swell and absorb the liquid.

3 Transfer the mixture to a large pot, add the salt, and cook over low heat, using a hand mixer on low speed to stir continuously until thickened. Add the rosewater and cardamom, whisking to combine. Divide the mixture among twelve 4-inch tart molds. Cover them with plastic wrap and place in the refrigerator to set for 1 to 2 hours.

4 Make the sour cherry gelée: Soak the gelatin sheets in a bowl of cold water to soften them, about 5 to 10 minutes. Gently wring out the excess water. Warm the sour cherry juice in a small saucepan over low heat, add the gelatin sheets, stir to combine, and set aside at room temperature.

5 Once the custard is set, gently pour the gelée over the custard to cover. Cover with plastic wrap and refrigerate for about 1 hour, until set. →

For the cookie crust

½ cup (48 grams) almond flour

1 cup (102 grams) graham cracker crumbs (from about 5½ sheets)

2 tablespoons granulated sugar

6 tablespoons (about ¾ stick, 85 grams) salted butter, melted

For the custard

1 cup (226 grams) wheat starch (see Resources, page 317)

1 cup (200 grams) granulated sugar

4 cups (1 liter) whole milk

Pinch of kosher salt

½ cup (120 ml) rosewater

1 teaspoon ground cardamom

½ cup chopped salted pistachios for garnish (optional) →

6 Make the brûlée: Sprinkle the superfine sugar over the top of the cherries and torch them with a kitchen blowtorch until well charred. Or spread the sugared cherries out on a baking sheet and broil until the sugar caramelizes. Garnish the custard with the sour cherry brûlée and serve.

Alternatively Although I think Ali's version is a more elegant presentation for Sofreh, you can also eliminate the cookie crust and make the custard, set it to chill, and garnish it with pistachios. Serve it humbly in a bowl. Also, feel free to cut this recipe in half.

For the sour cherry gelée

2 gelatin sheets, silver blooming strength

1 cup (235 ml) sour cherry juice

For the sour cherry brûlée

1 tablespoon superfine sugar

1 cup (155 grams) jarred sour cherries, drained of syrup

Sharbat and Sofreh Cocktails

Sharbat (from the Arabic word *shariba*, "to drink") are sweet syrups made from a base of fruits or herbs blended with honey or sugar. These syrups are then diluted with water to make a refreshing nonalcoholic drink, also called *sharbat*, that became part of Iranian culture when the Arabs brought Islam to Iran in the seventh century and forbade the consumption of wine. A love for drinking nonalcoholic *sharbat* still exists in Iran today, as does a centuries-old tradition of making distillates of flowers, herbs, and seeds, called *aragh* (from the Arabic word *rahiq*, meaning "nectar"), which are primarily used for medicinal purposes. At specialty medicinal herb shops called *attari*, you'll find floor-to-ceiling shelves stacked with every distillate imaginable—essence of orange, cumin, basil, and borage, and, of course, *golab* (rosewater), among them.

Following the establishment of the Islamic Republic in 1979, wine, spirits, and beer, which had been legal in modern-day Iran in most cities, were again outlawed. A vodka-drinking culture emerged at get-togethers behind closed doors; however, straight vodka, or our version of an Iranian vodka gimlet, is served with an array of savory, small bites.

While there has never been a cocktail culture in Iran, I took a culinary leap, using my knowledge of *sharbat* and *aragh* as the basis for the cocktails at Sofreh. Besides wanting the cocktails to be festive, delicious, and visually beautiful, I created the foundation of each from Persian flavor profiles— sun-dried lime, saffron, rosewater, dates, and many more that I continue to dream up and that organically pair with my dishes. Cocktail favorites come and go from my menu, but the recipes that follow are some of my favorites. You can also use the accompanying syrups to make nonalcoholic *sharbat* or in your own cocktail creations.

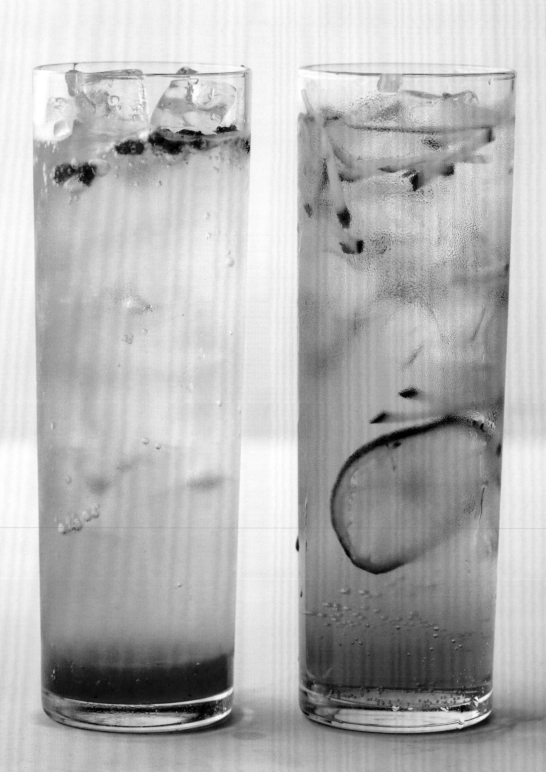

MINT and VINEGAR SYRUP

SHARBAT-E SEKANJABIN | *makes about 3½ cups syrup*

Sekanjabin, originally made with vinegar and honey, is one of Iran's oldest drinks, and has become a national summertime beverage. Because this syrup has such a long shelf life, my mother always made a big batch to last us the entire summer. The thickness and the color of this syrup vary according to preference. Some people use white vinegar (undistilled) and others add a touch of Saffron Water (page xxxiv) for a deep golden color. I make my *sekanjabin* with good-quality red wine vinegar for the deep amber color that I love. Besides being a beverage, the syrup is also enjoyed in spring as a dipping sauce with fresh romaine leaves for a lovely afternoon snack. I make a nonalcoholic *sharbat-e sekanjabin* with sparkling water, using a ratio of one to five syrup to water, adding grated cucumber and fresh mint. Or use the syrup for my *Sekanjabin* "Martini" (page 303).

1 Bring the sugar, salt, and 3 cups (¾ liter) water to a boil in a nonreactive container, stirring with a wooden spoon to mix. Just as the sugar is melted, cook on high for 10 minutes.

2 Add the vinegar and bring back to a boil, then lower the heat to medium-high and simmer for 15 to 20 minutes. Add the lemon juice, stir, and cook for 5 minutes more. The syrup should be moderately thick—sticky enough to stick between your fingers.

3 Cool the syrup down for about 30 to 40 minutes and then add all the mint leaves and stems. Leave overnight, lightly covered with plastic wrap.

4 The next morning, squeeze the mint leaves and strain the liquid. Store in a glass jar with a lid and keep in a dark, cool place for up to 6 months.

2 pounds (907 grams) granulated sugar

Pinch of kosher salt

¾ cup (180 ml) red wine vinegar

⅓ cup (80 ml) fresh lemon juice

A big bunch fresh mint leaves with stems (about 10 to 12 ounces/ 280 to 340 grams), washed and well dried

BARBERRY SYRUP

SHARBAT-E ZERESHK | *makes about 2 cups syrup*

During the short season for fresh barberries in Iran, street vendors sell fresh barberry juice to enjoy raw as a cleanse or for making barberry syrup. You can create a delicious *sharbat* using dried barberries at home. If not used within one week, freeze it in small batches for cocktails.

1 Clean the barberries by soaking them in cold water for at least 10 minutes and up to 25 minutes to remove any dust. Change the water a few times, until you can't see any dust on the bottom of the bowl. Transfer the barberries, along with 2 cups (470 ml) water, to a container and soak, uncovered, for 4 to 8 hours.

2 The next day, strain the barberries, reserving the liquid. Combine the barberry water with the sugar in a saucepan and cook over medium heat for about 10 minutes, until the sugar dissolves. Add the lemon juice and salt and cook on low for 2 minutes more. Add the barberries to the pan and continue cooking in the syrup on low for 5 minutes more.

3 Transfer the mixture to a blender and process until very smooth. Pass the puree through a fine-mesh strainer and add the rosewater. Blend with still or sparkling water, or use as a base for a cocktail. Store in a glass jar with a lid and keep in the refrigerator for up to 1 week.

10 ounces (140 grams) dried barberries

2 cups (400 grams) granulated sugar

⅓ cup (80 ml) bottled lemon juice

Pinch of kosher salt

Splash of rosewater

CRANBERRY SYRUP

makes about 3½ cups syrup

I often recommend cranberries to replace dried barberries in my recipes. If you would like to save your precious barberries for other dishes, use this cranberry syrup for *sharbat* and cocktails.

Note Cranberries contain a lot of pectin. Before each use, add a bit of water to the syrup to loosen it.

1 Place the cranberries in a small pot with a tight-fitting lid. Cover and bring to a boil for 20 minutes. Strain the liquid, reserving the cranberry pulp.

2 Transfer the pulp to a blender and starting on low speed, puree, stopping now and then to slowly add the reserved liquid in batches and gradually increasing the speed.

3 Pass the pureed cranberry mixture through a fine-mesh sieve and discard any bits of pulp that remain.

4 Return the pureed cranberry mixture to the same pot and add the sugar, lemon juice, and salt. Stir to combine and cook, uncovered, for 15 to 20 minutes, until the mixture coats the back of a spoon.

5 Remove the syrup from the heat and add the rosewater. Store in a glass jar with a lid and keep in the refrigerator for up to 2 weeks.

10 ounces (137 grams) frozen cranberries

2 cups (400 grams) granulated sugar

⅓ cup (80 ml) bottled lemon juice

Pinch of kosher salt

Splash of rosewater

SUN-DRIED LIME SYRUP

SHARBAT-E LIMOO AMANI | *makes about 4 cups syrup*

I combine this syrup with mezcal to become *Limoo* Mezcal (page 304), Sofreh's most popular drink.

1 Add the dried limes and 4 cups (1 liter) water to a medium saucepan with a tight-fitting lid. Cover and cook over low heat for about 1½ hours, until very soft. Pass the mixture through a fine-mesh strainer to remove the seeds, and reserve the liquid. Next, puree the liquid and the limes in a food processor, and set aside.

2 Bring the sugar and 2 cups (470 ml) water to a boil in a medium saucepan and cook until the sugar dissolves, about 10 minutes.

3 Add the dried lime puree to the syrup, mix well, and cook for 5 to 7 minutes, until well combined.

4 Freeze in small batches for a last-minute cocktail or use in a *limoo* mezcal.

7 sun-dried limes, halved

2 cups (400 grams) granulated sugar

RHUBARB SYRUP

SHARBAT-E RIVAS | *makes about 3½ cups syrup*

The beautiful tartness of rhubarb is complemented by floral rosewater in this syrup. You can use this for your own cocktail creations or for a *Rivas* Sour (page 307).

1 Bring the sugar, salt, and 1 cup (235 ml) water to a boil in a medium saucepan.

2 Add the rhubarb to the syrup and continue cooking for 10 minutes more.

3 Transfer the mixture to a nonreactive container and set aside to come to room temperature, then transfer to the refrigerator to chill for 1 hour.

4 Once the mixture is chilled, puree in a blender. Add the rosewater and lemon juice to taste. Store in a glass jar with a lid and keep in the refrigerator for 1 week.

1 cup (200 grams) granulated sugar

Pinch of kosher salt

1 pound (454 grams) rhubarb stalks, trimmed of leaves, chopped into 1-inch pieces

¼ cup (60 ml) rosewater

⅓ cup (80 ml) bottled lemon juice

DATE SYRUP

SHARBAT-E KHORMA | *makes about 4 cups syrup*

I use this sweet cardamom- and rosewater-perfumed date syrup in my
Sofreh Date Night cocktail (page 311) or for *sharbat*. If you make a big batch,
as I do, and portion it out to freeze in small containers, it's terrific drizzled
over pancakes or added to your smoothies (see Persian Street Smoothie,
page 18).

1 Combine 2 cups (470 ml) water with the dates in a medium saucepan, bring
to a simmer over medium heat, and cook until very soft, about 20 minutes.
Transfer the mixture to a blender and puree.

2 In a separate saucepan, bring the sugar and 1 cup (235 ml) water to a boil,
and cook until the sugar dissolves, about 10 minutes.

3 Lower the heat to medium, add the date puree to the syrup, and cook
for 10 minutes more. Remove from the heat and add the cardamom and
rosewater. Stir to combine. Allow the mixture to come to room temperature.
Store in a glass jar with a lid and keep in the refrigerator for up to 1 week.

1 pound (454 grams) Medjool
dates, pitted and chopped

¾ cup (150 grams) granulated
sugar

1 teaspoon ground cardamom

¼ cup (60 ml) rosewater

SAFFRON TINCTURE

makes about 3 cups tincture

This gorgeous saffron and rosewater tincture is great to have on hand to
make a martini or for a Saffron Vesper (page 308).

1 Mix the bloomed saffron and rosewater with 2 cups (470 ml) filtered water
in a medium bowl.

2 Store in a glass jar with a lid and keep in the refrigerator for up to 2 weeks.

½ teaspoon saffron powder,
bloomed over 3 to 4 ice cubes

1 cup (235 ml) rosewater

SEKANJABIN "MARTINI"

makes 1 cocktail

Before Sofreh even existed, I kept *sekanjabin* (see page 297) on hand.
Because I love gin, I created a cocktail by mixing it with the syrup for guests
when I hosted parties in our home. This is a sour play on a gimlet-style drink
that includes the fresh cucumber typically served with *sharbat-e sekanjabin*.

1 Wrap the cucumber ribbon around the inside of a rocks glass.

2 Muddle the cucumber in a cocktail shaker. Next, add the syrup, lime juice,
and gin. Shake with ice and double strain into the glass.

Three ¼-inch-thick cucumber
slices, and 1 thin cucumber ribbon

½ ounce (14 ml) Mint and Vinegar
Syrup (page 297)

½ ounce (14 ml) lime juice, fresh
or bottled

2½ ounces (70 ml) gin

LIMOO MEZCAL

makes 1 cocktail

The distinctive smoky flavor of agave-based Mexican mezcal, along with a bright herbal liquor, such as Dolin Génépy le Chamois, takes a traditional margarita to another level. I adore the musky complexity of the dried lime syrup and the sourness of a bit of dried lime powder on the rim.

1 Combine the lime juice, salt, and lime powder, if using, in a small bowl. Dip the lip of a rocks glass into the lime mixture for a sour rim, if you like.

2 Fill a cocktail shaker halfway with ice. Add the lime syrup, Dolin Génépy, and mezcal. Shake and strain over a large ice cube into an old-fashioned glass.

1 teaspoon fresh or bottled lime juice (optional)

Kosher salt for rim (optional)

Dried lime powder for rim (optional)

½ ounce (14 ml) Sun-Dried Lime Syrup (page 300)

½ ounce (14 ml) Dolin Génépy le Chamois or other herbal liquor

1½ ounces (42 ml) mezcal

RIVAS SOUR

makes 1 cocktail

The warm vanilla, spices, and malty notes in scotch get a wonderful tang from the Rhubarb Syrup (page 300) in my take on a whiskey sour. The garnish of rosebud and rosewater spray is a lovely touch.

1 Fill a cocktail shaker halfway with ice. Add the rhubarb syrup, lemon juice, and scotch. Shake and strain into a coupe glass.

2 Garnish with a small rosebud and rosewater spray.

1 ounce (28 ml) Rhubarb Syrup (page 300)

1 ounce (28 ml) fresh lemon juice

2 ounces (56 ml) blended scotch

Rosebud (see Resources, page 317) for garnish

Rosewater spray (see Resources, page 317) for garnish

SAFFRON VESPER

makes 1 cocktail

This cocktail is a super-dry spin on a classic Vesper martini. Lightly sweet and floral, Lillet Blanc pairs beautifully with the earthy and floral notes of the Saffron Tincture (page 301), and the color is so beautiful.

1 Fill a cocktail shaker halfway with ice. Add the saffron tincture, Lillet, gin, and vodka. Stir and strain into a coupe glass.

2 Garnish with the rose petals.

¾ ounce (21 ml) Saffron Tincture (page 301)

¾ ounce (21 ml) Lillet Blanc

¾ ounce (21 ml) gin

1 ounce (28 ml) vodka

3 rose petals (see Resources, page 317) for garnish

DATE NIGHT

makes 1 cocktail

This drink makes a terrifically creamy, fun dessert beverage. For the aquafaba in this cocktail, I save the liquid from cooking beans for my Sofreh Herb and Noodle *A'ash* (page 208). Or you can drain one can of chickpeas, reserve the liquid (save the chickpeas for something else), and use a hand mixer to whip it into peaks.

1 Add the aquafaba, cream, date syrup, port, rum, and ice cubes to a cocktail shaker for a wet shake.

2 Strain the ice, dry shake, and strain into an ice-filled Collins glass.

3 Finish with a splash of club soda to increase the foam, and garnish with rose petals and crushed pistachio "crumbs."

1 ounce (28 grams) aquafaba (see headnote)

1 ounce (28 grams) heavy cream

1 ounce (28 ml) Date Syrup (page 301)

1 ounce (28 ml) port

2 ounces (56 ml) rum

Splash of club soda

Rose petals (see Resources, page 317) for garnish

A few salted pistachios, finely crushed into "crumbs" using a mortar and pestle, for garnish

SAFFRON PUDDING
for NEW MOMS

KACHI | *makes 12 or more servings*

In our first week of being open, a pregnant Iranian woman came through our doors with her American husband. She reminded me of myself when I was expecting Soshy and Noony, and sure enough, she was expecting twins— a girl and a boy—and wanted to have a last dinner out before her babies arrived. I was moved to give my card to her husband, telling him that when his wife went into labor, I'd be honored to make *kachi* for her. In Iran, women make this fragrant, sweet halvah pudding of toasted flour, butter, and sugar for new mothers after childbirth to give them nutrition and energy. Her husband showed up at Sofreh a few days later with such an exhausted face. I understood just what they were going through!

What began as such an organic, casual gesture grew into a tradition of making *kachi* for soon-to-be new mothers. I will not sell *kachi,* and I cannot make *kachi* on demand. It transcends what money can buy and is deeply personal to me and to those women whom I've connected with in my dining room. (All I ask in return is a picture of the new baby and mom to keep on my phone.)

Note In the north of Iran, people make *kachi* with rice flour, and I like mixing in wheat flour, too. If you'd like, swap out the fragrant rosewater and saffron with black pepper, cardamom, turmeric, or even ginger for an expression that is all your own. Just add the spices when stirring the flour.

1 Combine the sugar and 8 cups (2 liters) water in a large saucepan and bring to a boil until slightly thickened, about 5 to 10 minutes. Add the saffron and rosewater, stir, remove from the heat, and set aside.

2 In a large pot, toast the all-purpose flour over medium heat until the color is a uniform light cream. Add the rice flour and butter and toast a little longer. Add the slivered almonds and stir, then lower the heat and slowly add the reserved saffron-rosewater syrup, whisking vigorously, being careful not to burn yourself. If the pudding is too thick, add a bit of water to thin it out and continue cooking, stirring continuously, for about 5 to 10 minutes.

3 Transfer the pudding to a pretty container or serving dish with a lid, garnish with pistachios and dried rose petals, cover, and send with love to a new mom.

2 cups (400 grams) granulated sugar

½ teaspoon saffron powder

¼ cup (60 ml) rosewater

1 cup (120 grams) all-purpose flour

1 tablespoon rice flour

About 6 tablespoons (about ¾ stick/85 grams) salted butter, cut into small pieces

1 cup (108 grams) slivered almonds

½ cup salted pistachios, chopped, for garnish

Dried rose petals for garnish

From
My Father

My daughter,
in the time of rain, you are like a gentle breeze.
In the time of a storm, you stand strong like a mountain.
You fly high and straight like an eagle.
I pray for the higher powers to have your back.

You have always moved through life so quickly.
Look in the mirror
at your fast-moving reflection
and slow down.

—Excerpted from a poem handwritten by my father.
He wrote it for me in the spring of 2018,
as we were planning to open Sofreh,
and I hung it at the restaurant's entrance.

Golé Yakh

In my father's garden,
I saw an old shrub standing as tall as I am now.
(When I was little, I could leap over it.)
That shrub grew, along with me, across the years
and the parting tears,
of *"Khoda-negahdar"* ("May God keep you safe").

This winter, I returned to the barest moment in my father's garden,
and I saw this shrub again, as I have seen it hundreds of times before
across the years
and the returning tears,
of *"Beh khanneh khosh aamadee"* ("Welcome home").

Its spindly branches
enveloped me with its intoxicating aroma, drawing me closer
to reveal lemon-yellow flowers,
all in bloom.

What offers up a flower on the coldest day of the year?
Golé yakh—"the flower of ice"—in Farsi.
And in that moment, I saw the soul of Iran.

Resources

Many of the ingredients mentioned in this book are available in good markets everywhere, as well as Middle Eastern and Persian stores. Here are several more sources for you to visit or order from online.

In New York

SAHADI'S   Has two locations, both in Brooklyn. The first is at 187 Atlantic Avenue, Brooklyn, NY 11201, and the second is in Industry City, 34 35th Street, Brooklyn, NY 11232. They are open every day and carry exquisite spices, ancient grains, nuts, dried fruits, and most every product mentioned throughout this book. Order online at sahadis.com. Or call (718) 624-4550.

KALUSTYAN'S   Located at 123 Lexington Avenue, New York, NY 10016, it carries many of the products featured in this book. Spices such as saffron, turmeric, sun-dried limes, nigella seeds, coriander seeds, dried fenugreek, sumac, dried herbs and prepackaged dried herb mixes labeled as *sabzi a'ash*, *sabzi ghormeh*, and *sabzi polo*, as well as rosewater, rosebuds and rose petals, dried barberries, basmati and jasmine rice, grains, and liquid and dried *kashk* are available. Order online at kalustyans.com. Or call (212) 685-3451.

Online

PERSIANBASKET.COM   Stocks a huge variety of spices, including dried lime powder and hogweed seeds, as well as Persian delicacies including excellent-quality nuts (walnuts, pistachios, slivered almonds), sour cherries in brine, tamarind blocks, *reshteh* wheat noodles, wheat starch, rice flour, and chickpea flour. Other products include preserved fruit *lavashak* and *samanu* for *sofreh haft-seen* for Nowruz, and fresh seasonal fruit and produce, including *goje sabz*, Seville oranges, unripened almonds, and pomegranates. You can also find the Sadaf brand of *kashk* that I use, as well as prepackaged dried herb mixes labeled as *sabzi a'ash*, *sabzi ghormeh*, and *sabzi polo*. They also carry date molasses, grape molasses, and bitter orange molasses.

KALAMALA.COM   This Persian online grocery store carries a wide selection of Persian pantry and fresh produce items and ships across the United States from Los Angeles for a flat rate. They also carry both wooden and aluminum *ghusht kub* meat mashers.

AMAZON.COM   Carries the Al Wadi brand of pomegranate molasses that I prefer for Sofreh Duck *Fesenjan* (page 285) and Pomegranate *A'ash* with Meatballs (page 201), but you can experiment with other brands. They also carry miscellaneous items, such as the *tawa* pan, food-grade pickling lime, and gelatin sheets.

MERCATO.COM   My source for grapevine leaves for making Stuffed Grapevine Leaves (page 133). They offer delivery in major U.S. cities and national shipping from select merchants. Order online or call (844) 699-2776.

SARZAMINE MAN

MY HOMELAND

AHMAD BELBASI

MAHSHAD JALALIAN

HAMID RAHMATI

KHALED MARDANI

ZOHREH SABAGHNEJAD

NASRIN ABRISHAMI

SONA MOAYEDZADEH

MAHDI RAZAVI

SAEED NIKPOUR

JAVAD REZAEI

HAMIDREZA MOHAMMADZADEH

ZHALEH BAHRAMI

AREZOO SADEGHI NAJAFABADI

ALI JAHANARA

NIMA BIGDELY

MASOUD DELAVARI

MEHRAN MAFI BORDBAR

MOHAMMAD GHAEDI

MOHAMMAD NAZARI

REZA ZANGENEH

MAHDI HOSEINI

IMAN SAMADY

KEYVAN FIRUZEI

SOURCED AND CURATED BY ROZHIA TABNAK, THESE IMAGES ARE PART OF NASIM'S COLLABORATION
WITH PERSIAN PHOTOGRAPHERS WHO CAPTURE A BEAUTY THAT IS UNIQUE TO IRAN.

Acknowledgments

Throughout giving birth to my restaurant, Sofreh, and working on this book, I found new meaning in my roots and identity, and for that, I am humbled and grateful. First, I must acknowledge the role of women in my circle of family and friends, especially my mother, Giti Joon. You supported, cared for, and fed your loved ones quietly as if your lives depended on it. Your presence seemed invisible until everything around you collapsed when you weren't there! You taught me about generosity, perseverance, and food.

Baba, dear father, you continue to be a beacon of light, quietly strong. You showed me how to find joy in your simple gestures of caring for all living creatures. You taught me that actions are stronger than words.

Thank you, "Aki," my husband and partner in life for nearly forty years. You helped me grow my wings and fly. And to my twins, Soshyan and Orpheas: I wouldn't be here without cooking for both of you. You provided me with a sense of calm and purpose that I had not known since I left my home in Isfahan.

Minoo Joon, you are the sister I never had. Your unconditional support throughout our friendship is thicker than blood, and your wisdom is a compass that I refer to when in doubt.

My gratitude for Rozhia Tabnak. You pushed me to write my recipes years ago, even before realizing my restaurant, Sofreh. I owe Sofreh's beauty and the authenticity of my voice to your talent, artistic vision, and creative direction.

Thank you, Theresa Gambacorta. Your ability to listen allowed me to share my life. You not only became my trusted partner in writing this book but you taught me that wisdom has nothing to do with age.

Soroosh Golbabae, thank you for trusting me and agreeing to work with me as I practiced my dishes in the months before opening Sofreh. Remember when we fed ninety people for a party by cooking with propane?

Ali Saboor, thank you for bringing your culinary expertise to Sofreh and helping to make "the new kid on the block" a success. Also, thank you for your perspective on my book's structure and your presence at Sofreh, which allowed me to write while running a restaurant.

Thank you to my newfound Sofreh work family in both the front and back of the house. I appreciate your dedication and your helping me understand the meaning of teamwork.

Rozanne Gold, thank you for your timely advice and for setting me on the right course for my book's journey.

My love and thanks to my neighbors and Brooklyn community for embracing Sofreh, notably Melissa Clark, for putting us on the map during our first weeks of opening.

Thank you to my agent, Janis Donnaud. You are a powerhouse, and this book would not be possible without you.

Thank you to my editors, Tom Pold and Peter Gethers, for your expertise and guidance. Peter, your big heart allowed me the freedom to express my life and my culinary experience as authentically as possible on the page.

And finally, my love and gratitude to you, my little brother Amir. No matter what happens in life, I always know you have my back. Sofreh would not be Sofreh without your generosity, hospitality, sweetness, and warmth, which you extend each night working with me.

Index

Page numbers in *italics* are photographs.

A NOTE ABOUT THE AUTHORS

NASIM ALIKHANI was born and raised in Isfahan, Iran, and is the executive chef and co-owner of the Persian restaurant Sofreh in Prospect Heights, Brooklyn. Nasim's cooking has traversed a lifetime: from Isfahani summers spent by her mother's side to help with pickling projects to her arrival in New York City, at twenty-three years old, following the 1979 Iranian revolution. And later, in her marriage to Akis Petroulas and in the raising of their twins in New York City, Nasim's journey in the kitchen has been one of a prolific home cook, expressing her life's calling to nourish others through the foods and the deep warmth of Persian culture. With each return visit to her native Iran, Nasim deepened her connection to the ancestral voices and regional Iranian recipes of the women in her family and circle of friends and neighbors. While raising her children in New York City, Nasim undertook massive catering projects for her kids' schools, churches, fund-raising events, and homeless shelters. By the time she opened her first restaurant, Sofreh, in June 2018, she had spent more than two decades cooking, honing, and dreaming of sharing the extraordinary flavors, traditions, and communal spirit of Persian home cooking with the world. In 2021, she was selected as one of ten chefs, and the first ever Iranian chef, to create the menu for guests at the Met Gala in New York City. *Sofreh* is her debut cookbook.

THERESA GAMBACORTA is a food journalist and playwright, and the coauthor, with Joey Campanaro, of *Big Love Cooking*.

A NOTE ABOUT THE ILLUSTRATIONS

The photographs in the *Sarzamine Man* (My Homeland) section were curated by and are the result of a collaboration between Sofreh's creative director, Rozhia Tabnak, and amateur and professional Iranian photographers. Each photograph evokes awe: in some, it's for the simplicity and immediacy of everyday life; in others, it's for the sublime beauty that is often under-represented in Western culture. Together they depict just a sliver of the vast land, the differing climates, cultures, and people from all walks of life, that make up my unique and beautiful homeland.

Calligraphy is an ancient art that is as fundamental to Persian culture as are our food and hospitable warmth. And I owe my appreciation for calligraphy to my father's love and knowledge of it. From the beginning, I knew I had to incorporate it into the design of my restaurant, Sofreh's, interior and into my book. Iranian artist Nazanin Vaziri created the one-of-a-kind calligraphy chapter titles and designs, also in collaboration with Rozhia Tabnak.